TIME
ANNUAL
The Year in Review 1997

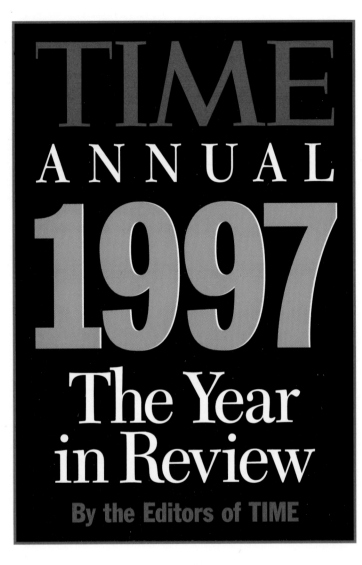

TIME
ANNUAL
1997
The Year in Review

By the Editors of TIME

TIME ANNUAL 1997

TIME ANNUAL 1997

EDITOR	Edward L. Jamieson
MANAGING EDITOR	Kelly Knauer
ART DIRECTOR	Gigi Fava
RESEARCH DIRECTOR	Leah Shanks Gordon
PICTURE EDITOR	Deborah Pierce
PRODUCTION EDITOR	Michael Skinner
ASSOCIATE ART DIRECTOR	Sumo
RESEARCH ASSOCIATES	Anne Hopkins, Valerie Marchant
COPY EDITORS	Bruce Christopher Carr, Ellin Martens
PRODUCTION DIRECTOR	John Calvano

TIME INC. HOME ENTERTAINMENT

MANAGING DIRECTOR	David Gitow
DIRECTOR, CONTINUITIES AND SINGLE SALES	David Arfine
DIRECTOR, CONTINUITIES & RETENTION	Michael Barrett
DIRECTOR, NEW PRODUCTS	Alicia Longobardo
GROUP PRODUCT MANAGERS	Robert Fox, Michael Holahan
PRODUCT MANAGERS	Christopher Berzolla, Stacy Hirschberg, Amy Jacobsson, Jennifer McLyman, Dan Melore
MANAGER, RETAIL AND NEW MARKETS	Thomas Mifsud
ASSOCIATE PRODUCT MANAGERS	Louisa Bartle, Alison Ehrmann, Carlos Jimenez, Nancy London, Dawn Perry, Daria Raehse
ASSISTANT PRODUCT MANAGERS	Meredith Shelley, Betty Su
EDITORIAL OPERATIONS DIRECTOR	John Calvano
FULFILLMENT DIRECTOR	Michelle Gudema
FINANCIAL DIRECTOR	Tricia Griffin
ASSOCIATE FINANCIAL MANAGER	Amy Maselli
MARKETING ASSISTANT	Sarah Holmes

CONSUMER MARKETING DIVISION

PRODUCTION DIRECTOR	John E. Tighe
BOOK PRODUCTION MANAGER	Jessica McGrath
BOOK PRODUCTION COORDINATOR	Joseph Napolitano

This book is dedicated to the memory of Rose Keyser

THE WORK OF THE FOLLOWING TIME STAFFERS AND CONTRIBUTORS IS INCLUDED IN THIS VOLUME:
Kathleen Adams, Edward Barnes, Jonathan Beaty, Ginia Bellafante, Lisa Beyer, Elizabeth L. Bland, Cathy Booth, Margaret Carlson, George Church, Howard Chua-Eoan, Adam Cohen, Patrick E. Cole, James Collins, Richard Corliss, Michael Duffy, Philip Elmer-DeWitt, John F. Dickerson, Tamala M. Edwards, Daniel Eisenberg, Christopher John Farley, Kevin Fedarko, Nancy Gibbs, Frank Gibney, Elizabeth Gleick, Christine Gorman, Lisa Granatstein, Paul Gray, John Greenwald, Anita Hamilton, Bruce Handy, Janice M. Horowitz, Robert Hughes, Walter Isaacson, Rahul Jacob, Leon Jaroff, Daniel Kadlec, Jeffrey Kluger, Charles Krauthammer, Nadya Labi, Richard Lacayo, Michael Lemonick, Belinda Luscombe, Scott MacLeod, J.F.O. McAllister, Johanna McGeary, J. Madeleine Nash, Bruce W. Nelan, Richard N. Ostling, Priscilla Painton, Joshua Cooper Ramo, Romesh Ratnesar, Christopher Redman, Elizabeth Rudulph, Thomas Sancton, Alain L. Sanders, Bill Saporito, Richard Schickel, Michael S. Serrill, Elaine Shannon, Hugh Sidey, John Skow, Anthony Spaeth, Ron Stodghill II, Karen Tumulty, David Van Biema, Bruce Van Voorst, Douglas Waller, James Walsh, Michael Weisskopf, Robert Wright, Steve Wulf, Adam Zagorin, Richard Zoglin

SPECIAL THANKS TO:
Gerry Abrahamsen, Ames Adamson, Ken Baierlein, Robin Bierstedt, Sue Blair, Andy Blau, Rick Boeth, Wayne Chun, Anne Considine, Urbano Delvalle, Dick Duncan, Elena Falaro, Linda Freeman, Alex LeVine, Steve Hart, Arthur Hochstein, Raphael Joa, Kin Wah Lam, Joe Lertola, John Meyer, Donna Miano-Ferrara, Amy Musher, Rudi Papiri, Hillary Raskin, Anthony Ross, Christina Scalet, Barry Seaman, Ken Smith, Robert Stevens, Michele Stephenson, Miriam Winocur, Anna Yelenskaya, Karen Zakrison, Carrie A. Zimmerman
Special thanks to the TIME Imaging staff.

SIX YEARS AFTER THE COLLAPSE OF THE SOVIET UNION, old forms of empire continued to give way to new ones. When Britain at last handed over control of Hong Kong to China, it was a quaint reminder that people once dreamed of straddling the globe politically—rather than through business and science, data and culture. In 1997 communication was global: when Diana, Princess of Wales, died in a car wreck, the entire world mourned, for people everywhere had been exposed to 17 years of media coverage of the royal superstar. Finance was global: when Asian economies tottered, markets around the world registered the after-shock. Science was global: the year's most significant event, the cloning of an adult sheep, took place in rural Scotland. Culture, too, was global: the year's two great architectural debuts took place in Spain and Los Angeles. And the new Broadway hit *The Lion King* married African imagery to American stagecraft, shaping a multihued masterpiece that caught the increasingly converging spirit of the age.

THE YEAR IN REVIEW

"If you think you can whup me, do it with the gloves on. You had a chance to fight back. Why did you bite?"

—HEAVYWEIGHT
BOXING CHAMPION
EVANDER HOLYFIELD,
TO MIKE TYSON

In Round 3 of his title bout with Evander Holyfield, Mike Tyson bit off more than he could chew: a sizable chunk of Holyfield's right ear

Images

PIONEERING PHOTOGRAPHER HENRI Cartier-Bresson called them "defining moments"—those instants when fact meets film, and history's flight is indelibly captured. From a close-up of a title fight to a vision of Princess Diana shot through a telephoto lens, such defining moments, while merely recording facts, may also serve as invocations of our deepest emotions.

"What we know is that a sheep named Dolly has written a whole new page in the history of our knowledge about genes."

—NATIONAL SCIENCE FOUNDATION DIRECTOR NEAL LANE

Could science make
another you? A cloned
lamb, Dolly, became the year's
most controversial lab animal

"Women, children, the elderly, they don't know anything about four-party talks. They want to eat. They want to live."
—OHIO CONGRESSMAN TONY HALL

Hungry children await the future at a kindergarten in Sinch'on, North Korea. The World Food program said nearly 2.5 million people in that country were at risk of starvation

"It's a spiritual experience. It touches the very heart of your being."

—AMATEUR ASTRONOMER THOMAS BOPP, ON FIRST SEEING THE COMET HALE-BOPP

Rivaling the moon in the
night sky, the Hale-Bopp
comet reappeared 4,200
years after its last passage

The arrival of Kenneth Robert and the other McCaughey newborns brought the world a septuplet of fragile wonders whose survival was a medical miracle

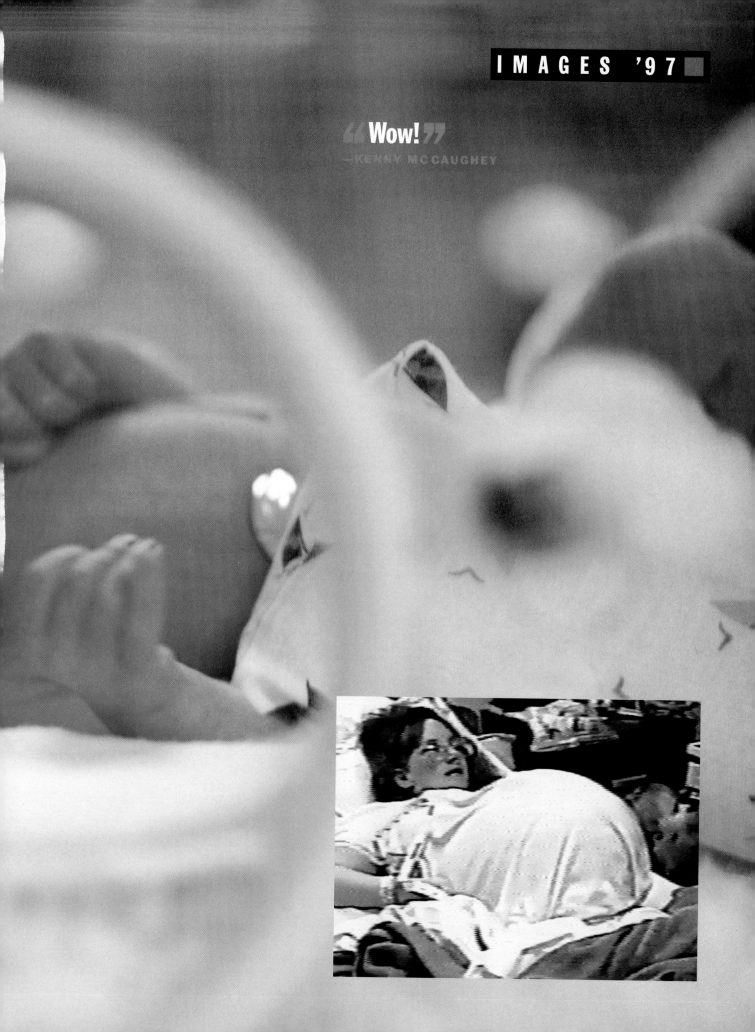

"Wow!"
—KENNY MC CAUGHEY

“Age cannot wither her.”

—WILLIAM SHAKESPEARE

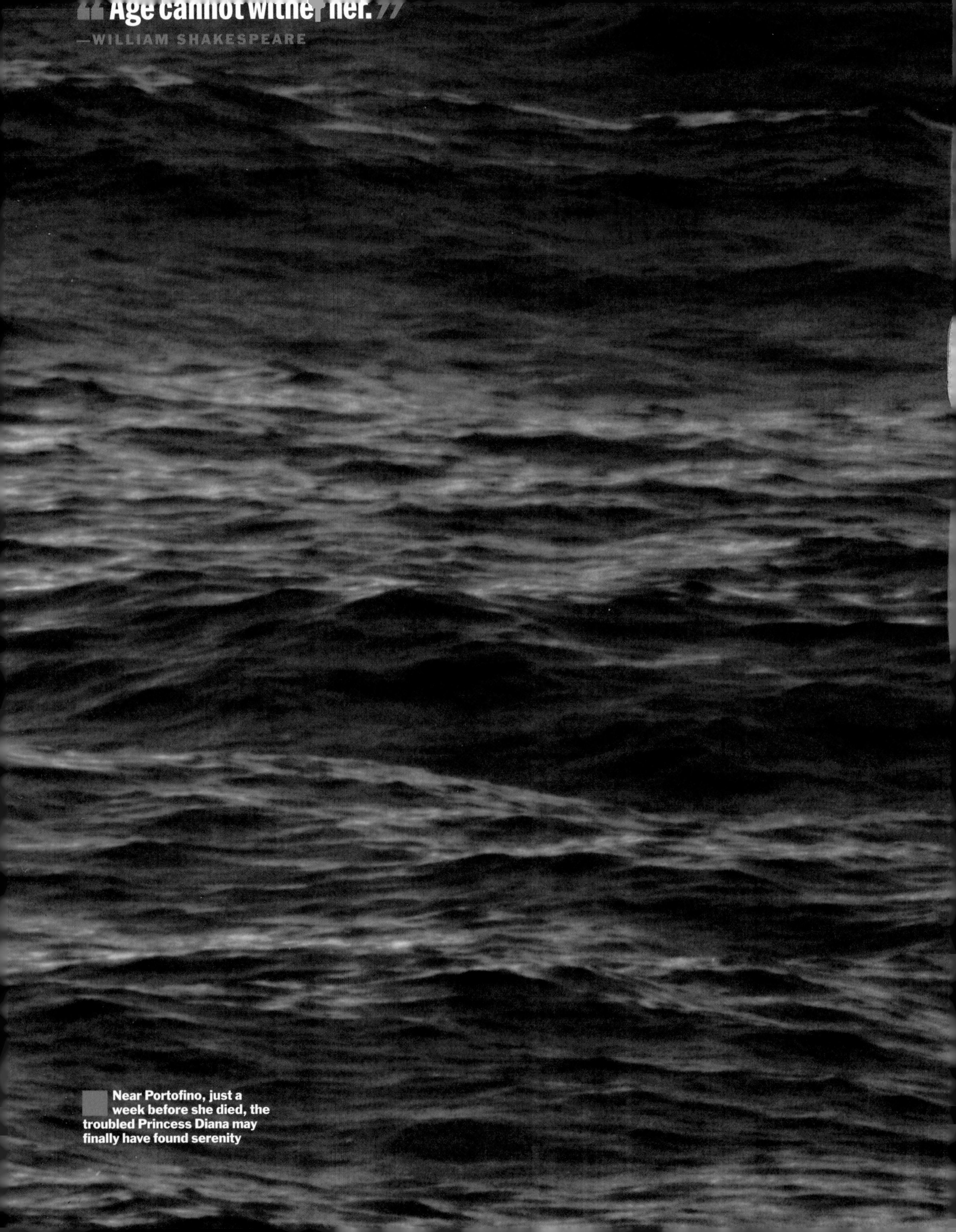

Near Portofino, just a week before she died, the troubled Princess Diana may finally have found serenity

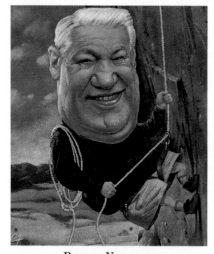

BORIS YELTSIN

He bounced back from heart surgery—but Russia still had an uphill climb

THE GOVERNOR & THE PRINCE

Rue, Britannia! Chris Patten and Prince Charles sail into Hong Kong's sunset

BILL CLINTON & BUDDY

What's a guy to do when his daughter leaves the nest? Get a dog, of course!

DEAN WITTER & J.P. MORGAN

Morgan Stanley met Main Street, taking over Dean Witter, the little guy's friend

NEWT GINGRICH

Still Speaker by a squeaker, he survived ethics woes and in-House foes

ALAN GREENSPAN

Toro! The Manolete of the money markets kept the bull stampeding

EVANDER HOLYFIELD

Move over, Vincent: the heavyweight champ took a chomp from a chump

EBBERS & SIDGMORE

WorldCom's country boys snatched MCI and began rafting the global data stream

RICHARD JEWELL

The "wrong man" had the last laugh as Big Media fessed up—and paid up

BOBBI McCAUGHEY

Just in time for Thanksgiving, the septuplets' mom hit seventh heaven

MARV ALBERT

A loud No! for the Yesss! man, his dirty laundry and his talk-show rehab tour

LAURENT KABILA

He ousted Zaïre's Mobutu. Did he hate dictatorship—or just want to be dictator?

AL GORE

"No controlling legal authority"? The Veep's verbiage didn't ring true

CHELSEA CLINTON

Free at last! So close to the Pacific— and so far from the Beltway

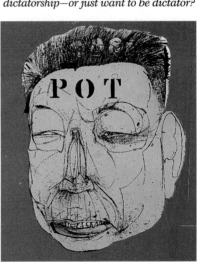

POL POT

The mastermind of the killing fields was purged by his own Khmer Rouge

BOB DYLAN

Mixed signals: he went knockin' on heaven's door before playing for the Pope

DAYTIME DIVAS

Roseanne planned to tussle with Rosie and Oprah for TV's talk tiara

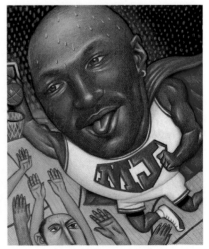

MICHAEL JORDAN

Ho-hum! Another season, another championship for b-ball's greatest ever

"Please—no one should tell them Clinton stopped for pizza on the way over."
—PRESIDENTIAL PRESS-POOL MEMO, *asking reporters not to tell the Kennedys that the vacationing president had a snack before dinner with the family*

"I thought that it is a people's matter—food."
—MIKHAIL GORBACHEV, *explaining to the New York Times why he filmed a commercial for Pizza Hut*

"The Lord had the wonderful advantage of being able to work alone."
—New U.N. Secretary-General KOFI ANNAN, *when asked why he had not yet reformed the U.N. after five months, given that God had taken only seven days to create the universe.*

"I never had so much body."
—SUSAN STILL, *astronaut, on the effect of zero gravity on her hair*

"I really thought I'd be seeing Elvis soon."
—BOB DYLAN, *of his bout with a potentially fatal infection*

"We are the meanest, nastiest bunch of jealous, petty people who ever lived. You think I wouldn't sell my mother for My Lai?"
—SEYMOUR HERSH, *on the profession of investigative reporting*

"If you hear of me getting married, slap me."
—ELIZABETH TAYLOR *to ABC's Barbara Walters on 20/20*

"I blew it."
—GEORGE BUSH, *on choosing Dan Quayle as his running mate in 1988, in a new biography*

"I have not seen a ten dollars bill green american and I would like to have one."
—FIDEL CASTRO, *at age 12, in a letter to Franklin Roosevelt, released by the National Archive*

"In the morning … I need 20 minutes to cry … To wake up and to make that shift, you know, and to just say, 'This really sucks.'"
—CHRISTOPHER REEVE, *explaining on 48 Hours how he copes with his paralysis*

"Giving up butter ... means that in about two years you will be covered with dandruff."
—JULIA CHILD, *praising the moisturizing quality of fat, in the Washington* Post

"Next time I'll give $600,000."
—ROGER TAMRAZ, *at the campaign-finance hearings, on whether he got value for his $300,000 contribution*

"My conscience is clear."

—POL POT, *Former Cambodian strongman and Khmer Rouge leader, charged with killing millions of his countrymen in the 1970s*

"Goddammit, get in and get those files. Blow the safe and get it."
—RICHARD NIXON, *to chief of staff H.R. Haldeman on breaking into the Brookings Institution to steal classified documents.*

"I'd love to have two so that I could have more time for myself."
—Supermodel CLAUDIA SCHIFFER, *explaining why she'd like to be cloned*

"I have to confess that it has crossed my mind that you could not be a Republican and a Christian."
—HILLARY RODHAM CLINTON, *addressing the National Prayer Breakfast*

"If you don't consider what happened in Oklahoma, Tim was a good person."
—MICHAEL FORTIER, *testifying about Oklahoma City bombing suspect Timothy McVeigh*

"It's golf, golf, golf—interspersed with politics."
—SEN. JOHN BREAUX, *discussing President Bill Clinton's agenda in his second term*

"Elizabeth's back at the Red Cross, and I'm walking the dog."
—BOB DOLE, *on his life after losing the presidential election in 1996*

Microchip eyes, right; and above, cat, happy face, emerald, spiral and dollar sign

Iris Magic! Technology Creates A Girl with Kaleidoscope Eyes

I**F THE EYES ARE THE WINDOWS OF THE SOUL** ... there are some strange souls out there. In 1997 custom-designed soft contact lenses made zany irises the latest accessory. "It's a statement," said optometrist Richard Silver, designer of the cool orbs worn by Arnold Schwarzenegger in *Batman & Robin*. ("These make the Terminator look like a baby sitter," the star boasted.) And now for the bad news: the painted lenses were costly ($800 and up), had to be professionally prescribed and fitted, and were not readily available due to FDA restrictions.

MR. FREEZE: Penetrating peepers

W.H.A.T. (When Horrid Acronyms Thrive)

R**EMEMBER THOSE SIMPLE DAYS OF** yore, when abbreviations did not have to spell out some silly word? Think N.A.A.C.P., AT&T, TWA. Now, it seems, the name of every new organization is contorted to spell out an annoying acronym. A small sampling of 1997's worst monikers:

ACHE American Council for Headache Education

SAFETY Sun Awareness for Educating Today's Youth

CONVINCE Consortium of North American Veterinary Interactive New Concept Education

MUSE Medicated Urethral System for Erection

The Lis Have It

IMAGINE THE PHONE BOOKS! THE Xinhua news agency announced that the family name Li (the Chinese character is at right), which belongs to some 87 million Chinese mainlanders, including hard-line Premier Li Peng, has surpassed Zhang as the surname most widely used in the world.

李

THE DRAWING BOARD

THE HOUSE PASSED A BILL ALLOWING STATES TO **REPLACE** THE EAGLE ON THE BACKS OF QUARTERS WITH A DESIGN OF THEIR OWN...

IN ODDS WE TRUST — NEVADA

IN POT WE PUFF — CALIFORNIA

OUT GAYS WE MARRY — HAWAII

CONCEALED WEAPONS WE CARRY — TEXAS

ROSWELL OR BUST — NEW MEXICO

ROBERTS & SILERDER

COMING IN 1998: Corporate logos on change? Look for Nike nickels, Disney dimes—and hang on to those J.C. Pennies.

Time Is Uncle Sam's Money

The nonpartisan Tax Foundation reported that the average American spends almost two hours of each workday just to pay federal taxes. Here's how your day breaks down, based on where the money goes:

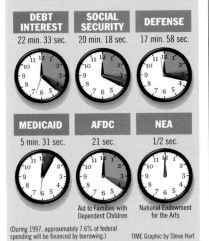

DEBT INTEREST	SOCIAL SECURITY	DEFENSE
22 min. 33 sec.	20 min. 18 sec.	17 min. 58 sec.

MEDICAID	AFDC	NEA
5 min. 31 sec.	21 sec.	1/2 sec.
	Aid to Families with Dependent Children	National Endowment for the Arts

(During 1997, approximately 7.6% of federal spending will be financed by borrowing.)

TIME Graphic by Steve Hart

What Was That Again?

HE'S THE NATION'S FIRST BABY BOOMER President, and in the fall Bill Clinton endured a boomer malady: he was fitted for hearing aids. Earlier in the year, Clinton injured his knee after tripping at golfer Greg Norman's home in Florida and had to use crutches for months.

DEAF EAR: The Prez needed aid

Mars Attack in Our Backyards

AFTER THE U.S. PATH-finder probe landed on Mars, Newt Gingrich remarked, "It's going to be a bummer if Mars turns out to be like us." A series of pictures—shot for far less expense than the eerie Martian landscapes transmitted by Pathfinder—show that any Martian who lands on Earth is going to feel very much at home, whether it's a bummer or not.

The surface of a leaf

Crumb cake

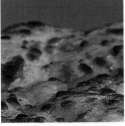

Rusted metal

Cantaloupe

Slice of pizza

STAMP ACT

MAIL CALL: The average American household receives 24 pieces of mail each week:

17 are advertisements

4 are bills & statements   3 are personal mail

Source: Arthur D. Little, Inc.

FED WEBS

YOUR TAX DOLLARS AT WORK—VIRTUALLY A close scrutiny of budgets revealed that 42 Federal Government agencies shelled out about $349 million to maintain 4,515 Websites and bulletin boards for fiscal years 1994-96. Uncle Sam's biggest spenders (in millions of bucks):

DEPT. OF DEFENSE	$147.8
NASA	$30.8
DEPT. OF COMMERCE	$30.8
EPA	$30.8
DEPT. OF AGRICULTURE	$30.8

WASHED UP

WHAT, NO BOTTLE OF BUD? A poll asked Gen Xers: If you were stranded on a desert island, what would you most like to have with you?

TV
Books
MY PARENTS
10%
15%
29%
21%
24%
A computer
Music

Due to rounding, numbers do not equal 100%
Source: BMG Entertainment TIME Graphic by S. Hart

Seinfeld Bows Out ... From Yada to Nada

CALL HIM THE GRINCH: DURING THE holidays Jerry Seinfeld announced that his long-running eponymous sitcom would end following the 1997-98 season. The news came half a year after Seinfeld's three supporting cast members, Julia Louis-Dreyfus (Elaine), Jason Alexander (George) and Michael Richards (the supremely nutty Kramer), had successfully lobbied for major pay increases, asking for $1 million per episode each—and settling for $600,000. With the artful use of a VCR and a calculator, TIME reckoned that, in a typical 30-minute show, the new pay scale awarded Louis-Dreyfus $1,863 and Richards $1,333—per word.

NUMBERS

100%: Increase in the amount of food imported into the U.S. since the 1980s

50%: Reduction in food inspections at the border since 1992

3: Number of serious outbreaks of diseases caused by uninspected imported food during 1997

- -

44% of college students are presumed to be binge drinkers

86% of college fraternity residents are presumed to be binge drinkers

- -

$125 million: Amount of the six-year contract signed by Kevin Garnett of the NBA's Minnesota Timberwolves, the richest contract in the history of professional sports

$36.5 million: Amount by which Garnett's contract exceeds the price paid for franchise in 1995, when Garnett was playing ball in high school

- -

8 years: Median age of a vehicle on the road in the U.S. (the oldest it has been since the 1950s)

$6,000: Increase in the average price of a new car over the past eight years

Sources: The New York *Times*, Associated Press, Minneapolis *Star-Tribune, American Demographics*

That's the Story of, That's the Glory of...

BIRDS DO IT, BEES DO IT, BUT THE FRENCH (*MAIS, BIEN SÛR!*), CLAIM they do it more often than anyone else. In a recent global survey of the frequency with which people have sex, the nation of Brigitte Bardot indeed led the amorous pack: the researchers found the French have intercourse an average of 151 times each year. Here is the list of how often the citizens of the world's top nations united:

FRANCE	151	CANADA	112
USA	148	AUSTRALIA	110
RUSSIA	135	ITALY	105
GERMANY	129	MEXICO	98
SOUTH AFRICA	117	SPAIN	90
POLAND	116	HONG KONG	77
BRITAIN	113	THAILAND	69

EMPTY NEST

WHAT DO (MARRIED) MEN WANT? Marriage has its ups and downs (the low point for both sexes is when kids are teens), but a 1997 study found a further discrepancy between male and female happiness: husbands are much less satisfied than wives before the kids arrive.

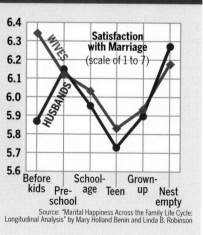

Satisfaction with Marriage (scale of 1 to 7)

WIVES

HUSBANDS

6.4 6.3 6.2 6.1 6.0 5.9 5.8 5.7 5.6

Before kids / Pre-school / School-age / Teen / Grown-up / Nest empty

Source: "Marital Happiness Across the Family Life Cycle: Longitudinal Analysis" by Mary Holland Benin and Linda B. Robinson

CALLING CARD

PAY PHONE OF THE FUTURE The idea of E-mail pay phones has been around for a decade; now telcos hope Net fever will finally make the idea go. If planners have their way, smart terminals (like the GTE at right) will replace pay phones everywhere. Cost, to check E-mail and surf the Web: 35¢ for a minute.

Say It With a :)

YOU CAN CHAT ONLINE UNTIL your fingers are raw, but you still can't convey the emotional subtlety of tête-à-tête conversation. That's why emoticons were invented: these sideways keyboard images are designed to punctuate online palaver with a fillip of feeling. Some have become well known: ;-) is a wink and a smile. But the art form has become increasingly complex—hence this signing dictionary:

:'-)	(I'm shedding a tear of joy)
:-X	(My lips are sealed)
:-0	(I'm shocked)
3;-}	(I'm giving you a devilish leer)
@}-->--	(Please accept this rose)
%*}	(I'm drunk)
-:(	(I have a Mohawk)
:-P	(I'm sticking my tongue out at you)
+0:-)	(Bless you—I'm the Pope)

A quick quiz. Translate the following conversation:

Boy : 3;-}	What happens after that is no- body's business but their own!
Girl : -P	
Boy : @}-->	
Girl: :'-)	

MORPHING BILL'S MOPTOP To make over the Microsoft maven, we scanned in his mug (above, right) pulled a few styles off *Cosmo's* hair palette and used the highlighter brush to add a goatee (be-low). Where do you want to go today, Bill? Gelled? Grunge? You decide.

Virtual Makeover: From Geek to Chic

THIS MAY NOT BE WHAT BILL GATES had in mind when he promised that computers would change the way we live, work and play. *Cosmopolitan* magazine's new Virtual Make-over CD-ROM ($39.99) may be geared to women looking for a quick, non-committal way to experiment with their hair and makeup, but it's being sold by Sega Soft as a coed toy. And once America's proto-geek sees what a good stylist can do to spruce up his look (those bangs! that pallor!), we're sure it will find a home on his hard drive. Next subject: Janet Reno.

RACE AND PERCEPTIONS

HANDICAPPING 2000 An early October TIME/CNN poll asked: If the presidential election were held today and you had to choose between Democrat Al Gore and Republican Colin Powell, for whom would you vote?

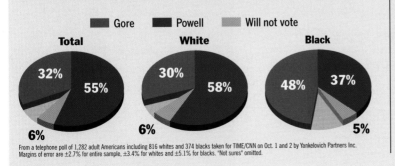

■ Gore ■ Powell ■ Will not vote

Total
32% 55% 6%

White
30% 58% 6%

Black
48% 37% 5%

From a telephone poll of 1,282 adult Americans including 816 whites and 374 blacks taken for TIME/CNN on Oct. 1 and 2 by Yankelovich Partners Inc. Margins of error are ±2.7% for entire sample, ±3.4% for whites and ±5.1% for blacks. "Not sures" omitted.

TROUBLES IN AMERICAN SOCIETY The second question: What do you think is the main problem facing the United States today?

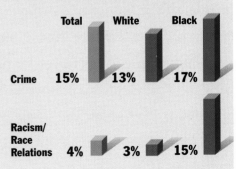

	Total	White	Black
Crime	15%	13%	17%
Racism/ Race Relations	4%	3%	15%

Johnny Chung's 49 White House visits showed how politics marries influence to affluence. Who will reform the system?

FOLLOW THE MONEY

BILL CLINTON'S RADIO broadcasts on Saturday mornings feel like messy family reunions. White House aides bring their kids and visiting in-laws over for happy snapshots with the President. No one wears a tie. For a few brief hours each week, the whole stuffy place feels more like a home than an office. So if six Chinese businessmen in dark suits standing near the back

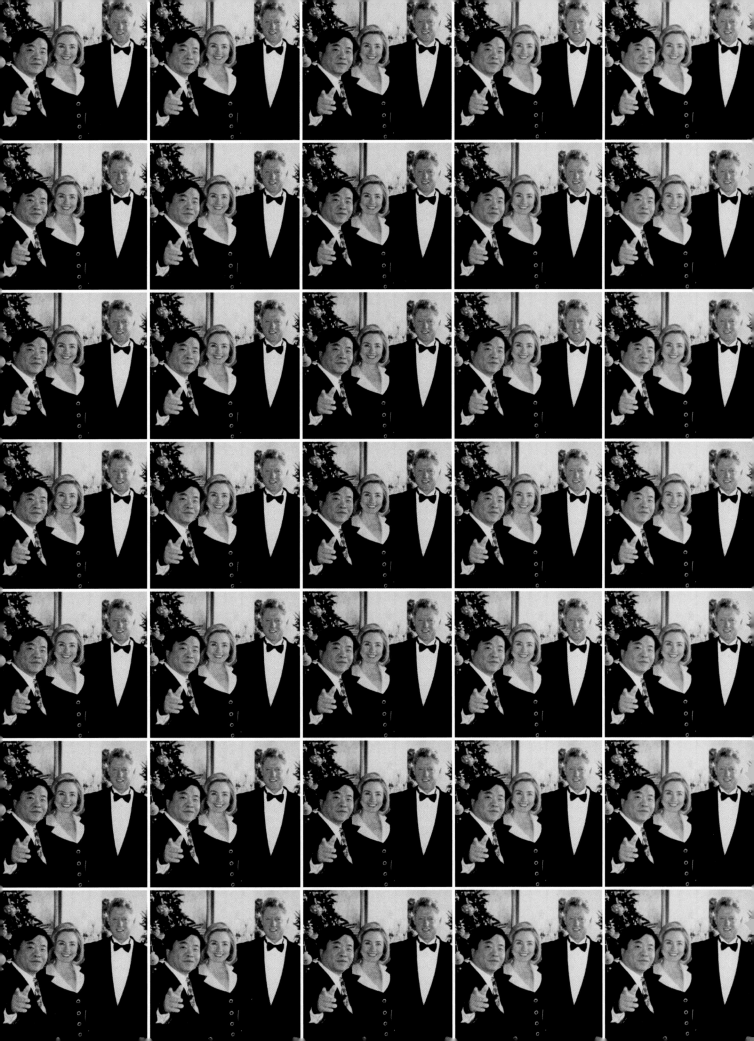

Al's Buddhist Pals

It was the most embarrassing moment of Vice President Al Gore's political career. At the Thompson hearings on illegal campaign practices, three shaven-headed Buddhist nuns, wrapped in nutmeg-colored robes and blanket immunity, recounted how they were badgered into laundering campaign money when Gore visited their temple in Southern California in April 1996.

The damage to Gore's presidential hopes may not come from the event itself, but from the shifting, legalistic and often contradictory versions of the occasion that he offered in his defense. Having built a reputation for rectitude and fastidiousness, Gore found himself pleading ignorance, naiveté and inattentiveness. For once, Dudley Do-Right seemed to have done wrong.

of the Oval Office looked a bit out of place on March 11, 1995, they were. Their admission had been bought and paid for. Johnny Chung, 42, a Taiwanese entrepreneur who had befriended Hillary Clinton during the 1992 election—and who dropped by the White House 49 times to visit the Clintons—paid $7,000 a head for his special friends to watch Clinton's eight-minute radio address.

The visit of Chung and his delegation from China was only one of the most blatant examples of a scandal that dominated headlines in 1997. "Donorgate" involved the alleged trading of access to America's top officials (of both political parties) in return for campaign contributions.

"Sometimes," President Clinton mused early in 1997, "there is a difference between what is legal and what ought to be done." And with that he offered a guided tour of Washington's favorite hideaway—the fertile, foggy valley that lies somewhere between what is wrong and what is illegal. Throughout the year, instance after instance that seemed to represent high-level influence peddling—and inquiry after inquiry that seemed prepared to prove it—disappeared into that foggy valley of uncertainty.

Republican Senator Fred Thompson of Tennessee chaired hearings he claimed would expose a Chinese government scheme to buy White House favors. They petered out in failure. Attorney General Janet Reno vowed to pursue every lead into questionable fund raising by the President and Vice President. Ultimately, she decided not to name an independent counsel to investigate the case. Republicans who denounced Democrats for illegalities turned out to be besmirched themselves. "Secret" White House videotapes that were expected to catch the President red-handed caught him glad-handing. And the McCain-Feingold bill, designed to clean up the messy process of fund-raising, died a tidy death in the Senate at the hands of majority leader Trent Lott.

By year's end, it was clear that America's system of raising campaign funds, which is based on reforms instituted after the Watergate scandals of the mid-1970s, was badly broken. But no one in Washington seemed prepared to fix it—especially when public opinion polls revealed that the issue was not a major priority for most Americans.

The most prominent inquiry to vanish into the valley was the Thompson committee hearings. They were touted as the congressional inquest of the decade, a journey deep into the addled soul of American politics. More FBI agents were onboard than tracked down John Dillinger. Enough big donors were under oath to fill a fund raiser. Even a man from Watergate was swinging the gavel (Thompson had served as chief Republican counsel during those hearings). It would be must-see TV: Big Fred Thompson and his Donorgate posse, bringing law 'n' order to the capital.

On the first day of the hearings, Thompson waved a large red flag in front of the TV cameras, charging he had information that the Chinese government was trying to subvert American democracy. The problem was, it was mostly classified, and he couldn't give any details. On the second day, the Republicans' lead witness was docile and

unresponsive. By the third day, so much time had been spent learning so little that CNN packed up its cameras, and there were empty seats in the spectators' gallery.

The hearings soon degenerated into party squabbling. When Thompson warned of Chinese influence peddling, ranking Democrat John Glenn raked over former G.O.P. chief Haley Barbour for funneling foreign money through his National Policy Forum. Majority whip Don Nickles hammered away about White House coffees as fund raisers; Dick Durbin, Democrat from Illinois, read a 1990 Nickles letter inviting Republican donors who pledged $1,000 to a reception at Vice President Dan Quayle's home.

THE EARLY PART OF THE HEARINGS FOCUSED ON the extent to which Asian contributors to the Democratic National Committee might have been rewarded by White House favors. But the evidence meant to show that foreign money had worked its way into Democratic coffers was circumstantial at best, and without further proof could be explained away as routine investment and consulting fees. And the key bankrollers of the alleged scheme were living in Asia, beyond the reach of subpoenas.

In the fall the Thompson committee turned its attention to Vice President Al Gore, examining his appearance at a fund-raising event at a Buddhist temple in Southern California [see box]. More ominous were new revelations about the dialing-for-dollars effort that Gore mounted from his White House office in 1995 and 1996, which was potentially a violation of an 1883 law that prohibits fund raising for political purposes on federal property. A smaller number of calls made by President Clinton also came under suspicion. Following the revelations, Attorney General Reno ordered a formal 30-day review to determine whether an outside investigation was warranted. A

90-day preliminary inquiry followed. On Dec. 2, Reno announced her decision not to name an independent counsel. But she swore that her conclusion—which was opposed by FBI Director Louis Freeh and denounced by Republicans— did not signal the end of her department's investigations into the campaign-finance scandals.

Behind the brouhaha over Donorgate lurked the issue of "hard money" and "soft money." Under the arcane laws of campaign finance, hard money refers to funds donated to individual candidates, and is restricted to $1,000 or less per donor. Soft money refers to money donated to the parties to fund general-election campaigns. Since these distinctions were put in place in the 1970s, both parties have managed to flout the intent of the laws by raising many millions of dollars in soft money, which party bosses then channel into individual campaigns.

The chief attempt to clean up the process of political fundraising through legislation was the McCain-Feingold bill. The act was sponsored by an unlikely pair of political bedfellows: conservative Republican Senator John McCain of Arizona and liberal Democratic Senator Russell Feingold of Wisconsin. But their bill posed a problem for Senate majority leader Lott, who didn't think a system in which Republicans raised $549 million in Campaign '96, at least 50% more than the Democrats, needed all that much reforming. In October, Lott saw to it that the McCain-Feingold bill—already heavily watered down from a failed 1996 version—met a swift death. The moral of the story: an America dazzled by a rampant bull market on Wall Street is prepared to tolerate a lot of bull out of Washington. ■

> **The Thompson hearings lost CNN, lost spectators and lost their way**

Sip with Bill, Sleep with Abe

The allegations that President Bill Clinton was selling access to the White House—even charging Democratic donors specific sums to spend the night in the Lincoln bedroom—first appeared during the 1996 election campaign. However dingy the process, Democrats correctly pointed out that Republican incumbents had also offered entrée to the White House in return for political cash.

In 1997 the issue of trading access for dollars heated up, as the Thompson hearings explored the presence of donors at the White House, including Johnny Chung's 49 visits, John Huang's frequent drop-bys and the series of coffees

with Clinton as host to reward fat-cat Democratic donors. After a typical stalling action by the Clintonites, the Thompson committee hoped it had struck pay dirt in October, when videotapes of the donor coffees taken for posterity were finally released to committee investigators.

But the content on the tapes failed to capture criminal minds at work. Watching them was a bit like sitting through *Groundhog Day*, the movie in which Bill Murray keeps repeating the same 24 hours of his life. In almost any segment, you see the President entering a room or in a receiving line. Now he charms, now he mixes, now he makes small talk ("Nice tie!"). He delivers some

cheerleaderish remarks and shakes every hand that looks capable of signing a check. Then comes another segment in which he does it all again. And then again. And again. Good to the last drop!

More than 100 hours of tape of the Panhandler in Chief were made public. Aside from the central question of what was illegal and what was just unseemly, the tapes proved that the most powerful nation on earth can operate on autopilot while its President chases campaign money. What they didn't appear to do is show whether the Democratic Party had a scheme to channel foreign cash into Campaign '96, and if so, whether Clinton was in on it.

WINGS OF DESIRE

When a star pilot crashes her career, sex in the military suddenly becomes a hot issue

THE MILITARY DEMANDS FROM ITS SOLDIERS an old-fashioned marriage: a vow to love, honor and obey. Love, expressed through sacrifice and hardship, to the point of risking your life and taking other people's lives in your hands. Honor, shown through every large and small token of respect: keep your hair short, press your shirt, shine your shoes, salute your superior. And above all, obedience without question, even to the rules that break your heart. It's a stern morality, a morality at odds with American culture, which exalts love first and then negotiates honor and obedience. In 1997, following the previous year's reports of sexual harassment in basic training at two army bases, a number of celebrated cases brought the conflicting codes of conduct into battle.

The case that attracted the most attention was that of First Lieut. Kelly Flinn, 26, an Air Force star who committed adultery, lied about it, disobeyed orders to stop and finally was discharged from the service. After graduating as most distinguished in her training class, Flinn became the Air Force "showgirl," as she put it, the first woman ever to pilot a B-52, which she flew from her post at Minot Air Force Base in North Dakota.

Flinn's troubles began with the arrival at Minot of Airman Gayla Zigo and her husband Marc, who was hired as the base youth-sports director. Soon after meeting in late June 1996, the star pilot and the charismatic Marc Zigo commenced an affair. "Less than a week after we arrived at the base," Gayla would later charge, "Lieut. Flinn was in bed with my husband, having sex." Flinn insists the relationship was not "consummated" until August.

After Gayla found one of Flinn's love letters to Marc in her husband's car, she took the letter to her supervisor, First Sgt. Kathleen Blackley. She included others, one of which had come with a key to Flinn's apartment attached. It was at this stage that Flinn was offered her first escape hatch. Blackley confronted Flinn with the evidence and warned her to halt the affair or Blackley would report it to Flinn's commanding officer. Air Force prosecutors later claimed

that Flinn had promised Blackley she would "cease contact" with Marc. Blackley decided to let the matter drop.

Had that been the last of it, the affair might have ended like most adultery cases: privately, discreetly, without official sanction. Of the 67 Air Force court-martial cases in 1996 that involved adultery, only one did not include other counts, such as sexual assault or disobeying orders. When an officer is involved in an adulterous affair with a civilian, officials tend to look the other way. If Marc and Gayla had been separated—as Marc had convinced Flinn they were—there would probably have been little intervention. But

once Gayla, an enlisted airman, told a superior that an officer was trying to steal her husband, the Air Force had to go on alert.

The affair boiled over in November, when another officer charged with sexual misconduct pointed a finger at Flinn, who made a pact with Zigo to deny their affair. She then gave base police several sworn statements that she and Zigo had never had a sexual relationship.

But Zigo didn't stick to the script. Instead, he gave investigators the full tour of Flinn's privacy, a map of where and how and how often they had had sex. Four days later, on Dec. 1, he tried to kill himself by taking sleeping pills and stuffing a rag in the exhaust of his car. But he left the garage door open and called Gayla from the car phone. In the hospital, he finally admitted the affair to her, and she announced that she was through with him. When Marc Zigo left the hospital, Flinn took him in. She bought a new car—the Jeep he'd always wanted. He was living in her house on Dec. 13 when Flinn's commander ordered her to cease any contact with him. Flinn signed a statement acknowledging she understood. One week later, she took Zigo to Georgia for Christmas to meet her parents.

It was not until the end of January that Flinn finally learned how much Marc had told the investigators. She also learned that he had lied about where and when he was born, his life, his career, practically everything. She threw Marc out of the house and found a lawyer. On Feb. 25, Flinn was ordered to stand trial at a court martial. She and her lawyers submitted a request to resign instead, on the condition that it be an honorable discharge.

Once the case became public, it was the Air Force and its rules that went on trial. Even though Flinn had been given several chances to extricate herself from the whole business, the case soon became one of sex discrimination in the service. Flinn launched a public relations blitz: her family made the rounds of TV talk shows "to convey our story" and opened a Website to solicit contributions for her legal-defense fund. Letters, phone calls and editorials were running heavily in Flinn's favor; politicians from both parties were blasting the Air Force brass for conducting a witch-hunt.

GROUNDED: First Lieut. Kelly Flinn broke the rules and lost her wings

But Air Force Secretary Sheila Widnall, 58, the first woman to hold the post, held firm. She refused to honor Flinn's request for an honorable discharge, and Flinn left the service in May with a general discharge, given in cases when "significant negative aspects of the member's conduct or performance of duty outweigh positive aspects of the member's military record."

NO SOONER HAD THE AIR FORCE COMPLETED ITS awkward ejection of Lieut. Flinn than allegations of wrongdoing by officials high and low began landing in the Pentagon's backyard. Army Major General John Longhouser, commanding general of Aberdeen Proving Ground, decided to retire after a telephone tipster told Army investigators of an affair Longhouser had had five years before. Army Brigadier General Stephen Xenakis was relieved of the command of all Army medical operations in the Southeast region in May because of an apparent "improper relationship" with a civilian nurse who was caring for his ill wife. In October Sergeant Major of the Army Gene McKinney, the Army's top enlisted soldier, was arraigned on 20 charges of assault, maltreatment and "soliciting adultery" following testimony in hearings from six women officers that McKinney had harassed them. The Army stripped him of his title.

The grim crusade reached the top military post in the land in June, when Defense Secretary William Cohen was rebuffed in his nomination of Air Force General Joseph Ralston to replace retiring General John Shalikashvili as head of the Joint Chiefs of Staff. Ralston withdrew when it was revealed that he had engaged in an adulterous relationship 13 years before. Secretary Cohen then came under fire for not prosecuting Ralston and allowing him to continue in uniform, but he noted that Ralston's affair had occurred while he was separated from his wife, from whom he was later divorced, and that his lover had not been a member of the armed forces.

The spate of cases encouraged civilians who like to meddle in the military's treatment of the

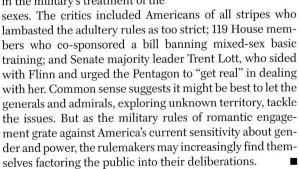

Six women officers testified Sergeant Major McKinney had harassed them

sexes. The critics included Americans of all stripes who lambasted the adultery rules as too strict; 119 House members who co-sponsored a bill banning mixed-sex basic training; and Senate majority leader Trent Lott, who sided with Flinn and urged the Pentagon to "get real" in dealing with her. Common sense suggests it might be best to let the generals and admirals, exploring unknown territory, tackle the issues. But as the military rules of romantic engagement grate against America's current sensitivity about gender and power, the rulemakers may increasingly find themselves factoring the public into their deliberations. ■

VITAL CENTER?
Al Gore is at
left, Gingrich is
on the right

Uncle Sam's Balancing Act

A strong economy—and party self-interest—finally put the U.S. budget in order

NOTHING MAKES POLITICIANS HAPPIER THAN MAKING people happy, especially when those politicians can say they've made history at the same time. And so on July 28 both political parties convened—separately, after a bipartisan Rose Garden photo op—to celebrate the passage of a long promised gift: a U.S. budget that was balanced for the first time in 30 years. Interns whooped on the White house lawn as President Bill Clinton basked in the ultimate triumph of his long march to the center, which almost none of the cheering Democrats behind him had backed. Down the street on the Capitol steps, G.O.P. lawmakers gathered around House Speaker Newt Gingrich and an elated Senate majority leader Trent Lott, who declared, "Today we celebrate the beginning of a new era of freedom." And his was about the most modest toast of the day.

Such are the blessings of a booming economy. In the year when the stock market landed on Mars and inflation became a fugitive, Washington embraced a new politics of abundance, enacting a five-year budget deal that gave away something to just about everyone. Republicans finally realized their cherished goal of cutting capital gains and estate taxes; in return Democrats got to spend more on education, more on cities, more on welfare, more on children's health—more in general.

The historic deal balanced the budget while it made the biggest tax cut in 16 years, managing both without bloodshed. It was left to sober economists to swat away all the confetti and note that the economy was going to reduce the deficit anyway, and that the big, important issues—like fix-

ing Social Security and Medicare—had all been tabled. In a rare moment in history when so much more was possible, the leaders did *only* what they had promised to do, and privately admitted it. Said a White House official: "They took care of their contributors. We took care of our voters."

The budget deal was the capstone legislation of a year that saw both parties in Washington declare war on themselves. The Republicans in the House fired the first salvos, as a batch of insurgents tried—and ignominiously failed—to oust Gingrich. Depending on whose story you believed, the anti-Gingrich schemers included one, two or all three of the other House leaders directly below the Speaker: majority leader Dick Armey of Texas, conference chairman John Boehner of Ohio and leadership chairman Bill Paxon of New York. But the leaders deserted the cause, and a weakened Gingrich stayed in office. Paxon, a trusted Gingrich lieutenant, was the only player who lost his position in the wake of the dustup, but the deep divisions the imbroglio exposed in the G.O.P. ranks would be a long time healing.

Not to be outdone, Democrats staged their own internecine war in the fall. Heeding a powerful lobbying effort by organized labor, a strong majority of Democrats rejected President Clinton's full-court press to approve his "fast track" authority to negotiate foreign trade deals. Emboldened Republicans piled on the President, who was immediately declared a lame duck. By November, the bipartisan effort that had passed the budget deal seemed a wistful memory in a capital whose intrigues and squabbles reminded one Republican of "a circular firing squad." ∎

All the World's Her Stage

New Secretary of State Madeleine Albright plays both good cop—and bad

THE FIVE U.S. ARMY BLACKHAWKS SWOOPED DOWN ON the Croatian village of Prevrsac, and out of one climbed U.S. Secretary of State Madeleine Albright. She had just given President Franjo Tudjman a public lecture in Zagreb for failing to live up to the peace accord that had ended the Yugoslav civil war 18 months earlier. In Prevrsac, standing in front of a burned-out Serb home, with cameras rolling, she dressed down one of Tudjman's ministers over Croatian attacks against returning refugees. "It's disgusting," Albright snapped. Secretaries of State usually make their protests to foreign leaders in private. She delivered hers with a two-by-four, watched by the whole world.

In her inaugural year as America's first woman Secretary of State, Albright confirmed her reputation as a person who confronted both issues and people head on— including some surprising news about her own heritage. Throughout her professional life, Albright had worn her biography like a brooch, a shiny tale of the daughter of a Czech diplomat who became a refugee— first from Adolf Hitler, then Joseph Stalin—and fell in love with America, the country that saved her. But she had had reason to suspect for some years that even she didn't know the whole story. During her Senate confirmation hearings, the Washington *Post* confirmed that her parents were not raised as Catholics, as she had been told growing up. They were born Jewish and converted. And her grandparents did not die of natural causes during the war. They died in the concentration camps.

"My mind-set is Munich," says Albright. "Most of my generation's was Vietnam." That orientation explained her willingness to confront bullies with force. In a meeting with Slobodan Milosevic in Belgrade, she began reciting a list of Serbian violations of the peace accord. Milosevic broke in with a patronizing smile: "Madame Secretary, you're not well informed." Albright, who had spent three years in Belgrade as a child, retorted, "Don't tell me I'm uninformed. I lived here." Milosevic's smile disappeared.

Albright didn't always play the bad cop; she was care-

MUNICH'S CHILD: Albright wears her history like a brooch

ful to cultivate those whose help she needed, from Russian Foreign Minister Yevgeni Primakov, who greets her with flowers when she flies to Moscow, to Senator Jesse Helms, the Foreign Relations Committee's curmudgeonly chairman. Visiting his home state of North Carolina, she spoke at Helms' alma mater and attended a birthday dinner for his wife. On the Air Force jet for her return to Washington, a bag of barbecue was waiting, courtesy of Helms.

The charm offensives pay dividends. With the barbecue came a promise from Helms not to block a Senate vote on a treaty banning chemical weapons. With the Russian flowers came Primakov's promise to drop an objection on NATO troop levels, which opened the way for Russia to agree to the alliance's expansion.

But she didn't win every battle. Even Albright wasn't tough enough to force Milosevic or Tudjman to surrender war criminals or allow hundreds of thousands of war refugees to return. And with a show of power rarely seen in the modern Senate, Jesse Helms easily blocked the White House nomination of Massachusetts Governor William Weld to be ambassador to Mexico.

Albright's first year on the job brought frustrations all around the world. The talks between Israel and Palestine broke down, and China ignored her calls to stop jailing dissidents. In her toughest test, she managed to conclude a deal with Iraq early in December that defused a serious crisis and put U.S. weapons inspectors back in the country. But critics claimed she had caved in to Saddam Hussein, trading concessions to resolve the crisis. Compared with her courtly predecessor, Warren Christopher, "she clearly has a sharper and more public style," Richard Haass, director of foreign policy studies at the Brookings Institution, told TIME. "But if this were a report card, at best you'd give her an incomplete." The final grade depends on results. ∎

> **Albright can talk tough to a Milosevic, then turn on the charm for a Jesse Helms**

NETWORK

In a bizarre suicide pact, 39 members of a UFO cult kill themselves—with kindness

PEOPLE WHO DECIDE TO COMMIT SUICIDE AS A group ought to begin with a master plan: proper burial outfits, packed suitcases, lists, farewell videotapes, even recipes for death. The members of the People's Temple cult who killed themselves in Guyana in 1978 provided a stark lesson in how not to do it: they left behind a ghastly jumble of bodies piled upon bodies. That mass suicide was a disorderly, ungracious way to meet your maker, a study not in serenity but in chaos.

This one was different. When 39 bodies were found on March 26, in a spacious Rancho Santa Fe, Calif., mansion, with the bougainvillaea in full bloom outside, they were laid out on their backs on bunk beds and mattresses, looking like so many laboratory specimens pinned neatly to a board. Each was dressed in black pants, flowing black shirt, spanking-new black Nikes. Their faces were hidden by purple shrouds, the color of Christian penance. Eyeglasses were neatly folded next to bodies, and all, conveniently, had identification papers for the authorities to find. The house was immaculate. It was as if, in preparing for their death, the members of the Heaven's Gate cult were heeding the words of the prophet Isaiah: "Set thine house in order; for thou shalt die, and not live."

But though the victims may have believed their bodies were merely irrelevant "containers," to be left behind when they were whisked away by extraterrestrials, the corpses were most certainly the real thing to the sheriff's deputies who first encountered them. The 21 women and 18 men, ranging in age from 26 to 72, were in varying stages of decomposition, and a putrid smell permeated the house. As the San Diego medical examiner reported, the cultists died in three groups: a first round of 15, then the next 15, then seven, all apparently by ingesting phenobarbital mixed with a bit of applesauce or pudding, kicked by a shot of vodka, then helped along by the asphyxiating effect of a plastic bag over the head. The final two men had only bags, no shrouds. Alone in the master bedroom was the master of the cult himself: Marshall Herff Applewhite, 65, a charismatic onetime music teacher from Texas who had been attracting followers to his bizarre spiritual potpourri of UFOs and religion since the early 1970s.

The cultists left far more than suicide notes—they left suicide press kits

The carefully choreographed mass suicide was made more astonishing by the rich trail of video and Internet information about the cult left behind by the victims. Do and Ti, or Bo and Peep, or the Two, as Applewhite and his former partner Bonnie Lu Trusdale Nettles were known, plucked bits of this and pieces of that doctrine like birds building a nest, intertwining New Age symbols and ancient belief systems. And for scores of spiritual seek-

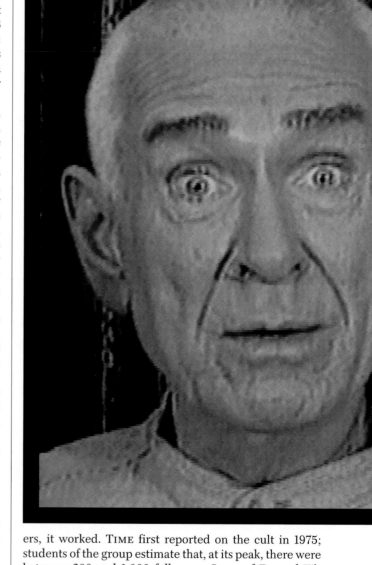

ers, it worked. TIME first reported on the cult in 1975; students of the group estimate that, at its peak, there were between 200 and 1,000 followers. Some of Do and Ti's followers had been with them as long as 20 years; they were rich and poor, black, white and Latino—people who shared little more than a willingness, or a need, to suspend disbelief, and in the end to come together in a common death.

The Heaven's Gate victims did more than leave suicide notes; they left suicide press kits. One of the first to receive the materials was a former cult member using the name Rio D'Angelo (police say he is really Richard Ford), who got a Federal Express package containing two videotapes, a letter and two computer discs. After watching the tape at home, he told his boss, Nick Matzorkis, at the Interact

OF DEATH

But on the tape it is hard to tell the victims apart: since each of them had close-cropped hair and unlined skin, police originally thought all the dead were young men. But shedding any signs of sexuality was integral to the cult, and six of the men, including Applewhite, had gone so far as to get castrated years before. By renouncing sex, drugs, alcohol, their birth names and all relationships with family and friends, disciples could become ready to ascend to space, shedding their containers to enter God's Kingdom.

THE GROUP ESTABLISHED A PRESence on the Internet through its glossy Heaven's Gate Website and energetic postings to various newsgroups. The Website proclaimed Applewhite's teachings, while a "Red Alert" message described the Hale-Bopp comet as the "marker" the cult members were waiting for, triggering the mass suicide. In this belief, at least, the Heaven's Gate cultists were not alone. According to a popular theory that circulated on the Internet, a spaceship was tucked away behind the comet—whether inhabited by benign or evil aliens was unclear.

The cult's work space in the Rancho Santa Fe mansion was decorated with posters of alien beings from *The X-Files* and *E.T.* Cult members paid $7,000 a month in cash for the 9,200-sq.-ft. house, complete with pool and tennis court, in the gated community of million-dollar homes. And although many locals knew their new neighbors were involved in some sort of religious activity, they did not investigate any further. The house was for sale, and prospective buyers, who were asked to remove their shoes and put on sterile surgical slippers before they traipsed through, described

MANSION OF MYSTERIES: Applewhite, left, had been preaching a gospel that combined UFOs and religion since the 1970s. In well-to-do Rancho Santa Fe, a walled enclave of some 2,500 homes, neighbors knew that the people who lived in the rented

Heaven's Gate mansion, top right, were members of a cult, but were impressed by their cleanliness and friendliness. The bodies, above—which the cult members regarded as "containers"—were thoughtfully prepared, with official papers at hand to speed their identification.

Entertainment Group in Beverly Hills, Calif., which had employed the cult's Web-page design service, that he believed the cult members had killed themselves. D'Angelo and Matzorkis drove to the house, and Rio went inside. When he came out, says Matzorkis, he was "white as a sheet." They notified the San Diego sheriff's office, whose deputies came in expecting a minor emergency at most and found themselves removing 39 corpses.

The cult members were not just unthreatening in life; they were mild in death. The farewell tape looks like a garden party of the apocalypse, with the California sun shining and the trees in the mansion's backyard blowing in a gentle breeze. The speakers talked as if they were anticipating a holiday, not a vodka-phenobarb cocktail of death.

seeing a lot of androgynous people hunched over computers. The tenants appeared to be odd but not dangerous.

Cult experts warned that the public should not be taken in by the cheerful departures, or by the notion that it was a small number of people exercising their own free will. "I don't consider it suicide. I consider it murder," said Janja Lalich, a cult expert who has been monitoring Heaven's Gate since 1994, when several distraught parents contacted her with their worries about their missing children. "[Applewhite] controlled it; he called the shots. These people were pawns in his personal fantasy." But Marshall Herff Applewhite died with his followers. And they seemed so happy to have gone with him. You can see that, over and over again—after all, the evidence is on videotape. ∎

TAGGED FOR

Gianni Versace, who sold the world rich dreams of opulence, falls victim to a fantasizing sociopath on a nationwide killing spree

WHEN GIANNI VERSACE walked down the street in Miami Beach, he walked through a world he had dreamed into being. Born to middle-class parents in the small port city of Reggio di Calabria in southern Italy, Versace came of age in the downtrodden years after World War II. But from these humble beginnings he rose to build a $1 billion global fashion empire, based on the breakthrough notion that there should be no barriers between the worlds of high culture and low. He finished his $20,000 couture gowns with accoutrements of denim and plastic, designed costumes for Milan's fabled La Scala opera house, outfitted the cast of *Miami Vice*.

It was Versace who helped fashion join Hollywood and sports among the great public spectacles of our time. And it was Versace who helped turn Miami Beach into a city of sexy sybarites, full of clubs and in-line skaters and muscle guys with deltoids like the gas tanks on a Harley. In the early 1990s, when the city was threadbare, Versace fell in love with it, and soon began converting a hotel and a crumbling apartment building into a comically scrumptious mansion, one of his four homes around the world. And where Versace went, comically scrumptious models and movie stars always seemed to follow.

Andrew Cunanan created dream worlds too. They just didn't work out. For years he had insinuated himself into

"NICE BOD": Cunanan flashes his style in his 1987 high school yearbook

MURDER

the lives of well-off, older gay men. An adroit and tireless liar, he told friends in San Diego he was Andrew DeSilva, a man with a factory in Mexico or with wealthy parents in the Philippines. In reality, Cunanan's father Modesto was a Philippine-born U.S. Navy veteran who later became a stockbroker. Andrew grew up in middle-class Rancho Bernardo, Calif., a San Diego suburb; in high school he was popular, openly gay and a little outrageous. Later his wealthy lovers gave the young bon vivant the money for his expensive clothes and the $1,000 restaurant tabs he would ring up with friends.

TRAIL'S END: Above, police at the cordoned-off murder scene, the steps just outside the villa's ornate wrought-iron gates. Right, eight days later, Cunanan would claim his final victim—himself.

But by April 1997, when he started a cross-country killing spree that claimed four victims before it climaxed in the fatal shooting of Versace, all Cunanan's worlds were collapsing. His last older rich guy—and his favorite young guy—had dropped him. He was gaining so much weight that few would give him a second look. And he may have learned he had the AIDS virus. His aggressively social personality had turned murderously sociopathic.

CUNANAN HAD TOLD FRIENDS THAT DAVID MADSON, 33, a Minneapolis, Minn., architect, was "the love of my life." But Cunanan appears to have thought Madson was involved with one of Cunanan's best friends, Jeffrey Trail, 28, a former Navy officer who had moved to Minnesota. On April 29, Trail's body was found in Madson's Minneapolis apartment, beaten to death with 25 to 30 furious blows from a claw hammer. Four days later, police found Madson's body dumped near a lake 50 miles away. He had been shot several times in the head and back with Golden Saber .40-cal. bullets.

In early May, Madson's missing red Jeep Cherokee was noticed collecting parking tickets near the home of Lee Miglin, 72, a millionaire Chicago developer. Days earlier, Miglin's body had been found in the garage of his home. His killer had stabbed him with pruning shears, sawed through his throat with a gardening saw and made off with his green 1994 Lexus. The car was found May 9 in rural Pennsville, N.J., near the body of William Reese, 45, a cemetery caretaker who had been shot in the head—again with a Golden Saber .40-cal. bullet. His red 1995 Chevrolet pickup was gone.

Just days after the New Jersey murder, on May 12, Cunanan apparently resurfaced in Miami Beach and began working his way into Versace's world. Later, reports would circulate that the two men had met years before at the opera in San Francisco, but no convincing proof of an earlier encounter between them ever emerged.

Versace lived on busy Ocean Drive, a 15-block strip of Art Deco hotels and sidewalk cafés facing the oceanfront. On Tuesday, July 15, the designer headed out around 8:30 a.m. for his regular morning walk to the News Cafe, four blocks from his home, to buy magazines and a coffee. On his return to the house, just as he was opening the ornate wrought-iron gate, Versace was suddenly approached by Cunanan.

Some witnesses reported seeing an ambush-style murder in which Cunanan pumped one bullet into Versace's head from behind, then another as he fell to the ground. Others said Versace first struggled briefly with his attacker. At the sound of the gunfire, Versace's longtime companion Antonio D'Amico rushed outside to find the designer face up on the pavement in a spreading pool of his own blood. He was pronounced dead at the hospital.

Pursued briefly by one witness, Cunanan ran to a public parking garage, got into the red pickup, changed clothes, then fled again on foot. Though the pickup now had stolen South Carolina plates, it was soon identified as the one that had been taken from the murdered William Reese. Inside it were Cunanan's passport, several belongings of Lee Miglin and a ticket stub soon traced to a shop where Cunanan had pawned one of Miglin's gold coins. Ballistics tests would later show that the gun that killed Versace had also killed two of the earlier victims.

Cunanan became the subject of an intense manhunt—yet he never got two miles beyond the crime scene. After leaving the pickup, he broke into a 25-ft. sailboat docked in Miami Beach. When its owner returned on July 16, Cunanan fled to an unoccupied two-story houseboat that had electric power but no water. Then, at 3:30 p.m. on July 23, caretaker Fernando Carreira and his wife came by to check on the boat. When they noticed that the wrong lock was secured, Carreira drew his gun. He then heard a shot, ran away and, while watching the door, had the police called. Quickly tear-gas-launching SWAT teams descended, and bullhorns brayed, "Andrew, come out; the whole world is watching!" But Cunanan had already claimed his last victim—himself. His body lay lifeless in the houseboat, the pistol by his groin. As for his face, one source said it still bore a resemblance to the photos in his wanted posters. ∎

Taken Before Their Time

A trio of killings—one still unresolved—belies America's dwindling crime rate

THE YEAR 1997 SAW A CONTINUING AND WELCOME REduction in the national rates of violent crime and murder. But the headlines of America's newspapers belied the good news, for the year was also marked by an unusual number of sensational deaths: the killing of Gianni Versace, the mass suicide of the Heaven's Gate cultists, the multiple murders in two Southern high schools, the deaths of college students due to binge drinking, the "nanny trial" in Massachusetts [see related stories]. In addition to those cases, three other murders brought homicide to the nation's attention:

JONBENET RAMSEY. Christmas season 1997 marked a sad anniversary in Boulder, Colo. On Dec. 26, 1996, six-year-old beauty queen JonBenet Ramsey was found dead in her parents' lavish home. The child had been beaten and strangled; her body was found by her father after her parents discovered a ransom note in the house. Yet after the passage of a year police had made no arrests in the case, and the inquiry had bogged down in a bitter rivalry between Boulder police chief Tom Koby and district attorney Alex Hunter.

JonBenet's father, John, was a wealthy businessman. Her mother, Patricia, herself a former beauty queen, had pushed JonBenet into the surreal world of underage beauty pageants when the girl was only four. Some observers believed one or both of the child's parents were involved in the crime. Yet the parents stonewalled police until May before consenting to be interrogated.

Many legal insiders—not all of them partisans of Hunter's—believe that, as one Boulder police source put it, "the case went down the toilet in the first five hours." From the beginning, it was clear that the cops who were called to investigate what was initially reported as a kidnapping had allowed contamination of evidence that might have been found at the crime scene. Detective Linda Arndt waited hours for a ransom call that never came before ordering a search of the house. She gave that order not to other cops but to John Ramsey, who found his daughter's body in a basement room and carried it upstairs—a complete violation of police procedure. Meanwhile, Arndt allowed Ramsey friends and neighbors to wander in and out; coroner John Meyer, arriving to examine the body, pushed through a crowd to enter the house. As the months went by with little new evidence, those initial blunders loomed larger than ever. "I'll be surprised if the Ramseys are ever charged," said Bob Miller, a former U.S. Attorney in Denver.

ENNIS COSBY. On Skirball Center Drive in Los Angeles, just off the freeway ramp, the body sprawled next to the Mercedes-Benz convertible might have been just another victim of random murder and robbery. But when a shocking identification was made, America shuddered.

The body on the roadside was Ennis William Cosby, 27, the only son of beloved comedian Bill Cosby. Ennis had been shot while trying to change a flat tire. "He was my hero," said a grieving Cosby, referring to his son's battle with dyslexia as a student and his decision to become a teacher of children with learning disabilities. In March L.A. police arrested Mikail Markhasev, 18, a Ukranian immigrant, and charged him with the murder. Police believed that the killing was the result of an unplanned attempt to steal Cosby's $130,000 Mercedes that went fatally awry.

JONATHAN LEVIN. The predominantly black and Latino students at Taft High School in New York City's tough South Bronx revered Jonathan Levin, 31, a gifted teacher of English. Few of them knew that Levin was a scion of one of America's most powerful media titans, Time Warner chairman Gerald Levin. The young teacher was found dead in his apartment; a few days later, New York City police arrested Corey Arthur, 19, a former student of Levin's, and charged him with the murder, claiming he had tortured Levin with a knife to obtain the password to his automated teller card. The killer had raided the account after the murder. The price of Levin's life: $800. ∎

JON BENET: After a year, no answers—but many questions

> Early bungling by the police is the reason JonBenet's killer hasn't been nabbed

Death Sentence for McVeigh

Just over two years after the bombing of a federal office building in Oklahoma City killed 168 people, a jury found Timothy McVeigh, 29, guilty of the deed after a five-week trial in Denver. Despite pleas for mercy from McVeigh's parents, the jury unanimously sentenced the U.S. Army veteran to death. Appeals will probably delay McVeigh's execution for many years. In the second trial in the case, federal prosecutors argued to a different Denver jury that Terry

ACCOMPLICE? Nichols is escorted into court

Nichols, 42, who first met McVeigh in the Army, was an accomplice in the bombing. But in a blow for prosecutors, late in the year the jury found Nichols guilty of involuntary manslaughter and conspiracy—but not guilty of taking part in the bombing itself.

When Drinking Turns Deadly

Senseless deaths set off a round of soul searching about binge drinking on U.S. college campuses. In August, Benjamin Wynne, 20, died of alcohol poisoning after a fraternity drinking party at Louisiana State University, and three of his fraternity brothers were hospitalized. An autopsy showed that Wynne, who had downed the equivalent of about 24 drinks, had a blood-alcohol level six times the amount at which the state considers a person intoxicated. Excessive drinking was blamed for at least six college student deaths in the 1995-96 school year. Binge drinking was every school's problem: in a survey

PAYBACK Richard Jewell, the FBI's mistaken suspect in the bombing of a park at the 1996 Olympic Games in Atlanta, savored his revenge. Jewell sued an Atlanta paper and garnered an apology from Attorney General Janet Reno, cash settlements from CNN and NBC—and a clarification from TIME. But don't speed in Georgia: Jewell is now a cop in Luthersville.

BAD BEEF After the U.S. Department of Agriculture traced some 15 cases of food poisoning to a meat processing plant in Nebraska, its owners, Hudson Foods, recalled 25 million lbs. of possibly tainted beef, the biggest meat recall ever.

SPOILED? Hudson Foods closed the faulty plant

of 18,000 Harvard undergrads, 44% said they had engaged in binge drinking—four to five drinks in a row—in the past two weeks.

When Bad Guys Wear Badges

New York City had been celebrating a steep drop in crime rates—until Aug. 9, when Haitian immigrant Abner Louima, 30, was arrested mistakenly after a fight in a Brooklyn night club. Louima claimed New York police department officers beat him in their car on the way to the precinct house,

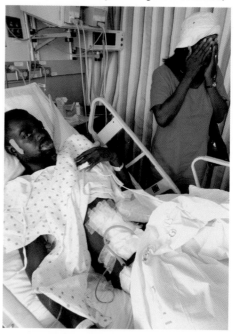

VICTIM: Louima, with his wife, in the hospital

where another shoved a wooden pole into his rectum. Louima said an officer then forced the stick into his mouth, breaking his front teeth. The charges against Louima were dropped. Officer Justin Volpe, 25, was arrested and charged with aggravated sexual abuse and first-degree sexual assault; three other officers were arrested, and 12 more were punished less severely.

Color Blind—or Just Blind?

School enrollments reflected the decline of affirmative action. After the Supreme Court let stand an appeals court's 1996 ruling in favor of four white students who sued the University of Texas law school for racial discrimination, the number of entering Hispanics dropped from more than 50 to 14. In California, where color-blind Proposition 209 passed in 1996, law schools at both Berkeley and UCLA saw black admissions drop 80%, while the numbers of Hispanic students fell 50% and 32%, respectively.

Horror in the High Schools

In a pair of killing sprees, two teenagers toted guns into high schools in the South and a total of five students were murdered. **MISSISSIPPI.** In tiny Pearl, Luke Woodham, 16, bookish and overweight, opened fire with a 30-.30, wounding seven schoolmates and killing two, Lydia Kaye Dew, 17, and Christina Menefee, 16, a girl he once dated. Three hours earlier he had stabbed his mother to death with a butcher knife. Six friends of Woodham's were later held

WOODHAM: Was there an occult connection?

on murder-conspiracy charges, amid town rumors of secret cults and Satanism. **KENTUCKY.** In West Paducah, Michael Carneal, a good student and the son of a prominent lawyer, opened fire on an informal prayer service, killing three students and wounding five with a .22 Ruger before a preacher's son persuaded him to disarm.

HIGH-WATER MARK The Grand Forks, Neb., Yellow Pages lists 143 churches and only three psychiatrists, and it would take all 146 of them to explain how a place with so much faith could lose a turn-of-the-century downtown to nearly biblical disaster while the Wal-Mart on the edge of town stayed high and dry. A 500-year flood of the Red River forced the evacuation of 50,000 residents of Grand Forks and sparked fires that destroyed half the historic business district. Plucky townspeople vowed they would rebuild.

JONES: A strong "no" to a cash settlement

Paula Jones vs. Bill Clinton

Lighting the fuse for a trial that promised to dominate headlines in 1998, the Supreme Court decided 9 to 0 that a sitting President has no immunity against civil suits involving his nonofficial actions, and so a trial of Jones' allegations of sexual harassment by Clinton when he was Governor of Arkansas need not be delayed until Clinton's term as President has ended. Jones, a former Arkansas state employee, accuses Clinton of making a crude sexual advance in 1991, when he was Governor of the state. A federal judge set the trial date for May 1998. Meanwhile, after an attempt to reach a monetary settlement broke down, lawyers Joseph Cammarata and Gilbert Davis, who had represented Jones for three years, quit the case, citing "fundamental differences" with their client. Jones hired a new lawyer, Donovan Campbell, and vowed to pursue her case.

GRAND FORKS: Buildings drenched, spirit unquenched

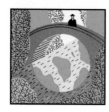

Millions around the world join grieving Britons when Diana, Princess of Wales, is killed in a car crash and buried at her family home

DEATH OF A DREAM

Her final ceremonial progression through the streets of London raised haunting memories of her first, on a brilliant morning 16 summers before. That was when a watching world fell in love with the beautiful young princess, her royal new husband by her side, being borne in a carriage toward an enchanted future. Her return journey carried her, alone, moment by moment, step by cadenced step, inexorably into the past.

In one sense, though, Diana, Princess of Wales, was not gone. The day before she was buried, her former mother-in-law, Queen Elizabeth II, made a rare, hastily arranged televised statement putting, after days of puzzling silence, the royal seal on the pain that so many people had already registered so sharply: "No one who knew Diana will ever forget her," the Queen said, looking directly into the camera lens. "Millions of others who never met her, but felt they knew her, will remember her."

Princess Diana's death was one of those large events that happen in an instant, like the explosion of the space shuttle *Challenger*, leaving everyone to grope for explanations of how a world of certainties can be undone so quickly. Everywhere that Diana's name was known, which is most places on earth, people were trying to comprehend the events that led to her death and wishing they could reach back somehow to change them.

Diana died in a car crash with her new beau, Dodi Fayed, the 41-year-old heir to a great Egyptian fortune, in an auto tunnel by Paris' Place de l'Alma on the Left Bank of the Seine. Eyewitnesses reported seeing a black Mercedes with silver trim enter the tunnel at high speed at around 12:30 a.m., feverishly pursued by a swarm of paparazzi on motorcycles and scooters, then hearing an explosion. Just inside the 660-ft. tunnel, the car struck the concrete divider that separates the eastbound lanes from the westbound and then cartwheeled, rolling over a full 360 degrees and spinning around nearly 180 degrees.

The car's roof was crushed, its windshield smashed and its air bags deployed. The chauffeur, Henri Paul, 41, an employee of the Hotel Ritz, which is owned by the Fayed family, was killed instantly. He was found slumped over the wheel, the weight of his body pressing the ruined car's horn. In front of the wreck, witnesses saw a paparazzo—the last Diana paparazzo—raise his camera and begin to snap. It took only minutes for the Paris police to arrive, cordoning off the area with red-and-white crime-scene tape and leaving the lights of their cruisers flashing as they rushed into the tunnel. The officers broke into two groups: one headed straight for the wrecked car; the other fanned out to nab the photographers, who at the time were believed to have caused the accident. Five of them were quickly arrested and led out in manacles. In all, nine paparazzi and a photo-agency motorcycle driver would eventually be placed under investigation by the French police, not only for perhaps helping cause the wreck, but also for failing to assist the injured accident victims, a felony under French law.

> "Millions who never met her, but felt they knew her, will remember her."

In the tunnel, the scene was grim. It was clear that the chauffeur, Paul, and Fayed, both sitting on the car's left side, were beyond help. But both Princess Diana and the bodyguard, Trevor Rees-Jones, 29, who were sitting on the vehicle's right, appeared to be clinging to life. The rescue team cut through the buckled roof and doors of the Mercedes, removed the two survivors and rushed them by ambulance to a public hospital, the Pitié-Salpêtrière, one of the best in the city. Diana was suffering from extensive chest injuries, a massive wound to the left lung and numerous broken bones. Doctors struggled to stabilize her, eventually opening her chest and applying direct massage to her heart for two hours. But the loss of blood and the system-wide trauma proved too much for Diana. At 4 a.m. Paris time, doctors declared the princess dead.

DIANA'S FAMILY—AND MUCH OF THE WORLD—was outraged at the paparazzi's behavior. Diana's only brother, Charles, the current Earl Spencer, bitterly declared, "I always believed the press would kill her in the end. Not even I could imagine that they would take such a direct hand in it, as seems to be the case." But he may have rushed to judgment: police lab tests later showed that Paul was taking Prozac and had nearly four times the legal limit of alcohol in his blood, the equivalent of nine shots of whiskey.

Bodyguard Rees-Jones survived, but he suffered from amnesia concerning the moments before the crash and could not assist the inquiry into its causes. The French police investigation soon focused on finding a small dark-colored Fiat Uno, which several witnesses described as being in front of the Mercedes as the two cars entered the tunnel. Pieces of an Uno were found inside the tunnel, and police believed the Mercedes may have sideswiped the smaller car before swerving into the support pillar.

Unlike Diana's brother, her former in-laws kept a regal silence. Members of the royal family, including Queen Elizabeth and Prince Charles, vacationing with his sons—her sons—William and Harry at Balmoral Castle, were notified by phone. None made any public statement at first, until the pressure of public opinion led to the Queen's unusual televised remarks the day before the funeral.

Actually, for several weeks before the crash, Britain's first family had been maintaining a studied silence on the topic of Diana. Almost a year to the day after a final divorce decree ended her arid marriage to Prince Charles, the princess had exploded back onto the pages of the tabloids, on the arm—and in the arms—of the wealthy

The courtship began correctly enough in mid-July, when the senior Al Fayed invited the princess and her two sons to vacation with his family at his villa in St.-Tropez. It may or may not have been mentioned that the younger Fayed would be there as well, but it was clearly understood. Tabloid reporters began scenting a story when they learned that Diana and her children would be spending a holiday at the home of the elder Al Fayed, a man sniffed at by the British élite. Rumors flew of an engagement to be announced in August. The week after the St.-Tropez jaunt, Diana joined the younger Fayed at Paris' Hotel Ritz, then spent a five-day vacation aboard his family yacht in the Mediterranean. Photographers again tagged along, hurrying home with fuzzy photos of the princess and her maybe beau rather unremarkably kissing. One tabloid boasted that it had paid $200,000 for those pictures—a bounty that may have driven the celebrity hunters wild.

For most royal watchers on both sides of the Atlantic, such a public and unapologetic courtship was sign enough that Diana was finally putting her palace past behind her. Only a week before her death, in an interview with the French newspaper *Le Monde*, she had said forthrightly, "Any sane person would have left [Britain] long ago."

But how could she truly leave when, for the previous 16 years, she had in a sense embodied Britain, proving that despite the demise of its empire, the country was capable of youth and vigor and charm. After generations of imported brides, she was the first Englishwoman to marry an heir to the throne in more than 300 years.

The world had watched as Charles and Diana cooed and wed. In Diana the House of Windsor found a new star—

Fayed. The photographs were the purest paparazzi stuff—grainy images furtively snapped through telephoto lenses the size of bazookas. The story they told, however, was unmistakable. After years of smiling bravely and brittlely by the side of a man she was no longer in love with, the princess just may have found one she did love.

Diana Spencer and Dodi Fayed had been indirectly linked even before they were romantically linked, mostly as a result of a long-standing friendship between their fathers, the late Lord Spencer and the wealthy Mohamed al Fayed. The children of these men met 10 years ago, when the younger Fayed and Prince Charles played on opposing polo teams. It would not be until the summer of 1997, however—after a brief, bad marriage for Fayed and a long, bad one for Diana—that the two would be free to see each other socially.

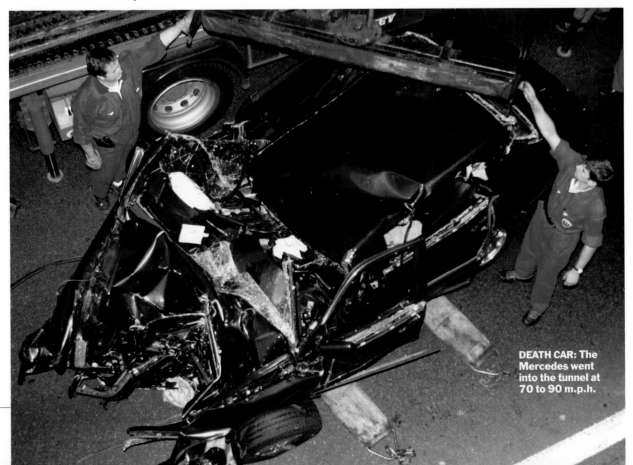

DEATH CAR: The Mercedes went into the tunnel at 70 to 90 m.p.h.

with a warm smile and soulful eyes—and the public obsession with the princess who would be Queen began. But in Diana's case, public and private lives collided with the grit of soap opera—for that was indeed what she had married into, a very grim fairy tale that had come true. When she walked down the aisle of St. Paul's Cathedral on July 29, 1981, to take the hand of her prince, there was no inkling of a doomed denouement. The bells that pealed in celebration drowned out any fears of future trouble; Britain and the world beyond it rejoiced. Here indeed was a union to gladden hearts.

"Irreconcilable differences" was the catchall phrase used in the divorce petition that finally brought the fantasy to a finish, after years of ugly rumors and backbiting, of private phone calls captured on tape, of infidelity on both sides. But the chasm between Prince Charles and Diana Spencer should have been clear from the start. Looking back, it seems impossible that the shy 20-year-old in the sumptuous dress could somehow have seen a future with the dutiful, tweed-clad monarch-in-waiting.

Despite the divorce, the war of the Windsors was expected to go on. After all, Diana was the mother of the heir to the heir. And when her son William became King, how could she not wield influence as the unofficial Queen Mother? For all Diana's honest enthusiasm for her charitable causes, the latest of which was a ban on the use of land mines, many saw her highly publicized good works as a weapon in her ongoing battle with the royal family for the affections of the public.

But on the morning of Aug. 31, Britons woke to find their nation's future irrevocably altered and their darling dead, stolen away during the night by an inexplicable fate.

As Elton John began to sing "Goodbye, England's rose," Prince Harry wept

New Prime Minister Tony Blair seemed to be close to tears as he declared, "She was the people's princess, and that is how she will stay in our hearts and memories forever."

Princess Diana's final public appearance proved his point. More than 1 million people lined the route of her funeral procession through central London; 2,000 mourners who had been invited to attend her funeral service filled Westminster Abbey. Tens of thousands more gathered along roadsides to say farewell as her coffin was driven roughly 70 miles northwest of London to Althorp, her family's ancestral home, where she would be buried. And across the globe, hundreds of millions gathered around television sets to watch the services.

On the way to the abbey, Diana's cortege was joined by five of the men in her life: her ex-husband and her former father-in-law, Prince Charles and Prince Philip; her broth-

er Charles, Earl Spencer; and her two sons, Prince William, 15, and Prince Harry, who would turn 13 only a few days later. They walked behind her coffin, followed by five representatives from each of the 110 charities with which Diana had been associated. The route was lined with flowers: London was awash with floral tributes, and dealers reported there were no more blooms to be found in the city. Outside Westminster Abbey, spectators quietly applauded the celebrities they spotted, among them Hillary Clinton, Steven Spielberg and Luciano Pavarotti.

The service was memorable for two moments of high drama. First, pop star Elton John sang *Candle in the Wind*, a song he had originally written to celebrate Marilyn Monroe, with the lyrics revised to honor his friend Diana. When John began to sing the words "Goodbye, England's rose," Prince Harry, who like his brother had kept his composure while walking behind their mother's coffin, buried his face in his hands and sobbed.

THEN DIANA'S BROTHER CHARLES DELIVERED a remarkably pointed tribute. He described his sister as "someone with a natural nobility who was classless, who proved in the last year that she needed no royal title to continue to generate her particular brand of magic." The statement seemed to refer directly to Queen Elizabeth, sitting nearby, who had seen to it that the appellation Her Royal Highness was taken from Diana when she was divorced from Prince Charles. When Earl Spencer concluded, applause could be heard outside the abbey. Those inside at the rear then began clapping, and the tide of approval swept forward toward Diana's coffin.

Services in Westminster Abbey are not supposed to generate applause. But then so many of the events following Diana's death seemed unprecedented. At one point Tony Blair said, "It is something more profound than anything I can remember in the totality of my life." Many people might disagree with that sentiment, but few could doubt that something remarkable was going on. Men were swayed by Diana's poise and beauty, but her hold on women was stronger still. Little girls are still taught to dream that someday their prince will come and take them away to the castle. Grown women, no matter how bruised by reality, remember those romantic dreams.

Diana lived them. Her prince really came. She grew famous beyond measure, bore two healthy sons and acquired a regal platform for her generous heart. She translated her own pain not into bitterness and withdrawal but into a desire to acknowledge and comfort the suffering of others. She could have done far worse with her fortune and acquired fame.

But then she and her prince went their separate ways, and her story grew more fascinating still. Diana alone became a work in progress, an inspiration to every woman anywhere who faced the trauma and challenge of sudden independence. Even those—men and women—who did not follow her every zig and zag over the past few years found themselves weeping at her funeral. We have some sense of what she was, but we will never know what she might have become. ■

The Irreplaceable DIANA

Charles, Earl Spencer recalls his sister in a moving eulogy

I STAND BEFORE YOU TODAY THE REPRESENTATIVE of a family in grief, in a country in mourning, before a world in shock. We are all united, not only in our desire to pay our respects to Diana but rather in our need to do so. For such was Diana's extraordinary appeal that the tens of millions of people taking part in this service all over the world via television and radio, who never actually met her, feel that they too lost someone close to them in the early hours of Sunday morning. It is a more remarkable tribute to Diana than I can ever hope to offer her today.

Diana was the very essence of compassion, of duty, of style, of beauty. All over the world she was a symbol of selfless humanity, a standard-bearer for the rights of the truly downtrodden, a very British girl who transcended nationality, someone with a natural nobility who was classless and who proved in the last year that she needed no royal title to generate her particular brand of magic.

Today is our chance to say thank you for the way you brightened our lives, even though God granted you but half a life.

Today is our chance to say thank you for the way you brightened our lives, even though God granted you but half a life. We will all feel cheated always that you were taken from us so young, and yet we must learn to be grateful that you came along at all. Only now that you are gone do we truly appreciate what we are now without, and we want you to know that life without you is very, very difficult …

There is a temptation to rush to canonize your memory. There is no need to do so; you stand tall enough as a human being of unique qualities not to need to be seen as a saint. Indeed, to sanctify your memory would be to miss out on the very core of your being—your mischievous sense of humor, with a laugh

I stand before you in a country in

today the representative of a family in grief, mourning, before a world in shock...
—*Charles, Earl Spencer*

A girl given the name of the ancient goddess of hunting was, in the end, the most hunted person of the modern age …

For all the status, the glamour, the applause, Diana remained throughout a very insecure person at heart …

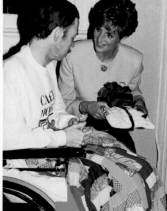

Diana was the very essence of compassion, of duty … she was a symbol of selfless humanity …

that bent you double, your joy for life transmitted wherever you took your smile, and the sparkle in those unforgettable eyes, your boundless energy which you could barely contain.

But your greatest gift was your intuition, and it was a gift you used wisely. This is what underpinned all your other wonderful attributes ... Without your God-given sensitivity we would be immersed in greater ignorance of the anguish of AIDS and HIV sufferers, the plight of the homeless, the isolation of lepers, the random destruction of land mines.

Diana explained to me once that it was her innermost feelings of suffering that made it possible for her to connect with her constituency of the rejected ... For all the status, the glamour, the applause, Diana remained throughout a very insecure person at heart, almost childlike in her desire to do good for others so she could release herself from deep feelings of unworthiness ... The world sensed this part of her character and cherished her for her vulnerability whilst admiring her for her honesty ...

I cherish the days I spent with her in March when she came to visit me and my children in my home in South Africa ... Fundamentally, she hadn't changed at all from the big sister who mothered me as a baby, fought with me at school and endured those long train journeys between our parents' homes with me at weekends. It is a tribute to her levelheadedness and strength that, despite the most bizarre life imaginable after her childhood, she remained intact, true to herself ...

I don't think she ever understood why her genuinely good intentions were sneered at by the media, why there appeared to be a permanent quest on their behalf to bring her down ... Of all the greatest ironies about Diana, perhaps the greatest was this: A girl given the name of the ancient goddess of hunting was, in the end, the most hunted person of the modern age ...

I pledge that we, your blood family, will do all we can to continue the imaginative and loving way in which you were steering these two exceptional young men so that their souls are not simply immersed by duty and tradition, but can sing openly, as you planned. William and Harry, we all care desperately for you today ... How great your suffering is, we cannot even imagine.

I would like to end by thanking God for ... taking Diana at her most beautiful and radiant, and when she had joy in her private life. Above all, we give thanks for the life of a woman I am so proud to be able to call my sister—the unique, the complex, the extraordinary and irreplaceable Diana, whose beauty, both internal and external, will never be extinguished from our minds. ∎

She hadn't changed at all from the big sister who mothered me as a baby, fought with me at school ...

[Her] beauty ... will never be extinguished from our minds.

TWO WHO WOULD BE KING

After Diana's death, Prince Charles and Prince William must reinvent the monarchy

D READFUL IRONY AS IT MAY BE, the untimely death of Princess Diana could become a moment of opportunity for the besieged House of Windsor. It may encourage the Windsors to take charge of the revolution in the British royal family that Diana, "the people's princess," pioneered. The monarchy will probably survive—it has, after all, endured wars and divorces, beheadings and exile. But in the wake of Diana's death, the House of Windsor must settle back down on its foundation quite differently.

If the monarchy is to survive and thrive in the new millennium, it will be because it has listened to its subjects and responded, not with mere tactical concessions—a waiving of protocol here, a letting slip of the mask there—but with the courage to think and act strategically. The Prince of Wales, who once said the realization that he was heir to the throne hit him as a "ghastly, inexorable sense," must lead the way. Britons want evidence that the chilly Charles is the right man for the job—the job not only of King but also of father to his two young sons, Prince William, 15, and Prince Harry, who marked a sad 13th birthday the week after his mother's funeral.

The trick for Charles will be to help his sons do what his ex-wife did so naturally: "walk with Kings—nor lose the common touch," as Kipling put it. Publicly, at least, Diana was the more ostentatiously devoted parent, and the boys, fair-haired and already casually handsome, appeared to take after her. With their father they hunted, fished and rode, while with their mother they jetted to the Caribbean or to theme parks, and shouting with laughter rode together down water slides. Diana insisted they make forays into the real world outside the confines of Kensington Palace, and took them along on visits to some of those less fortunate, even to a homeless shelter in the middle of the night. "I want them to have an understanding of people's emo-

LIKE FATHER, LIKE SON? The kilt-clad Prince Charles is a traditionalist, while Harry and William take after Diana

tions, of people's insecurities, of people's distress, of their hopes and dreams," she said.

That common touch is what the homely Charles—formal in attire and stiff of bearing—has sometimes comically seemed to lack. But royal insiders dismiss reports of Charles as a cold and distant father. For the heir to an ancient throne, he has been a fairly modern dad. He was present at the birth of both children; he changed their diapers and bathed them; and he would delay early-evening meetings to be with William and Harry before bedtime.

Charles and Diana may not always have seen eye to eye on the style of their sons' upbringing, but they agreed on the substance. Diana believed in the monarchy; she just wanted a warmer, sleeker, prettier version—much like herself. And Charles shared her desire to give the boys a less spartan education than his own gloomy days at Gourdonstoun in Scotland. The couple settled easily on the choice of Eton for Prince William—Diana's father and brother had attended the school. Eton offered something for everyone: tradition, discipline, discretion—and convenient proximity to the steadying influence of the Queen, just up the road at Windsor Castle.

Without their mother, of course, there is good reason to worry about what will become of the young princes. William, initially so bubbly and mischievous he was dubbed "His Naughtiness," has plainly hit adolescence, towering above his father, and is considered the sensitive one, a "deep thinker," as Diana called him. During his parents' separation and divorce, William took on the role of his mother's protector, reportedly slipping tissues under her door when he heard her crying. He is said to have suggested the charity auction of her frocks in June of 1997. Now it is Harry who is the impish one. To get a chance to mature a bit more, he will repeat a year at Ludgrove, the boarding school his older brother attended, before probably joining William at Eton.

There has been talk of installing the popular William after the death of the Queen—which may not be for decades, given that the Queen Mum is 97. But the one thing Charles will not do, according to people who study these matters, is step aside. He has spent his life waiting to be King. Even if he wanted to turn the throne over to William, the choice of succession is not his to make. Parliament would have to agree to allow Charles to leave, then pick a new King, and that could throw the entire idea of monarchy open to official, and perhaps fatally rancorous, debate.

> **Charles must prove he is up to the job of being King — and father to the princes**

This is a risk Charles—and his people—may not wish to take. Outsiders may regard the monarchy as a gilded anachronism, the mere guardian of a glorified theme park offering more pomp than circumstance. But that ignores the monarchy's role as part of the warp and woof of the fabric of British life. Opinion polls may show that the monarchy's popularity waxes and wanes, but there is no evidence that the country has turned decisively against its Queen or her heir. In death, Diana may have taught them both how to survive. ∎

Days of Hope and Glory

Goodbye, Tories! Tony Blair's revamped Labour Party sweeps to a landslide

RIGHT UP TO THE END, TONY BLAIR KNEW THAT IT WAS his election to lose. His reborn Labour Party remained consistently so far ahead in opinion surveys that the 44-year-old standard-bearer refused to risk the lead through complacency. "It's not over until it is over," he kept saying, when pestered to predict victory. Then he would head off to another constituency, more hand shaking and rallies in which he pounded away at the theme "Britain deserves better." The afternoon before election day, Blair and his wife Cherie campaigned in the marketplace of Stockton in England's northeast. Just across from a travel agency named Going Places, Blair called for a return of "the decent British values missing from this country for so long." The next morning the couple strolled in glorious spring sunshine to cast their ballots. Said Blair: "Now it is in the lap of the gods."

He could not know what breathtaking fortunes were in store. By the close of polling stations at 10 p.m. on May 1, the Conservatives of Prime Minister John Major began to get an inkling of why May Day is used as a distress signal. Across Britain, Blair's "new Labour" was wiping the Tories off the map, ending nearly a generation of governance in a resounding rout. From Scotland and Wales to England's major cities and chic suburbs, Labour was rolling up win after win, gaining even supposedly safe Tory seats and knocking down senior Conservative Cabinet ministers like ninepins.

Ordinary Britons were in a mood to throw the rascals out. The Tories were viewed as an arrogant collection of striped suits who had lost touch with the people. Sex and corruption scandals had hit one Tory M.P. after another, and Major's spotless reputation could not cancel out the blows. Even the fact that the British economy was purring along like a Bentley seemed to encourage voters to gamble on Labourites: After all, what harm could they do?

Tony Blair is Britain's youngest leader since the days of Jane Austen

The results left Blair's own faithful, partying in London's Royal Festival Hall, practically speechless with wonder. Labour won 419 of the House of Commons' 659 seats, the party's most impressive triumph in its history. The great political fighting machine of Margaret Thatcher, an establishment that thought of itself as the natural ruling party, held just 165 seats and 31% of the vote, the lowest share since the Duke of Wellington was trounced by the Whigs in 1832. And taking Major's place was the youngest Prime Minister since Lord Liverpool in 1812. Derided at times as "Tony Bland," the architect of Labour's towering new majority was now a man who could do no wrong.

After flying to London aboard "Blair Force One," Blair arrived at the Royal Festival Hall as daybreak was lighting Big Ben and the dome of St. Paul's to the east. "A new dawn has broken, has it not?" he told the gathered party faithful. The Oxford-educated barrister then entered 10 Downing Street to receive a thick briefing book from the Cabinet Secretary and to see how well the famed premise's cramped quarters might accommodate his barrister wife Cherie and their three children: Euan, 13, Nicholas, 11, and Kathryn, 9.

In renouncing Labour's old Marxist faith in nationalized industry and statism, Blair stressed continuity with Tory economic policies: boosting private enterprise and keeping within current tax and spending limits, though with altered budgetary priorities. "Don't expect things to change overnight," he cautioned. But they did. On the first working day of Labour's initial week in office, new Chancellor of the Exchequer Gordon Brown announced that the government was relinquishing its power to determine the base interest rates set by the Bank of England, Britain's central bank. The move, which brought Britain into line with other industrialized nations such as Germany and the U.S., was startling and bold—and warmly welcomed by the financial markets in the City of London. For at least one brief shining moment, the new dawn Tony Blair had promised Britain seemed anything but false. ■

NEW DIGS: Moving day for Blair and wife Cherie

NEW FISH TO FRY: Open-heart surgery in November 1996 restored Yeltsin's vigorous spirit—but how long can he stay healthy?

Holy Mackerel! Boris Is Back

Russia's boss rebounds from a long illness. But can he heal his ailing nation?

SINCE THE DECLINE AND FALL OF THE SOVIET EMPIRE in the early 1990s, Russia has become known as the sick man of Europe. According to a study released in 1997, the description is not simply a political metaphor; it is a scientific fact. The grim news report was delivered to Boris Yeltsin by a Presidential Commission on Women, the Family and Demography, a blue-ribbon panel of top government officials, academics and other luminaries. In 1997, the commission announced, official life expectancy in Russia—59 years for men and a little over 73 for women—slipped behind Europe, the U.S. and all of Asia, except Afghanistan and Cambodia.

Behind the statistics is the story of a country in turmoil. Once placid and dull, Russia has become an astonishingly sick and violent place. The murder rate is three times that in the U.S., and diseases virtually eradicated in most developed societies—tuberculosis, dysentery, pneumonia—are again ravaging Russian lives. The traditional scourge, alcohol, continues to take its massive toll. And with the opening of borders a new epidemic has entered Russia: AIDS.

Fittingly, the recipient of the study was himself a very sick man as the year began. Yeltsin lay in a Moscow hospital, recuperating from open-heart surgery and a battle with pneumonia that set in after the operation. In the first few months of the year, Russia's government—politically designed to place maximum power in the hands of the President—was barely functioning. But proving once again his surprising resiliency, Yeltsin not only recuperated from his surgery but also returned with newfound vigor. In May he fired two high-ranking military officials, Defense Minister Igor Rodionov, 60, a former army general, and General Viktor Samsonov, chief of the General Staff. The firings signaled that, after several years of apathy and illness, Yeltsin was back in charge. Even his renewed personal health, however, wasn't enough to spare Yeltsin the humiliation of having to accept the expansion of NATO into Poland, Hungary and the Czech Republic. The two sides went eyeball to eyeball at negotiating sessions in Moscow in May, and the Bear could only blink. NATO ceded nothing of substance to Russia to gain Yeltsin's assent.

At least Russians had something to celebrate in August, when Moscow Mayor Yuri Luzhkov staged a glittering international gala to mark the 850th anniversary of Moscow's founding. But in the fall Yeltsin's government was rocked by a fresh corruption scandal, as Anatoli B. Chubais, 42, the reformer charged with reshaping Russia's financial health, came under heavy fire for accepting a $90,000 book contract from a publishing house owned by a bank that had benefited from his privatization program. Yeltsin relieved Chubais of his duties as Finance Minister but left him in charge of the economy.

In December Yeltsin "rested" for 10 or 12 days in a sanatorium; he had a cold, Kremlin officials insisted. But the Kremlin has a credibility problem when it comes to Yeltsin's health—and the sick man of Europe will never recover with an unhealthy leader at the helm. ∎

Britain returns Hong Kong to China, transforming capitalism's outpost in Asia

RELINQUISHING A TERRITORY AND BIDDING farewell to 6.4 million imperial subjects in the dead of night is a disquieting scenario. Except perhaps in incandescent Hong Kong, where midnights, far from being dark, have a quality of brilliant luminesence—and never so much as the midnight of June 30, when Hong Kong ended 155 years of British rule and became the crown jewel of the People's Republic of China. High-rise buildings were wallpapered with extra neon; dragons soared, dolphins leaped and one skyscraper bore a rendering of those ultimate Hong Kong symbols: skyscrapers. Few apartment windows failed to display a tell-tale flicker of the televised ceremony at which the Union Jack was lowered by somber British troops just before midnight, the Chinese flag went up moments later, and Prince Charles, heir to the British throne, shook hands diplomatically and very briefly with a triumphant, beaming Jiang Zemin, President of China.

In Britain's prouder times the event might have taken place on a blazing field or a significant hilltop, with blowing bugles and firm jaws. Instead, Hong Kong was handed up in an air-conditioned convention hall with inky rain cascading outside. ("The tears of the British as their tyranny and colonialism in China come to an end," according to a report aired on Chinese TV.) Midnight was the official moment sovereignty changed hands, but beyond legalities there was an appropriateness to the night timing, the rain, the stiff ceremony and the opaque attitudes of the common folk on the streets, hurrying home with take-out food in seeming obliviousness to the epochal events occurring only blocks away.

The British touted their triumph in building Hong Kong into capitalism's nerve center in Asia and one of the most prosperous localities in the world; the Chinese emphasized their victory in reuniting a sundered motherland. But for the man in the rain-slicked street, it was a chancy and possibly precarious instant in time. After the ceremony, several generations of certainties sailed away with Prince Charles and outgoing Governor Chris Patten on the *Britannia*, Queen Elizabeth's massive, aging yacht. And a future drenched with imponderables crossed the border and entered the territory along with more than 4,000 troops of the People's Liberation Army, all young and iron-visaged.

True, there were splendid British fireworks before the handover and an even bigger pro-China extravaganza the

Once back in Beijing, Jiang Zemin zeroed in on his next target: Taiwan

LOST COLONY

ROCKETS' RED GLARE: British rule built Hong Kong into the sky. Will China turn out the lights?

following night. (Exponentially more was spent on the latter show, which sputtered out with alarming inauspiciousness when a fireworks barge caught fire in the harbor.) Families rented out living-rooms-with-views for celebratory parties, and at one $320-a-ticket ballroom soiree the guests and even the waiters changed from western to Chinese costumes at midnight.

Yet the chasm between Hong Kong and Beijing was evident on July 1. The cultural program for the morning swearing-in ceremonies had all the energetic cosmopolitanism of its Hong Kong hosts, including the world's hottest CantoPop stars, a symphony from a mainland composer who lives in New York and a soundtrack glitzy enough for Hollywood. Jiang Zemin himself, the first Chinese leader ever to set foot on Hong Kong Island, was consolingly statesmanlike during his visit, calling for "a new chapter in the annals of relations between China and Britain." But by that evening, when Jiang returned to Beijing, he was in a mood to party, joining nearly 100,000 people in Tiananmen Square to celebrate the "reunification." It was the largest crowd in the square since the 1989 pro-democracy student demonstrations, and, as a precaution, students in the capital were strongly encouraged to remain on campuses lest they get carried away.

Later Jiang addressed a crowd at Workers Stadium in a scene more akin to a propaganda production. Some 18,000 performers acted out the historical humiliations of China as well as its salvation under the guiding hand of the Communist Party. Jiang told the boisterous assemblage that the people of Hong Kong had "waged a heroic struggle against foreign aggression." Clearly in an expansive mood, Jiang then moved on to Beijing's next target. Taiwan, he said, should "take concrete steps toward ... complete reunification of the country."

Call it "one country, two rhetorics," but that was precisely the type of anomaly that made Hong Kong's epochal moment worthy of commemoration. Many Chinese residents expressed satisfaction that their home was becoming part of China again. "Hong Kong will take off like a rocket now," predicted a jubilant K.C. Tang, mayor of a village along the Chinese border. "On the one hand I am proud, on the other I am worried," said Lam Sui Por, who fled China in 1962 and has worked in Hong Kong for three decades as a vegetable hawker and factory worker. "Hong Kong has been very good. I've had freedom every day."

MANY IN HONG KONG TOOK THE EVENT WITH A characteristic blend of caution and eagerness. On Day One of Chinese rule, 31% of the people polled by the Social Science Research Center of the University of Hong Kong said they were positive about the handover, while only 5% described themselves as worried. An inscrutable 58% said they had "no special feeling." In Shek Kong, one of the border towns where troops entered China's newest territory, storefronts were festooned with the new Hong Kong flag. In conversation, however, the stores' owners conceded that they had serious qualms about their future. So why display the flag? Answered one merchant: "Insurance."

The question hanging in Hong Kong's muggy air was whether the future would offer the same kind of freedom— to protest, to cruise the Internet or to play tennis on a historic evening rather than attending an official rally at a workers stadium—and there were efforts during handover week to avoid an early, harsh answer. Democratic Party leader Martin Lee was allowed to address a crowd from the balcony of the Legislative Council, the body China had dissolved an hour earlier, at midnight. "We shall return!"

OUT WITH THE OLD, IN WITH THE NEW
Eight years after some 5,000 protesters were killed in Tiananmen Square, two youngsters, above, celebrate the reunification. At right, dragons dance while Hong Kong bids farewell to Britain's Union Jack—and Prince Charles

Yankee Noodle Dandy

Tourist Jiang happily talks trade—but avoids Tibet and Tiananmen

President Jiang Zemin, 71, a portly former mayor and party boss of Shanghai, has been a national figure in China only since 1989, when Deng Xiaoping called him to Beijing in the wake of the Tiananmen Square massacre. In his first years in power, he was dismissed as a lightweight and a weather vane who moved with the political winds; in fact, he has shown a lot of political savvy over time. With Deng's help, Jiang took on key party posts and went on to build a network beholden to him. He cemented his power over the party at a critical meeting in October, shortly before his state visit to America.

In the U.S. Jiang mugged for the cameras, donning a tricorn hat in Williamsburg, Va. At the White House, Jiang got a stiff lecture from Bill Clinton on human rights, but China's boss stood by his nation's actions, as he did to persistent questioners in a later appearance at Harvard. All told, Jiang got what he wanted: a 21-gun salute, a state dinner—and a historic, wide-ranging trade pact.

he vowed. Three activists demanded entry to the official handover ceremony to deliver a letter to Chinese Premier Li Peng. Police refused but did not arrest them, and they departed prosaically in a Hong Kong taxi—a cab-ride beamed around the world by drama-hungry journalists.

By autumn the mantra in the former colony remained "nothing has changed." The political system had been rejiggered, disenfranchising tens of thousands of formerly eligible voters. But Beijing was still handling Hong Kong with a relatively light hand. "It's business as usual," the city's new Chief Executive Tung Chee-hwa declared on his September visit to the U.S., and Jiang Zemin echoed the sentiment as he barnstormed through America in October.

In subtler ways, however, business—and much else—was already changing in Hong Kong. The sense Hong Kong people once had that the territory was sharply distinct from the mainland was fading. With Beijing ruling the former colony, the border itself was no longer such a dividing line. From motorists escaping Hong Kong's crowded streets for mainland highways to workers seeking to improve their lives, everyone was looking northward. "We are losing our enclave mentality," said Victor Fung, chairman of the Hong Kong Trade Development Council.

The burgeoning contacts weren't limited to business ties. They include building homes for Hong Kong retirees in southern China, welcoming academics from the mainland, and seeking mainland support for cultural and environmental projects on both sides of the border. Tung was already making plans for an ambitious network of roads and rails to link the territory's new airport and expanded container port with China's booming Pearl River delta.

The mainland offers that most precious of commodities for Hong Kong: room to grow. In colonial times, when the administration needed additional land, it had little choice but to fill in the territory's fabled harbor, at great commercial and aesthetic cost. Now planners were focusing on how to move Hong Kong-owned factories deeper into neighboring Guangdong province, where Hong Kong businessmen already employed millions of workers. And plans were moving forward to demilitarize the border.

China had rolled back some of the political reforms of the last days of British rule, but it had not undone everything: its prominent military headquarters still bore the unlikely name Prince of Wales Building. More important, though the new government had quickly introduced controversial controls on citizens' rights to stage protest marches after the handover, protesters calling for the release of mainland dissidents were able to assemble outside the Convention Center on Oct. 1, as Hong Kong officially celebrated Chinese National Day for the first time. For the present, Hong Kong remained a tale of two cities: one with a fabled past, the other with an uncertain future. ∎

THE LAST EMPEROR

Deng Xiaoping survived civil war, the Red Guards— and Mao—to rule China

THE BOY WAS VERY SMALL, BUT THE VILLAGE elders remembered him distinctly because his family was descended from a mandarin who had left the village and risen to serve the Emperor in faraway Beijing—the most famous citizen of the humble settlement of Paifangcun until, well, until the very small boy came along. But by 1904, when Deng Xiaoping was born, the great Chinese Empire of his celebrated forefather was moribund, preyed upon by the very foreigners it despised.

Young Deng was remembered for another reason: he liked to turn somersaults. He would roll out of his family compound, onto footpaths and into the countryside, turning and turning and turning. And his life would be one of many somersaults: away from home, over the seas, into politics, into war, in and out of power and, at last, into the role of Emperor of a China once again strong and swaggering.

In 1920, at age 16, Deng left his rural home in Sichuan for the port of Shanghai. There he learned basic French and won a scholarship for a work-study program in France. "We felt that China was weak, and we wanted her to be strong," he later said of his generation. "So we went to the West to learn." Deng spent most of the next five years working at various menial jobs: arms-factory worker, waiter, train conductor and rubber-overshoe assembler. As a member of the proletariat, he was exposed to communism, the doctrine spreading among French industrial laborers and the Chinese students among them.

In 1922 Deng joined the Communist Youth League; he earned his credentials in Moscow, where he studied Marxist-Leninist thought in 1926. Then it was back to a strife-torn China to propagate the faith. He was ordered to the backcountry of Guangxi province in the far south, where he met up with Mao Zedong. From 1931 to 1935, as the two worked to establish a Red Army base in the south-central province of Jiangxi, a mutual affection ripened that was almost brotherly. When Mao was denounced and demoted by pro-Russian elements of the party as an "es-

THE FRENCH CONNECTION: Deng, here at age 20, left impoverished China for France, where he found both work—and communism

capist" for advocating a hit-and-run campaign of attrition, Deng was ousted along with him. Subjected to psychologically brutal criticism sessions, Deng said just enough to save his life, and he soon rejoined Mao. Amid the purge, Deng's second wife (little is known of his first) divorced him and married his chief accuser.

The fortunes of Mao and Deng changed after October 1934, when the Red Army of Jiangxi joined the arduous Long March, threading through the hinterland to the caves of Yan'an in northwestern Shaanxi province a year and 7,500 miles later. The retreat cost the lives of more than 90,000 troops, but the Communists' spirit and self-sacrifice made heroes of them. Mao's guerrilla strategy had by then made him the movement's unchallenged leader.

In Yan'an, Deng met and married his third wife Zhuo Lin, and a family of three daughters and two sons followed. But the civil war, which was soon subsumed into the bloody conflict with invading Japanese forces, provided little time for family, and certainly no time for home. After Japan's defeat in 1945, Deng played an instrumental role in the rebels' victory in 1949.

Deng rose rapidly in the People's Republic; by 1956 he was General Secretary of the Communist Party and one of Mao's 12 Deputy Premiers. But in the next few years a devastating man-made catastrophe would strain the comradeship between Mao and Deng and wound the nation almost mortally. Perhaps 40 million Chinese died as a result of Mao's Great Leap Forward, the failed campaign he launched in 1958 to revolutionize Chinese industry. The Leap's unscientific agricultural practices and inane technologies turned China into an immense archipelago of unproductive communes racked by famine.

"It doesn't matter whether the cat is black or white, as long as it catches mice."

BY 1961 PEOPLE WERE STARVING BY THE MILLIONS, and the state was on the verge of collapse. Deng collaborated with President Liu Shaoqi's economic reforms, declaring, "It doesn't matter whether the cat is black or white, as long as it catches mice." It was his way of arguing that any method could be tried as long as it meant the people could eat. The words would later be used against him.

Mao ultimately made a strategic retreat and allowed Liu and Deng to restore order and the food supply, but he never forgave them for showing him up. His revenge came in 1966 with the Great Proletarian Cultural Revolution. With big-character placards crying BOMBARD THE HEAD-QUARTERS!, revolutionaries attuned to Mao—led by his fanatically leftist wife Jiang Qing—took over the party and ousted Liu and Deng. By August 1967, with China in tumult, the two outcasts were put on public trial. Though he was branded a "capitalist roader" and a "traitor," Deng was not put to death, because Mao recalled with some affection their old adventures together. Deng and his wife were sent back to the old revolutionary base of Jiangxi, where they were required to work at the tractor factory.

Deng's moment came in 1973, when the Chinese army had to intervene to stop the revolution and save the nation. The military trusted Deng's pragmatism, so Mao recalled him. Though still outside the party's inner circles, Deng resumed his post of Deputy Premier and helped develop Premier Zhou Enlai's Four Modernizations, the reforms that launched China's growth.

Mao died in September 1976, and within a month Deng's chief enemies, Jiang Qing and her radical Gang of Four, were put under arrest. Deng staged his third and last comeback the next year. He easily outmaneuvered Mao's official heir, the ineffective Hua Guofeng, and eased the Maoists out of power.

Now Deng launched his own revolution. He allowed millions of peasants to cultivate private plots, sell surplus crops and invest in village factories. Soon not only were China's peasants adequately fed, but also more than a few were able to build houses and fill them with TV sets, refrigerators and clothes washers. By the late 1980s, however, economic liberalization had spilled uncontrollably into political yearnings; labor unrest and student demonstrations for greater freedom panicked Deng. In April 1989 students launched protracted protests in Beijing's Tiananmen Square. In the early-morning hours of June 4, Deng called in the army, and the protesters were crushed. At least 5,000 Chinese citizens were brutally killed.

Deng's conservative rivals took advantage of the massacre to pull back the economic reforms—or at least slow their pace. But Deng, though increasingly frail, fought back. In February 1992 he led high officials on a tour of Shenzhen and Zhuhai, his prosperous economic centers, and urged Chinese to "seize the opportunity" of such free-market examples. The result was an explosion of economic growth and the elevation of "Deng Xiaoping Thought" to gospel, an ironic turn for a man who shuddered at "cults of personality." But it was the final somersault he had to perform to ensure the survival of his legacy. ■

No Partnership, No Peace

Suicide bombs rock Israel, and an end to strife in the Mideast remains elusive

WHEN YIGAL AMIR, A RIGHT-WING ISRAELI ZEALOT, took aim at Yitzhak Rabin at an outdoor rally in Tel Aviv in 1995, he was not simply drawing a bead on the prime mover of the Mideast peace process: he was aiming to stop the process itself. As 1997 brought one crisis after another to the region—suicide bombings, bungled assassinations, deadly raids, corruption in government—it seemed Amir may have succeeded in both goals. Rabin was dead. And the peace process, if not entirely dead, was moribund. The men charged with carrying it forward, Israeli Prime Minister Benjamin Netanyahu and Palestinian Authority head Yasser Arafat, were so distrustful, so hamstrung by extremist constituents, that they could not bear to talk to each other, much less carry on negotiations in good faith.

Palestinians were enraged and frustrated by Netanyahu's hard-line stands on carrying out provisions of the 1993 peace agreement and by his decision to approve the building of a new Jewish settlement in traditionally Arab East Jerusalem. Netanyahu in turn was stiffened by Arafat's failure to cooperate with Israeli agents in monitoring and arresting Islamic extremists— or at least to silence the rhetoric of violence that lent legitimacy to their acts.

MORE BLOOD: A March bombing killed three in Tel Aviv

Chief among the radical Islamist groups was Hamas. On July 30 two Hamas suicide bombers struck in Jerusalem's main food market. After each bomber detonated a device, 13 Israelis were killed and more than 170 were wounded. It was the worst terror strike since Netanyahu came to office 13 months before, when he had vowed he could deliver progress toward peace together with the security Israelis crave.

In September Hamas struck again, launching the 20th suicide attack since the peace accord was signed. This time there were three bombers; they targeted the Ben Yehuda promenade in the heart of West Jerusalem, where crowds shop at a pedestrian mall and sip drinks at outdoor cafés. The attack killed four Israelis and wounded almost 200 more. And it succeeded in its larger goal: making U.S. Secretary of State Madeleine Albright's first visit to the Mideast, which followed a few days later, entirely unproductive.

Netanyahu fought another major enemy throughout the year: himself. In the spring his government barely survived a sordid influence-peddling scandal that almost saw the Prime Minister indicted on criminal charges. The day after the second Hamas bombing, Israel lost 11 élite commando fighters and a military doctor in a failed raid into southern Lebanon whose objective remains unclear. It was Israel's worst one-time loss in the 12 years it has maintained a five-mile-wide "security zone" in southern Lebanon, supposedly to protect Israel's northern border from attack. Two Lebanese civilians died, and six Lebanese militiamen and two soldiers were wounded in the raid.

One month later, the Israelis botched a more delicate special operation. Two agents of Mossad, the Israeli spy agency, attempted to assassinate Khaled Meshal, the political chief of Hamas, in Jordan's capital city, Amman. Acting apparently in retaliation for the two bombings, the two Israeli agents contaminated Meshal with a deadly chemical substance. But they were nabbed, and Meshal survived.

The bungled hit almost severed relations between Israel and Jordan, the Jewish state's friendliest neighbor. The U.S. was angered by Israel's foray just as Washington was delicately trying to restart negotiations with the Palestinians. Moreover, to repair the damage they had caused, the Israelis were compelled not only to provide an antidote to save the life of the man they had meant to kill but also to release from one of their prisons Sheik Ahmed Yassin, the founder and spiritual leader of Hamas. Once again Netanyahu had fallen short of his pledge to provide Israelis with an answer to Hamas' terrorism. And once again the enemies of the peace process—on both sides—appeared to have the upper hand in the Mideast. ∎

> A bungled assassination attempt frays relations between Israel and Jordan

Saddam Acts Up Again

Iraq's dictator ejects U.S. weapons inspectors and strains the alliance of his foes

SADDAM HUSSEIN IS LIKE A PUNCHING BAG. NO MATTER how many times you hit him, he just keeps coming back in your face. In the fall, the Iraqi strongman was in the face of both the U.S. and the U.N., expelling American weapons inspectors from Iraq, threatening to shoot down U-2 surveillance planes and daring the world to do something about it—and thus precipitating the gravest international crisis of Bill Clinton's presidency. Though Clinton and his foreign policy team hung tough and forced the Iraqi dictator to back down, Saddam succeeded in exposing the fault lines that now strain the unusual coalition of allies that had opposed him in the Gulf War in 1991.

Though caught off guard by the crisis, Clinton was resolute in dealing with it. He kept his public comments pointed but brief while lining up unanimous support for a U.N. Security Council resolution condemning Iraq. He then turned to the harder task of enlisting allied support for military action. With the exception of Britain, America's key Gulf War allies—notably France, Russia and Egypt—all opposed the use of force this time around.

France and Russia had argued for a year that because Iraq had made progress toward eliminating its arsenals of missiles and chemical weapons (though not its biological stores), it should receive some kind of carrot—a partial lifting of economic sanctions—to go with all the sticks. Both countries would reap financial windfalls from such a decision. America's Arab allies in the Mideast were already voicing their disappointment at the U.S. failure to push Israel into serious peace negotiations with the Palestinians; the fractious, anti-American sentiment was building.

Undeterred by this lack of support, Clinton assembled a formidable armada in the Persian Gulf: the aircraft carriers *Nimitz* and *George Washington* (which hurriedly moved in from the Mediterranean), backed by more than a dozen cruisers, destroyers, guided-missile frigates and attack subs capable of delivering

100 strike planes and 600 cruise and air-to-air missiles. Saddam countered with a human armada: as the specter of a U.S. attack rose, obedient if bewildered Iraqis streamed into Saddam's presidential palace to act as human shields against bombing.

But with the world poised at the brink of war, Saddam blinked. On Nov. 20 he agreed to a Russian-led diplomatic effort, which began when Clinton telephoned President Boris Yeltsin to give him the green light to find a way out of the crisis. Eager to have the U.N. sanctions lifted so that Russia could trade with Iraq, Yeltsin and his Foreign Minister, Yevgeni Primakov, won an agreement from Iraqi Deputy Prime Minister Tariq Aziz that all the American inspectors would return to Iraq. In exchange, Russia would vigorously press Baghdad's case in the U.N. for lifting the economic sanctions and wrapping up the inspections.

Russia and France think Saddam likes carrots; the U.S. says he fears big sticks

After toughening up the details, Albright signed on to the deal at a 2 a.m. meeting in Geneva with top British and French foreign ministers in attendance. The crisis was defused for the moment, but few doubted Saddam would flex his muscles again.

American and U.N. officials believe Saddam blocked the inspection teams because they were closing in on his secret stores of biological weapons, perhaps located in the more than 50 "palaces" Saddam has built since the Gulf War. Iraq reportedly has some 900 lbs. of the anthrax bacterium, a single gram of which can kill millions. The U.S. also believes Saddam is continuing to develop nuclear-weapons capability and is trying to rebuild his ballistic missile program. The real issue was unresolved: weapons of mass destruction were in the hands of a regime prepared to use them. ■

HUSSEIN'S HIDEAWAY: One of Saddam's lavish palaces towers over the Tigris River

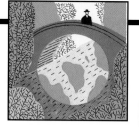

Twilight of a Tyrant

In a July show trial staged deep in the jungle by his own cadres, former leader Pol Pot was expelled from the Khmer Rouge movement, which was responsible for the death of more than 1 million Cambodians between 1975 and 1979. The onetime dictator received a lenient (by Khmer Rouge standards) sentence of life imprisonment. The ouster reflected a confusing year in which the nation found itself

THE END? Pol Pot endures his show trial

under two "official" regimes. Meanwhile a bloody power grab by Hun Sen, one of the competing Prime Ministers, left at least 65 people dead in Phnom Penh. Hun Sen's followers then rounded up more than 30 of his rivals, some of whom had their eyes gouged out before being executed.

Even Iran Votes for Change

Around the globe, restless voters rejected incumbent governments and elected new parties that promised to reshape national agendas. A round-up:
FRANCE. Voters rebuked President Jacques Chirac and his austerity program in June, demolishing the right-wing majority in the National Assembly and installing Socialist Lionel Jospin as Prime Minister.
MEXICO. July elections finally shook the hegemony of the all-powerful Institutional Revolutionary Party (P.R.I.). The P.R.I. lost its majority in the lower house of the national congress, as well as two key governorships and the mayoralty of Mexico City.

CHOOSING SIDES
In August U.S. troops directly intervened to aid Biljana Plavsic, the President of Republika Srpska, the truculent Serb statelet that vowed to cooperate in a "unified" Bosnia— but doesn't. Some 35,000 U.S. and NATO soldiers took Plavsic's side in her power struggle with indicted war criminal and Serb strongman Radovan Karadzic. But Karadzic hung tough: in November elections, his party lost its majority but remained the most powerful political faction.

FEUD: Plavsic, at top, couldn't oust Karadzic

IRAN. Moderate candidate Mohammed Khatami, who was once hounded out of the Cabinet by fellow clerics, handed the conservative Muslim theocracy a stunning upset as he swept to the presidency with 69.7% of the 29.7 million votes cast.
CANADA. Parliamentary elections in June further balkanized the nation. The Reform Party nearly swept the provinces of Alberta and British Columbia but failed to pick up a single seat east of Manitoba. In Quebec the separatist Bloc Québécois took a majority of the 75 seats in its home province. Even Prime Minister Jean Chrétien's Liberals depended for two-thirds of their majority on a single province, Ontario.

Growing Pains for NATO

At a historic July summit meeting in Madrid, the 16 member nations of the North Atlantic Treaty Organization

RSVP: NATO growth was by invitation only

enlarged and reshaped what is now often described as the most successful alliance in history. The expansion produced much friction, as the U.S. ruled that only three former Warsaw Pact countries would be admitted to NATO in the first round of expansion: the Czech Republic, Hungary and Poland. But France, Italy, Canada and others had championed entry for Romania and Slovenia. After the conference, President Clinton, Secretary of State Madeleine Albright and Defense Secretary William Cohen bustled across Europe to congratulate the newcomers and soothe the also-rans. Ahead: a fight to win approval of the plan by the U.S. Senate.

A Daring Rescue in Lima

After Túpac Amaru rebels held 72 hostages for 126 days in the Japanese embassy in Lima, the siege ended in a surprise raid; all but one of the captive Peruvians and foreign diplomats and businessmen survived. More than 140

SUCCESS! Cheering the siege's end in Lima

Peruvian army, navy and air force special-operations troops burst through a tunnel that had been secretly dug underneath the embassy and surprised the rebels, who were engaged in a makeshift soccer game. Only 15 minutes after the commandos blasted and shot their way into the building, all the guerrillas were dead. Only one prisoner and two of the raiding soldiers died in the siege, though a third soldier died several days later. The risky gambit was a triumph for Peru's embattled President Alberto Fujimori and his military.

Rumblings on Montserrat

In June, 19 residents of the scenic Caribbean island of Montserrat perished when the Soufrière Hills volcano spewed molten rivers of lava and ash down its flanks at 150 m.p.h. onto the villages below. An August eruption threatened previously safe areas. The volcano—dormant for four

FLIGHT TO DEATH The long reign of Africa's most durable dictator, Mobutu Sese Seko of Zaïre, finally ended in May when the ailing dictator, 66, was driven from the capital of Kinshasa by the approaching army of longtime rebel Laurent Desire Kabila. Mobutu died of cancer four months later.

EXPLOSIVE ISSUE Eighty-nine nations signed a treaty to ban antipersonnel land mines that kill or maim 25,000 civilians each year—but the U.S. did not join them. Later, American Jody Williams was given the Nobel Peace Prize for her anti-mine crusade.

centuries—had been belching and fuming since 1995, and continued to give hints of a cataclysmic blow to come. Two-thirds of the 39-sq.-mi. British colony was uninhabitable; two-thirds of the population of 12,000 had fled; thousands more had abandoned their homes; and Plymouth, the capital city, had been reduced to rubble.

No Corn, No Grain, No Hope

Alas for North Korea. In 1997 famine stalked its 24 million citizens, a famine that was not the sad by-product of war but the miserable result of chronic mismanagement, atrocious policies and three years of terrible luck. Catastrophic flooding over the previous two summers swept the Stalinist hermit state to the edge of famine. Now the unending drought and extraordinary heat of El Niño–troubled 1997 brought the real thing. Some 70% of the year's corn crop was lost, and half the nation's grain supply con-

VICTIMS: Starving children near Pyongyang

sists of corn. Relief agencies predicted that as many as 2 million to 5 million North Koreans could starve to death.

More Terror in Islamic Lands

Militant Islamist fundamentalists continued their campaign to undermine secular, Western-oriented governments across Muslim Africa. In Algeria, where the Islamic Salvation Front won the country's first free elections in 1991, only to have the military void the results, the secular government and Islamic militants remained locked in a civil war that has so far claimed an estimated 60,000 lives. Early on Sept. 23, the Armed Islamic Group, an extremist splinter faction, capped years of massacres and reprisals with a rampage of horror: as many as 200 villagers in a suburb of Algiers were shot, stabbed, dismembered and burned. On Nov. 17, terrorists in Egypt opened fire on sightseers at the historic site of Luxor in the Valley of the Kings. Of the 62 victims, 58 were foreign tourists.

STIRRING: The volcano devastated Montserrat

Wall Street's great bull market rolls on—but will the financial crisis that roiled Asia's "tiger" economies finally put an end to the market's long run?

ENDANGERED SPECIES?

Higher ... HIGHER ... higher! After thrilling investors with its inexorable climb in 1996, the Dow Jones industrial average, the most widely accepted proxy for the health of the Wall Street stock market, kept right on climbing in 1997. Cheering the surge was an enormous group of small investors, middle-class Americans who had staked their future on the strength of the Dow. Only

10 years after the market's most devastating one-day plunge in history, Americans were married to Wall Street to a confounding degree. The stock-obsessed masses, involved in mutual funds and investment clubs, trading online and standing in line a dozen deep at the corner Fidelity or Schwab office, had the trust of a newlywed that stocks would be a lifetime mate. The average person had more invested in the market than in the house that sheltered him. Stocks accounted for more than 40% of the average household's financial assets, more than in any period in history. In 1965, 10.4% of American adults owned stock; in 1997, 43% did.

Angry voters threw out Korea's long-time ruling party in December voting

Higher … higher … higher! The Dow passed the 7000 mark for the first time in history in mid-February—and TIME cautioned investors: "By all the conventional measures of Wall Street, the market seems ripe for a setback."

But the great bull market that began in 1990 might just as well have been called the bunny market: its tireless upward trend reflected an astonishingly resilient and inflation-free U.S. expansion that, like the Energizer Bunny, just kept going. In July, only five months after busting 7000, Wall Street's bull galloped right through the 8000 gate.

Finally, in late October, the much-predicted "correction"—Wall Street's euphemism for a market-wide price drop—seemed to have hit at last. In a horrific session that reminded veterans of the Street's major crash in 1987, the Dow plunged a record 554 points in one nauseating session; automatic "circuit breakers" kicked in twice to avoid panic, and trading was stopped for 30 minutes. The market drop was a one-day point record, although the 7% decline was only a third as bad as the 1987 crash.

But the long-awaited correction was short-lived indeed. The next day, Turnaround Tuesday, the Dow reared up to gain back 337 points of that loss. It was the small investors, the keep-the-faith individuals, this bull market's greatest ally, who ended what could have been a global catastrophe. At least for the short run, their faith was justified. Within weeks the market was growing again. But this time there were serious signs that the market's long ride might at last be coming to an end. The signs came rolling in from across the Pacific, in a tsunami of ill financial tidings.

In early July, just about the time Pathfinder was landing on Mars, Thailand's currency, the baht, plunged to earth like a wounded satellite; it fell more than 12% in value against the greenback on July 2. Then the selling wave crashed into the Philippines, Malaysia and Indonesia, where governments were forced to devalue their currencies. That triggered a region-wide crisis, in which stock markets gave up as much as 35% of their value; inflated real estate prices fell through the floor; banks collapsed; and hundreds of thousands of Southeast Asians, rich and poor, lost their jobs and fortunes.

The reverberations of that early July disaster reached Wall Street following a brief, awful stopover in Hong Kong. The former British colony had vowed to use its $88 billion in foreign reserves to fight off speculators and keep its highly valued currency pegged to the U.S. dollar at a rich 7.8-to-1 ratio. The gambit succeeded, but at a price: $42 billion of Hong Kong's wealth vanished as the Hang Seng index dropped 6% on Oct. 22, then 10.4% the next day.

Hours later Wall Street was in full retreat for the first of three days that culminated in the Oct. 27 drop. The global economy, once an abstraction to most people, had shown up front and center to deliver the bad news. U.S. companies earning high profits in Asia were faced with a potential double whammy. First, Asia's economic crunch would probably cause its consumers and companies to buy less from America. Second, sales by U.S. firms in Asia wouldn't add as much to their bottom line because Far Eastern currencies were worth 20% to 40% less than they had been just a few months before. At the same time, however, devaluation of Asian currencies might make Asian exports

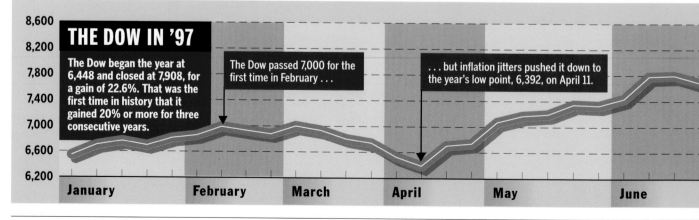

THE DOW IN '97

The Dow began the year at 6,448 and closed at 7,908, for a gain of 22.6%. That was the first time in history that it gained 20% or more for three consecutive years.

The Dow passed 7,000 for the first time in February . . .

. . . but inflation jitters pushed it down to the year's low point, 6,392, on April 11.

| 8,600 | 8,200 | 7,800 | 7,400 | 7,000 | 6,600 | 6,200 |

January   February   March   April   May   June

The Artful Manipulator

Federal Reserve Board Chairman Alan Greenspan is credited by many with being the steady force behind the American economy's 6½ years of expansion: his artful manipulation of central bank interest rates has fostered muscular economic growth while keeping inflation down. The day after the Dow sagged on Oct. 27, Greenspan appeared before Congress's Joint Economic Committee. Once there, he talked about the sell-off in such measured terms you'd think the words were wearing tuxedos. But his message was soon being shouted by traders around the world, as markets cheered his view of the U.S. economic performance as "impressive" and unthreatened by turmoil in Asia. Greenspan, who had long suggested that market prices were inflated, speculated that the downturn in stocks might produce an economic cooling off and thus "prolong our ... expansion." As usual, the chairman dressed his opinion in qualified verbiage—call it Greenspam—never using one syllable or one word when two or three could do the job. But the result spoke volumes too: the market bounced back.

cheaper, help keep inflation at bay in the U.S. and deter the Federal Reserve from raising interest rates.

The once grand gown of the "Asian miracle" was growing tattered. From Seoul to Bangkok, economies that earlier made annual double-digit growth look easy suffered skyrocketing interest rates, current-account deficits, shrinking budgets and rapid flight of the foreign capital that underwrote the miracle. How could things go so wrong so fast? One reason is that Asia's "tiger" economies had a virtually unlimited credit line from the world's bankers. The easy money had colluded with easy virtue in places like Indonesia, where an authoritarian government and crony capitalism led to corruption.

THE CRISIS WAS MADE WORSE BY THE DEMA-goguing of some of the affected leaders. As Malaysia's currency, the ringgit, and its stock market plummeted, mercurial Prime Minister Mahathir Mohamad implied that international financier George Soros—or (reviving an old canard) Jewish speculators—was responsible.

As the rows of dominoes tumbled, the Asian crisis spread to the region's two dominant economies, Korea and Japan. The signs of trouble had been building in Korea: a string of high-profile bankruptcies, beginning in January with Hanbo Steel and continuing in July with Kia Motors,

led foreign creditors to begin shying away from rolling over loans to Korea's ailing banks, which were burdened with short-term loans. Korea finally gave in, accepting a $57 billion bailout from the International Monetary Fund. But citizens of the proud nation resented the pain that an IMF-supervised restructuring of the economy was bound to cause: corporate cutbacks, lower wages, higher unemployment. In a stunning Dec. 19 ballot, they overturned Korea's long-time governing party to elect a legendary pro-democracy campaigner, Kim Dae Jung, as president.

Japan, the world's largest creditor nation—which had loaned Korean banks $24 billion—was the last link in the chain of Asian disasters. In November, Hokkaido Takushoku, one of Japan's 20 largest banks, collapsed; days later Yamaichi Securities, one of the nation's "Big Four" securities companies, toppled. In December the government announced it would cut taxes $16 billion and attempt a $77 billion bailout of its financial crisis.

As Asia's troubles hit home, America's stock markets grumbled and groaned. In one mid-December week, technology stocks on the NASDAQ composite index—the major market for many high-tech issues—plummeted 6%. As the year ended, the stakes involved in investing in stocks mounted. Would the great bull market finally be stopped? Or would it struggle through its financial problems and keep going higher ... higher ... higher? ■

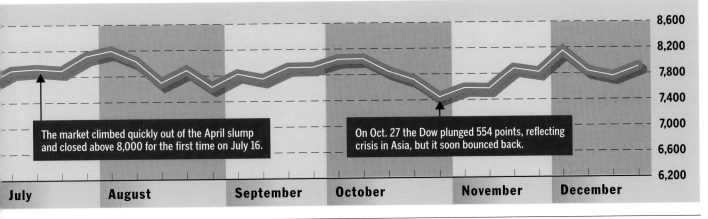

The market climbed quickly out of the April slump and closed above 8,000 for the first time on July 16.

On Oct. 27 the Dow plunged 554 points, reflecting crisis in Asia, but it soon bounced back.

8,600
8,200
7,800
7,400
7,000
6,600
6,200

July   August   September   October   November   December

Bernie's Deal

In the biggest merger in U.S. history, Bernie Ebbers' upstart WorldCom acquires MCI—and gets ready to run the Internet

A FTER BERNIE EBBERS, THE VOCIFEROUSLY acquisitive boss of WorldCom, acquired the cyberspace network CompuServe in September, TIME asked him whether he had any new deals up his sleeve. Ebbers shot back, "Are we alive?" Were they ever. Just ask MCI. Two months later, in the biggest corporate buyout in U.S. history, the country boy from Canada by way of Mississippi acquired MCI, the country's second largest long-distance carrier and a company four times the size of WorldCom, for $36.5 billion, mostly in WorldCom stock.

Ebbers had stunned the business world on Oct. 1, when he initially offered a $30 billion bid for MCI, demolishing British Telecommunication's $19.9 billion offer for the company just as the two phone giants were preparing to seal their transatlantic deal. In snagging MCI, Ebbers rode out a second challenge: this time from another phone giant, GTE, which had countered the WorldCom offer two weeks after it was made with an offer of $28 billion in cash. Critical to WorldCom's victory was gaining the support of the vanquished British Telecom, which agreed to sell to Ebbers its already large $7 billion stake in MCI.

A born dealmaker, Ebbers, 56, is a buccaneering presence whose 6-ft., 4-in. frame has begun to tower over the telecommunications world. His success stems from seeing early on that a global-communications industry was forming, which may seem like a blinding glimpse of the obvious. But he realized that the winners would be the companies that could mass enough capacity to serve the exploding growth of data and Internet traffic on a local, long-distance and international basis. So he got to massing.

When Ebbers bought CompuServe for $1.2 billion, he kept its Internet hookups and swapped its consumer sub-

scribers for the hookups of America Online [see related story]. That gave WorldCom a broader range of telecom assets—from local and long-distance lines to high-speed Internet-access networks—than even mighty AT&T. Adding MCI should balloon WorldCom's revenues from $4.5 billion in 1996 to nearly $28 billion, and make the company, based in Jackson, Miss., by far the leading challenger to the $52.7 billion colossus once known as Ma Bell.

Ebbers has traveled a long way from his birthplace in Edmonton, Alberta, to become the telecom industry's Southern-fried Paul Bunyan. His first job taught him that "delivering milk day to day in 30-below-zero weather isn't a real interesting thing to do with the rest of your life." A warmer clime beckoned in the form of Mississippi College, a Southern Baptist school in Clinton, Miss. After coaching high school basketball for a year, Ebbers bought a motel-restaurant on borrowed money—and before long he owned nine Best Westerns.

Not good enough. By 1983 Ebbers was ripe for the kind of transformation that business legends are made of. In a Days Inn diner, goes WorldCom lore, Ebbers and some partners scratched out on a napkin a plan for a phone company that would resell long-distance service to local businesses. Its name—Long Distance Discount Services—supposedly came from a helpful waitress. "The only experience Bernie had operating a long-distance carrier was that he used the phone," recalls an investor in the original enterprise, which changed its name to WorldCom in 1995.

LDDS faltered early on, and Ebbers took charge in 1985. Then, as now, he saw acquisitions as the fast-track growth alternative to banging away against the giants for one account at a time. His strategy was to string together local carriers that sold long distance to business users, cutting overhead and paying for the acquisitions with his

BUILDING AN EMPIRE

Before its MCI offer, WorldCom bought some 50 telecom companies, mostly by using its skyrocketing stock. Among the acquisitions:

1993

BOUGHT: Resurgens Communications Group and Metromedia Communications Corp in a $1.2 billion merger, adding long-distance capacity in new areas.

1995

BOUGHT: WilTel Network Services, which operates an 11,000-mile fiberoptic cable network, for $2.5 billion.

1996

BOUGHT: MFS Communications and its subsidiary, UUNet Technologies (world's largest Internet service provider) for $12.5 billion.

company's stock. His plan worked: anyone who invested $100 in WorldCom stock when the company went public in 1989 would have a holding worth more than $3,000 in 1997—by far the best showing in the telecom industry.

WorldCom's muscular stock is Ebbers' checkbook. He paid $2.5 billion in 1995 for a company called WilTel and its 11,000-mile network of fiber-optic cable, making WorldCom the fourth largest U.S. long-distance carrier. But he knew he needed local service to sell. So while driving to work on Aug. 12, 1996, he dialed up James Crowe, chairman of a local-service provider called MFS Communications, to propose a deal. By the time Ebbers hung up, he was ready to shell out $12.5 billion for MFS, which was itself acquiring UUNet, the world's largest source of trunk lines—or "backbones"—to the Internet.

THE MFS DEAL NOT ONLY ALTERED WORLDCOM'S DEStiny, but also brought a new superstar to its ranks in John Sidgmore, the technovisionary behind UUNet. Ebbers "sees the industry at a historic turning point," Sidgmore says. "That's why WorldCom [has] made big bets and moved faster than anybody else." In between buying CompuServe and bidding for MCI, WorldCom was unveiling a $2.9 billion buyout of Brooks Fiber Properties, which provides local phone service to businesses in more than 30 U.S. cities.

WorldCom won't put up a single penny to buy MCI. Instead, it will issue 820 million new shares and exchange them for MCI's. The one snag? Investors normally head for the exit in the face of this kind of dilution. Sure enough, WorldCom's stock, which had held steady throughout the bidding war with GTE, sank from a high of more than $36 in October to below $30 in the days following the conclusion of the deal. But many observers remained bullish on the company. No wonder: among other advantages, the merger will give WorldCom control of an estimated 60% of all U.S. lines to the Internet, ensuring that it will have the capacity to carry the volume of data—from E-mail to video clips—that Sidgmore sees as the key to growth in the telecommunications industry.

Across the road from Mississippi College, WorldCom is constructing a five-building, Microsoft-like corporate campus from which it will direct its global telecom conquests. Will Ebbers become the Bill Gates of the telephone line? WorldCom will have the size and scale to challenge anyone in the industry—and that includes AT&T and the Baby Bells. When they look into their rearview mirrors, Bernie Ebbers and WorldCom will be looming large. ∎

1997

BOUGHT: Brooks Fiber Properties, expanding WorldCom's U.S. fiber-optic networks and switching facilities. A $2.9 billion stock merger includes assuming Brooks' outstanding debt.

BOUGHT: CompuServe in a $1.2 billion stock swap with H&R Block, trading the subscribers to America Online for AOL's network services group.

The New World of Corporate Giving

Critics call CEOs greedy, but more companies and bosses are taking to philanthropy

TAKE YOUR PICK. CORPORATE CHIEFTAINS are: a) overpaid Scrooges; b) visionary philanthropists busily inventing a new kind of company with a social conscience. In 1997 both answers were correct. The year saw a broadcast mogul donate a fortune to the United Nations, a global financier promise half a billion to Russia, a former head of the Joint Chiefs of Staff chair a conference on volunteerism, more and more corporations engage in strategic philanthropy—and more and more of their CEOs receive mind-boggling pay packages, bolstered with stock options, that brought cries of condemnation.

In the springtime, when corporations issued their 1997 proxy statements, shareholder activists and Big Labor took up their favorite pastime: railing against runaway CEO pay. The new batch provided plenty of ammunition: they showed that in 1997 the corner office of a typical FORTUNE 500 company would come with annual total compensation of $7.8 million, an increase of roughly 50% over 1996. CEOs made at least 200 times more than the average factory worker, even if you threw in the paltry 3% raise that working stiffs gained. The pay disparity is five times greater than it was 30 years ago—and it's growing. You could almost hear the proletariat sharpening the guillotine.

But defenders of the system point out that the packages that give huge sums to CEOs are exactly the deals that corporate critics were clamoring for in the late 1980s. Then the bigwigs were pulling down huge salaries, out of proportion to company results. The solution? Link pay to stock performance. It seems to have worked—all too well. Corporate profits are at a record high, a task that is, after all, the CEO's job. Those lush profits have helped the stock market soar, as anyone with a mutual fund plainly knows. And it is that bull market that turned millions upon millions of stock options into pure CEO gold, in cartloads unforeseen by anyone. Nice work, if you can get it.

Now a growing number of CEOs get so-called megagrants, which are grants of stock options valued at more than three times the CEO's annual salary and bonus. Such grants are an increasingly large and irksome cost shared by all stockholders. The value of existing shares is diluted when new shares are created to hand over to the boss. Most visible in the land of megagrants was Walt Disney Co. chief Michael Eisner, who was given options on an astounding 8 million shares, a value that compensation experts fix at $196 million. And that's in addition to his salary, his bonus—and free rides at Space Mountain. Counting the options, his 1996 compensation came to $204 million. While Disney stockholders have done well under Eisner's long reign, Eisner himself has done even better.

Another lavishly rewarded CEO was Lawrence Coss of little known Green Tree Financial, a company based in St. Paul, Minn., that finances mobile-home purchases. In 1996 he was paid $102 million in salary and bonus. He was also given 2 million stock options valued at $35 million, presumably as an incentive. In his case too, shareholders have shared the earnings. Far more galling was exorbitant CEO pay at companies with laggard stocks. Gil Amelio, the CEO of struggling Apple Computer, received total compensation valued at $23 million in 1996, while Apple shareholders lost 40% on their investment. By July 1997, both Amelio and his paycheck were history at Apple.

But the examples of CEO jackpots belied another trend

A Time to Share ...

SHELLING OUT: George Soros, left, has made philanthropy a systematic element of his business. Among his recipients: Eastern Europe, Russia, U.S. drug reform. Ted Turner's gift to the U.N. came after a year in which he pestered other bigwigs to share the wealth.

A Time to Score ...

RAKING IN: Apple's ex-chief Gil Amelio, second from right, and Green Tree Financial's Lawrence Coss were among those most frequently charged with being overpaid. The difference: Coss made a profit for his shareholders, while Apple floundered under Amelio.

DREAM WORLD? Ben and Jerry are in the vanguard of the share-the-wealth crew

sweeping the nation's companies: personal and corporate philanthropy. At a September dinner in New York City, media magnate Ted Turner stunned an audience that included U.N. Secretary-General Kofi Annan by announcing that over 10 years he would give $1 billion to fund U.N. programs.

While other philanthropists have given more over the course of their lives, Turner's gift would be the largest donation ever made to a single organization. In the previous year, Turner had been hectoring the very rich to act more philanthropically. Among his complaints: he believes *Forbes* magazine's ranking of wealthy Americans discourages giving, because those on the list don't want to slip down. Turner claimed that one of his role models was the billionaire financier and philanthropist George Soros. And shortly after Turner's stunner, the Hungarian-born Soros pledged to pump up to $500 million of his personal fortune into health and education programs in Russia over the next three years.

WHILE TURNER AND SOROS WERE LEADING THE charge for individual giving, retired General Colin Powell convened a covey of U.S. Presidents in Philadelphia in April to embark on a well-publicized effort to turn corporate responsibility into a duty. Though his summit on volunteerism raised the bar for what passes as a socially responsible corporation, he was seeking to accelerate an old movement. Savvy CEOs began linking their companies to social causes a decade ago, seeing that as a way to stand out in a world of look-alike products. By 1997 caring capitalism, long practiced in seeming isolation by such companies as Vermont ice-cream maker Ben & Jerry's and a handful of others, was gospel in many boardrooms.

Today American Express is feeding the hungry. Alarm company ADT is giving away personal-security systems to battered women. Avon Products is helping fund the fight against breast cancer. Kimberly-Clark is building playgrounds in poor neighborhoods. Barnes & Noble is promoting literacy. Nike, Wal-Mart, Home Depot, MCI and Starbucks all have pet social causes, as do countless other companies. Some 800 companies belong to a group called Business for Social Responsibility, based in San Francisco.

Critics charged that companies have one duty: to increase returns to shareholders. But Ben Cohen of Ben & Jerry's responds, "You can't have the biggest force in society, business, concerned only with maximizing profits and still have a socially responsible society." His partner, Jerry Greenfield, elaborates, "When it's just trying to maximize profits, business lobbies for laws that would be most helpful, even if it means polluting the environment. That's not exactly in the best interest of society."

Ted Turner, never one to think small, gave $1 billion in stock to aid the U. N.

Closely related to strategic philanthropy is the movement toward "cause marketing," which is the fastest-growing segment in advertising. Companies will pay more than $500 million in 1997 for the right to sponsor various social programs, from research on AIDS to support for local fire departments. Typically, such sponsorships come with expensive marketing campaigns that promote the company while pushing the cause. By raising public awareness, these ads will help generate some $2.5 billion for the causes they champion, even as they publicize their donor.

Critics may not like profit-minded CEOs deciding which charities get all the loot—or the fact that backing causes moves corporations into social planning. But in an era of shrinking government responsibility for the welfare of its citizens, somebody has got to pick up the tab. ∎

McDonald's Fallen Arches

Long dominant in the burger wars, a lagging Mickey D's finds itself in a pickle

MCDONALD'S SERVES JILLIONS OF Happy Meals each year, but not many of them were being shared in 1997 at the company's pleasant headquarters in a Chicago suburb. "There's no question we've been under more stress than we're used to," said McDonald's USA chairman Jack Greenberg, who runs the company's 12,100 domestic restaurants.

The company's sales in U.S. stores have been as flat as a frozen beef patty for the past two years, with profit margins eroding. Some of the 2,750 franchisees were unhappy—some downright testy— because rapid store expansion had cannibalized sales; the company's advertising and promotion, although ubiquitous, had been ineffectual. Worst of all, though 22 million customers still showed up every day, they'd gladly take a bargain where they could get one.

McDonald's is still the king of convenience—nobody runs a better fast-food operation than Mickey D's—but it has become vulnerable, outflanked on such factors as price and taste. It's having a hard time playing ketchup. The company attacked the food issue with the 1996 Arch Deluxe introduction, and took on the price issue with 1997's Campaign 55 promotion. But Arch Deluxe featured weird, kid-unfriendly advertising and Campaign 55 fostered confusion at the counter. Both were flops.

By 1997, McDonald's had been raising some prices selectively for the previous year and a half or so, and consumers had begun to stray. "Comp sales," an internal company statistic that tracks performance in existing stores, turned negative for six consecutive quarters through the third quarter of 1996, an absolutely unheard-of reversal for a company that must grow to stay alive. Greenberg knew he had to improve McDonald's value equation fast. He called the media department and got out the price ax.

Campaign 55, which started in April, had a seemingly simple premise: Customers could buy a

WILL BK'S BIG KING...

May the best Mac win: Burger King's pretender aims for Big Mac's throne

Big Mac or other designated sandwich for 55¢ if they also bought any size beverage and fries. According to the theory, customers would love the cheap burgers. Owners would pocket profits on the soda and fries.

But in practice the plan proved less than simple. First, its details appeared in the pages of the *Wall Street Journal* before franchisees approved it. Fears of an all-out industry price war sent the stock tumbling, and some franchisees, already struggling against rising wages, worried openly about the cost. Worse, when the promotion rolled out, customers realized the deal wasn't such a good one. A Campaign 55 meal generally cost 50¢ to $1 less than one purchased à la carte, or 10¢ to 30¢ less than an Extra Value meal, except when…oh, never mind. The campaign was put out to pasture.

Then came the ultimate humiliation. On Labor Day, archenemy Burger King introduced its new Big King, a burly burger patently modeled on the Big Mac. It sold at nearly twice the rate Burger King expected—about 3 million a day—and stores in Dallas, Miami and elsewhere were selling out. One downtown Chicago outlet upped its order from 2,000 Big King patties the first week to 5,000 the second week, and manager Lolita Aldan said that lunch lines had doubled. The secret to the American stomach, circa 1997? The Big King has 75% more beef than the Big Mac, an extra 12 grams of fat (yum!) and no soggy third bun in the center. Most important, it was launched at a special introductory price: 99¢. A simple strategy—more food for less money—easily outflanked McDonald's off-putting pitch for the Arch Deluxe and the 55¢ campaign.

The good news for the embattled folks under the arches? Overseas sales remain robust: they kicked in 59% of the company's $2.6 billion in operating income in 1996. And, as Greenberg is quick to point out, McDonald's remains one of the most powerful brands in the world. "It's worth remembering that we've got this fabulous thing going," he says. Indeed. He's simply got to get it going a little faster. ∎

...TOP BIG MAC?

Why Levi's Has the Blues

In a year that saw most U.S. businesses thriving, two grand old brand names—and their employees—endured rocky times. **LEVI STRAUSS.** Fierce competition forced the jeansmaker into a round of belt-tightening measures. The company announced plans to close 11 factories in four states and lay off 34% of its North American work force—but cushioned the news with extended benefits for ex-workers. **KODAK.** Locked in a tough battle with Japanese giant Fuji in the film business, and reeling from the botched 1996 launch of its

WASHOUT: Levi's had to shrink its work force to fit

high-tech Advantix camera, Eastman Kodak sagged. In September the company said its 1997 operating earnings could fall as much as 25% below 1996 results—and its stock plunged $8.25 a share in two days.

Ron Carey's Bittersweet Year

When Ron Carey won the race for Teamsters president in 1991, he rode to power behind dissidents who had risked their jobs, and their lives, to fight Mob control of their locals. But in the Teamsters, power often seems to corrupt. In 1997

RIVALS: Hoffa, left, savored Carey's fall

Carey brought new vigor to his 1.4 million-strong organization, facing down United Parcel Service in a 15-day strike that found most Americans siding with Carey and the drivers against UPS. Yet even in Carey's moment of triumph, a federal overseer nullified his victory over James P. Hoffa—son of legendary Teamster kingpin Jimmy Hoffa—in a 1996 election for the union's presidency. Carey planned to run against

OUR GIDDY IRS After Congress stuck it to the Internal Revenue Service in brutal hearings in the fall, the agency made a strong effort to crawl out of the 1950s. It fished in the private sector to find a new commissioner, launched a Website —even was host of a Problem Solving Day "to provide effective relief from the headache, fever and that all-over achy feeling that accompanies long-standing tax problems."

AT&T UNPLUGGED Only eight months after he was plucked from printing giant R.R. Donnelley & Sons and named president of AT&T, John Walter left the company. Ma Bell's new boss: Michael Armstrong, late of Hughes Electronics

Hoffa in a new campaign, but in November federal monitor Kenneth Conboy banned Carey from the race, claiming the Teamster boss was a party to illegal schemes to funnel nearly $900,000 of union funds into his earlier winning campaign.

A Wave of Mergers Makes the Street's Big Guns Even Bigger

It's the law of the jungle (and thus, of course, of Wall Street): the strong get stronger, and big companies get bigger. The three biggest megamergers of the year:

WHEE! Sanford Weill finds room for Salomon Brothers under his big Travelers umbrella

TRAVELERS/SALOMON BROTHERS. Sanford Weill's monster insurance-and-everything-else conglomerate (1996 sales: $21 billion) devoured Salomon Brothers, one of the world's largest bond-trading houses and a player in investment banking, for $9 billion. The merger united Salomon with Travelers' Smith Barney brokerage, which is stronger in stocks. **MORGAN STANLEY/DEAN WITTER.** Showing an unprecedented interest in common folks for a concern founded by J.P. Morgan, Wall Street trading powerhouse Morgan Stanley (1996 sales: $7 billion) engineered a $10 billion merger with Dean Witter Discover. Dean Witter, once owned by Sears, has long been the everyday investor's best friend on Wall Street. **MERRILL LYNCH/MERCURY.** In the most expensive acquisition ever in the money-management business, Merrill Lynch (1996 sales: $25 billion) agreed to acquire Mercury Asset Management Group of Britain for some $5.3 billion. The combined firm will be the world's third largest active money manager, after Fidelity Investments and a French firm, AXA-UAP.

MAN *of the*

The microchip has become

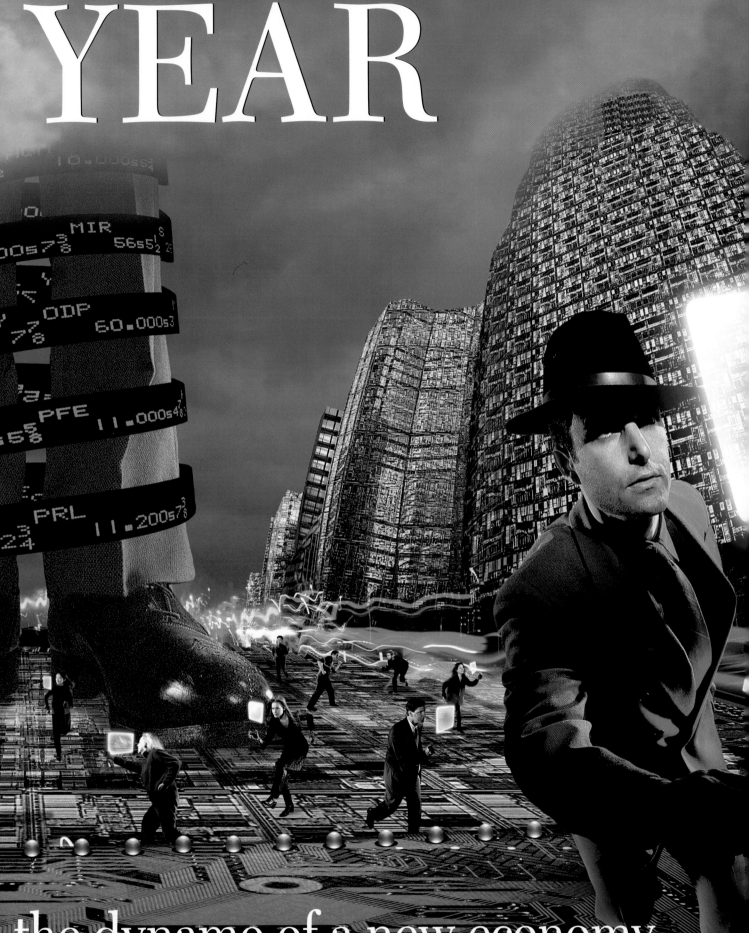

YEAR

the dynamo of a new economy

By **WALTER ISAACSON**

...driven by

IFTY YEARS AGO—SHORTLY AFTER lunch on Dec. 23, 1947—the Digital Revolution was born. It happened on a drizzly Tuesday in New Jersey, when two Bell Labs scientists demonstrated a tiny contraption they had concocted from some strips of gold foil, a chip of semiconducting material and a bent paper clip. As their colleagues watched with a mix of wonder and envy, the two researchers showed how their gizmo, which was dubbed a transistor, could take an electric current, amplify it and switch it on and off.

That Digital Revolution is now transforming the end of this century the way the Industrial Revolution transformed the end of the last one. Today, millions of transistors, each costing far less than a staple, can be etched on wafers of silicon. On these microchips, all the world's information and entertainment can be stored in digital form, processed and zapped to every nook of a networked planet. And in 1997, as the U.S. completed nearly seven years of growth, the microchip has become the dynamo of a new economy marked by low unemployment, negligible inflation and a rationally exuberant stock market.

It was a year of big stories. The death of Princess Diana tapped a wellspring of modern emotions and highlighted a change in the way we define news. The cloning of an adult sheep raised the specter of science outpacing our moral processing power and had a historic significance that will ripple through the next century. But the story that had the most impact on 1997 was the one that had the most impact throughout this decade: the growth of a new economy, global in scope but brought home in the glad tidings of personal portfolios, that has been propelled by the power of the microchip.

And so TIME chose as its 1997 Man of the Year Andrew Steven Grove, chairman and CEO of Intel, the person most responsible for the amazing growth in the power and innovative potential of microchips. His character traits are emblematic of this amazing century: a paranoia bred from his having been a refugee from the Nazis and then the Communists; an entrepreneurial optimism instilled as an immigrant to a land brimming with freedom and opportunity; and a sharpness tinged with arrogance that comes from being a brilliant mind on the front line of a revolution.

Like his fellow wealth builders of the digital age, Grove's mission is his product, and he shuns the philosophical mantle and higher callings often adopted by titans of an earlier era. Ask him to ruminate on issues like the role of technology in our society, and his pixie face contorts into a frozen smile with impatient eyes. "Technology happens," he clips. "It's not good, it's not bad. Is steel good or bad?" The steel in his own character comes through at such moments. He has a courageous passion alloyed with an engineer's analytic coldness, whether it be in battling his prostate cancer or in guiding Intel's death-defying climb to dominate the market for the world's most important product.

These traits have allowed Grove to push with paranoiac obsession the bounds of innovation and to build Intel, which makes nearly 90% of the planet's PC microprocessors, into a company worth $115 billion (more than IBM), with $5.1 billion in annual profits (seventh most profitable in the world) and an annual return to investors of 44% during the past 10 years. Other great entrepreneurs, most notably the visionary wizard Bill Gates, have become richer and better known by creating the software that makes use of the microchip. But more than any other person, Andy Grove has made real the defining law of the digital age: the prediction by his friend and Intel cofounder Gordon Moore that microchips would double in

Intel's Andy Grove

about history. We can pause to notice what Grove calls, somewhat inelegantly, "strategic inflection points," those moments when new circumstances alter the way the world works, as if the current of history goes through a transistor and our oscilloscopes blip. It can happen because of an invention (Gutenberg's printing press in the 15th century), or an idea (individual liberty in the 18th century), or a technology (electricity in the 19th century) or a process (the assembly line early in this century).

The microchip has become—like the steam engine, electricity and the assembly line—an advance that propels a new economy. Its impact on growth and productivity numbers is still a matter of dispute, but not its impact on the way we work and live. This new economy has several features:

▶ It's global. Money now respects no borders. With clicks of a keyboard, investors trade $1.5 trillion worth of foreign currencies and $15 trillion in stocks worldwide each day, putting errant or unlucky nations at the mercy of merciless speculators.

▶ It's networked. Handbags from Italy and designer shoes from Hong Kong are available to Web surfers throughout cyberspace; clerical work or software programming can be outsourced from anywhere to workers in Omaha or Bangalore; and the illness of a child in Bali can be diagnosed by a doctor in Bangor.

▶ It's based on information. In today's knowledge-based economy, intellectual capital drives the value of products. In addition, from 1990 to 1996 the number of people making goods fell 1%, while the number employed in providing services grew 15%.

▶ It decentralizes power. As the transistor was being invented, George Orwell, in his book *1984*, was making one of the worst predictions in a century filled with them: that technology would be a centralizing, totalitarian influence. Instead, technology became a force for democracy and individual empowerment. The Internet allows anyone to be a publisher or pundit, E-mail subverts rigid hierarchies, and the tumult of digital innovation rewards wildcats who risk battle with monolithic phone companies. The symbol of the atomic age, which tended to centralize power, was a nucleus with electrons held in tight orbit; the symbol of the digital age is the Web, with countless centers of power all equally networked.

▶ It rewards openness. Information can no longer be easily controlled nor ideas repressed nor societies kept closed. A networked world facilitates free minds, free markets and free trade.

▶ It's specialized. The old economy was geared to mass production, mass marketing and mass media: cookie-cutter products spewed from assembly lines in central factories; entertainment and ideas were broadcast from big studios and publishers. Now products can be individualized. Need steel that's tailored for your needs? Some high-tech mini-mill will provide it. Prefer opinions different from those on this page? A thousand Webzines and personalized news products are waiting to connect with you.

No one believes the microchip has repealed the business cycle or deleted the threat of inflation. But it has, at the very least, ended the sway of decline theorists and the "limits to growth" crowd, ranging from the Club of Rome

power and halve in price every 18 months or so. And to that law Grove has added his own: we will continually find new things for microchips to do that were scarcely imaginable a year or two earlier.

The result is one of the great statistical zingers of our age: every month, 4 quadrillion transistors are produced, more than half a million for every human on the planet. Intel's space-suited workers etch more than 7 million, in lines one four-hundredth the thickness of a human hair, on each of its thumbnail-size Pentium II chips, which sell for about $500 and can make 588 million calculations a second.

The dawn of a new millennium—which is the grandest measure we have of human time—permits us to think big

Cassandras to more recent doomsayers convinced that America's influence was destined to wane.

The U.S. now enjoys what in many respects is the healthiest economy in its history, and probably that of any nation ever. More than 400,000 new jobs were created in November, bringing unemployment down to 4.6%, the lowest level in almost 25 years. Labor-force participation has also improved: the proportion of working-age people with jobs is the highest ever recorded. Wage stagnation seems to be ending: earnings rose more than 4% in 1997, which is the greatest gain in 20 years when adjusted for inflation. The Dow ended the year at 7,908.25, more than doubling in three years, and corporate profits are at their highest level ever. Yet inflation is a negligible 2%, and even the dour Fed Chairman Alan Greenspan seems confident enough in the new economy to keep interest rates low.

Driving all this is the microchip. The high-tech industry, which accounted for less than 10% of America's growth in 1990, accounts for 30% today. Every week a Silicon Valley company goes public. It's an industry that pays good wages and makes both skilled and unskilled workers more efficient. Its products cost less each year and help reduce the prices in other industries. That, along with the global competition that computers and networks facilitate, helps keep inflation down.

Economists point out that the Digital Revolution has not yet been reflected in productivity statistics. The annual growth of nonfarm productivity during the 1980s and 1990s has averaged about 1%, in contrast to almost 3% in the 1960s. But that may be changing. During the past year, productivity grew about 2.5%. And in the most recent quarter of 1997 the rate was more than 4%.

In addition, the traditional statistics are increasingly likely to understate growth and productivity. The outputs of the old economy were simpler to measure: steel and cars and widgets are easily totted up. But the new economy defies compartmentalized measurement. Corporate software purchases, for instance, are not counted as economic investment. What is the value of cell phones that keep getting cheaper, or of E-mail? By traditional measures banking is contracting, yet there has been explosive growth in automated banking and credit-card transactions; the same for the way health care is delivered.

Even the cautious Greenspan has become a wary believer in the new economy. "I have in mind," he told Congress when not raising interest rates, "the increasingly successful and pervasive application of recent technological advances, especially in telecommunications and computers, to enhance efficiencies in the production process." Translation: Inventories can now be managed more efficiently, and production capacity can more quickly respond to changes in demand. A fanatic for data, Greenspan has soaked up the evidence of surging corporate investment in technology and says managers presumably are doing so because they believe it will enhance productivity and profits. "The anecdotal evidence is ample," he says.

Anecdotal? Economists are supposed to eschew that. Yet the most powerful evidence of the way the Digital Revolution has created a new economy comes from the testimony of those embracing it. A manager at a service company in Kansas talks about not having to raise prices because he's reaping increased profits through technology. An executive of an engine company in Ohio tells of resolving an issue with colleagues on three continents in a one-day flurry of E-mail, a task that once would have taken weeks of memos and missed phone calls. At a Chrysler plant in Missouri, a shop steward describes labor-saving technology that his union members embraced because they see how their factory, which had been shut down in the late '80s, is now expanding. And the greatest collection of anecdotal insight, the stock market, has spent the year betting on ever increasing profits.

Of course the microchip, like every new technology, brings viruses. Increased reliance on technology has led to the threat of growing inequality and a two-tier society. Workers and students not properly trained will be left behind, opening the way for the social disruptions that accompanied the shift to the industrial age. At a time when they are most needed, schools have been allowed to deteriorate, and worker-training programs have fallen prey to budget austerity. For all the spending on computers and software ($800 billion in the U.S. during the past five years), the most obvious investment has not been made: ensuring that every schoolchild has a personal computer. Grove himself says this would be the most effective way to reboot education in America, yet he and others in the industry have been timid in enlisting in such a crusade.

In addition, though wage stagnation seems to be easing, workers' insecurity remains high. The layoffs that have accompanied technological change have been burned into their minds like code on a ROM chip. The weakening of labor bargaining power, inherent in a global economy where jobs and investment can be shifted freely, has led to what William Greider in the *Nation* calls a "widening gap between an expanding production base worldwide and an inability of consumers to buy all the new output."

There are also more personal concerns. Computer networks allow information to be accessed, accumulated and correlated in ways that threaten privacy as never before. Unseen eyes (of your boss, your neighbor, thousands of marketers) can track what you buy, the things you read and write, where you travel and whom you call. Your kids can download pornographic pictures and chat with strangers.

But these challenges can be surmounted. Technology can even provide the tools to do so, if people supply the will. As Andy Grove says, technology is not inherently good or evil. It is only a tool for reflecting our values.

If the Digital Revolution is accompanied by ways to ensure that everyone has the chance to participate, then it could spark an unprecedented millennial boom, global in scope but empowering to each individual, marked not only by economic growth but also by a spread of knowledge and freedom and true community. That's a daunting task. But it shouldn't be much harder than figuring out how to etch more than 7 million transistors on a sliver of silicon. ∎

A Survivor's Tale

BUDAPEST: DECEMBER 1956. The Red Army had been streaming into the city for a month, brutalizing Hungary's October revolution. The foggy nights, filled all fall with the sounds of ecstatic students, were now split with the jostle of machinery—10 divisions of Soviet tanks—and the uneven light of Molotov cocktails thrown through the rain. Fear blossomed in the dampness. The Premier vanished.

The boy—lean, strikingly handsome at 20—hoped the tumult would pass. During the day he buried himself in schoolwork. Nights he passed at home. But over his books, across his strong Hungarian coffee, he heard rumors: the Russians were rounding up students. Children were disappearing. Trains were leaving for the frontier.

He longed to ignore the stories. He had already lived through the horror of the Nazis, outsmarting the SS, avoiding Budapest's brownshirts. One day his mother had bundled him into the house of a "courageous acquaintance," where they sweated out the pogroms of 1944. He saw his father return from the labor camps on the Eastern front, a proud, garrulous man shriveled by typhoid fever and chilled by pneumonia. Boys at school mocked him: before the war as a Jew, after the war because his father was a businessman (a dairyman, but that was enough). In his government file the boy was an "enemy of the classes." He wasn't going to wait for the Soviets.

So he ran. With his best school friend he hopped a train westward, as close to the Austrian border as they dared. The Russians were storming through the countryside, arresting everyone they could. Since no one would guide them, they gathered the last of their money, and their courage, and bought directions from a smuggler who spoke of secret byways the Russians hadn't yet discovered.

And so, hours later, he found himself facedown in a muddy field somewhere near the Austrian border—but how near? Soldiers marched by, dogs barked, flares lit the night. Then a voice cried out, in Hungarian, paralyzing him with fear: "Who is there?" Even 40 years later, as he laughs at the memory, his eyes harden; he shifts his neck under his collar. Had the smuggler betrayed him? The man shouted again, and the boy finally answered, "Where are we?" "Austria," came the reply. The relief poured cool as the rain. András Gróf, a name he would later Americanize to Andrew Grove, stood up and headed toward the future.

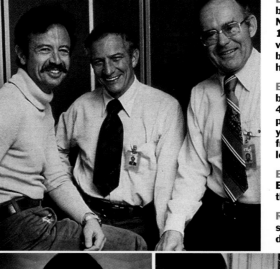

LEFT Intel was shaped by fire and finesse. Noyce, center in this 1975 photo, brought vision; Moore, right, had brainpower; Grove, left, had relentless drive

BELOW LEFT Grove, the budding scholar. At age 4, shortly after this photo was taken, the youngster nearly died from scarlet fever, which left him hard of hearing

BELOW Grove met wife Eva at a summer job; they married in 1958

RIGHT Grove doing research as a Ph.D. candidate at U.C., Berkeley

ANDREW GROVE HAS ALWAYS BEEN, IF

nothing else, a survivor. From that terrifying night, Grove, 61, has been pushed by a will to live as other men are fired by a taste for power or money. Intel, the firm that Grove built, has survived in one of the most tumultuous industries in history, emerging to become one of the most powerful companies of our age, with a stranglehold on one of the transformative technologies of the 20th century. And though Intel's spotless rooms and its brilliant engineers seem far removed from that Austrian hillside, few places better reflect the sense of urgency with which the firm operates. Grove has it boiled down to a mantra that is as fresh as it is chilling: "Only the paranoid survive."

Intel, of course, has done much more than survive. Founded in the summer of 1968 by Gordon Moore (one of the great chemists of the century) and Robert Noyce (a co-inventor of the integrated circuit), it has blossomed under Grove's leadership into the world's pre-eminent microprocessor manufacturer. From a standing start in 1981, when IBM introduced the first personal computers, the machines have populated the planet at an astounding rate. And of the 83 million machines sold this year, nearly 90% get their kick from an Intel chip. So do antilock brakes, Internet servers, cell phones and digital cameras. And who knows what products not yet invented will be powered by the chip 10, 20 years from now?

Intel has ceased being just a Silicon Valley wonder. It has become a weather vane for an entire digital economy, a complete ecosystem of drive manufacturers, software houses and Web programmers whose businesses depend on escalating PC growth. Because Grove and his firm control the blueprints of the PC, he is in the unique position of being able to tell customers what to do. Intel sets release dates for new chips, dictating the pace of the computer industry. It's the sort of ironfisted market grip that rarely exists outside economics textbooks: one superefficient firm with monopoly-like returns gliding past competitors and, not incidentally, racking up huge profits.

It has not been easy. Intel has endured crippling chip recessions, one Federal Trade Commission probe and a nasty public flogging over its flawed Pentium chips in 1994. Now the prospect of cheaper computers using cheaper chips, not to mention the threat of economic troubles in Asia, looms. But no firm does more reliable (or more profitable) work in the tiny molecular spaces that Intel has colonized. It is the essential firm of the digital age.

Grove's dogma of relentless change and fearless leadership echoes from IBM in Armonk, N.Y., to the Great Hall of the People in Beijing. Yet, as he insists in his usual point-blank locution, "I haven't changed." He is a protective father of two daughters, a spirited teacher (his Stanford business-school course is an annual sellout) and, almost incidentally, a man worth more than $300 million. His 5-ft. 9-in. frame—honed by hourlong morning workouts, coiled by nervous energy—seems as tightly wired as one of his microprocessors.

At work he operates from the same kind of cubicle that everyone else at the company gets. He keeps a support staff

His father disappeared in 1941 after being drafted into a work brigade at a time when Jewish men around Eastern Europe were vanishing like a morning fog. Then in March 1944, the Germans occupied Budapest and, Grove recalls, "began rounding up Jews." The Grófs, mother and son, living on stolen papers, pretended to be acquaintances of a Christian family that sheltered them. "They took us in at a very serious risk to themselves," he says.

After the war, Grove was determined to fulfill his parents' dream—his father, somehow, had survived the Eastern front—of his getting into college. After an early stint as a young journalist, he turned to science, in particular to chemistry. His innate curiosity made him a standout, especially after he discovered that he had an intuitive sense about molecules, an ability to manipulate mentally the tiny structures faster than most people could work them on slide rules and paper. "He was by no means a nerd," recalls Janos Lanyi, his best friend and the man who ran for the border with him. "You could always hear him singing—in gym class, in lab."

When the Soviets entered Budapest, Grove knew it was time to leave. After his dramatic escape to Austria, he made his way to New York City, where the apparent equality of American life astonished him. "I grew up to be 20 years old, and I was always told I was undesirable for one reason or another," he says. "I got to the United States, and I expected there would be some of the same because I was an immigrant. And there wasn't." From his spot in a cramped one-bedroom apartment in Brooklyn, Grove devoured Eisenhower's America. He enrolled at City College of New York, a free school that had become a kind of immigrant Oxford. He tore through the place—nearly all A's—and finished just shy of summa cum laude.

He was also in love. He met Eva, a refugee herself, at a New Hampshire resort where they both worked in the summer of 1957—he as a busboy, she as a waitress. In June 1958 they were married, and the couple soon moved to California, where Grove entered the Ph.D. program at the University of California, Berkeley. Again he was a star. When he graduated, he had the pick of American research corporations. Grove narrowed his choices: prestigious Bell Laboratories or Fairchild Semiconductor—a start-up staffed by a handful of brilliant engineers. Grove listened to the Berkeley buzz and came back with a sense of the future: Fairchild.

In the early 1960s, the computer industry was in the midst of a benign revolution—and Fairchild was a breeding ground for revolutionaries. Early computers were fast, but attempts to make them faster were running into a thermodynamic wall: every time you asked the computer to think harder, it got hotter. The heat came from vacuum tubes, which acted as giant on-off switches, holding and releasing electrical charges. But the tubes, which sucked up huge amounts of energy, represented a limit on the power of those early computers.

The logical solution was to replace the tubes with a device

of three busy. He has developed his own special "mail codes"—f/u for "follow up"—that let him zip through his In box. But Grove is not all work: he skis, bikes with his wife Eva, listens to opera.

Grove is a passionate, if disjointed, man. He is a famously tough manager who, late at night, can still fill Intel's offices with a rolling laugh. He lost most of his hearing when he was young, but won it back after five reconstructive operations over 20 years. And though Grove says he is a "whiner" about minor ailments, he coolly eyed a diagnosis of prostate cancer, researched the options and ignored his doctors' advice in favor of his own, so far successful, therapy.

ANDRAS GROF WAS BORN ON SEPT. 2, 1936, IN Budapest, the son of George the dairyman and Maria, a bookkeeping clerk. His father, a gregarious man with a strong, logical mind, left school early and taught himself business and accounting. Grove's mother, a spare, lovely woman, raised him in their two-room 19th century apartment. From an early age Grove was marked as the son of a capitalist and as a Jew.

At age 4 he nearly died. Budapest was swept by a scarlet fever epidemic, and young András succumbed. A raging fever left its mark: his eardrums were perforated like a colander, the result of a middle-ear infection. Grove refuses to discuss his childhood in Budapest during World War II and, though he travels the world, has never returned to the city.

that performed the same role—storing electrical charges—but was less temperamental. The device proved to be an electrical "switch" called a transistor, essentially a tiny electrical gate that controlled the flow of electrons that computers needed to do their math. Yet wrangling infinitesimally small electrons into place demanded phenomenally pure chemical surfaces that were beyond the capabilities of most scientists in the 1950s and '60s. What the world needed was a reliable base for these circuits. What would it be?

THE ANSWER, OF COURSE, TURNED OUT TO BE what gave Silicon Valley its name. Gordon Moore (who ran Fairchild's research arm and later became Grove's mentor as CEO of Intel) believed you could store those charges with an integrated circuit made by sandwiching metal oxide and silicon into an electrical circuit called a MOS transistor. Unlike trickier semiconductors, silicon is both a wonderful conductor of electrical charges and a nearly bottomless sink for heat, meaning it doesn't melt down as you push electrons under its surface at nearly light speed. In MOS, however, it is highly unstable. One day you'd run a voltage through a sample and see one thing; the next you could run the same voltage through the same sample and get a different reading. It was a nightmare. Of course, if you could fix that problem, you'd be onto something big.

On his first day of work, Grove knew none of this. He merely wanted to make a good impression. Nervous? Here he was, trained as a fluid dynamicist and going to work in materials chemistry. But when someone soon asked him to study the electrical characteristics of MOS, Grove delivered a sharp, comprehensive report. His bosses were impressed.

Grove and two colleagues—Bruce Deal and Edward Snow—then set out to make silicon usable. After months of work, they discovered that most of the MOS instability was traceable to an impurity—sodium—introduced when the chips were cured. The discovery solved a fundamental problem in materials science and set the stage for the semiconductor revolution. Grove and his team won one of the industry's most prestigious awards for the work.

BY 1968, FAIRCHILD WAS UNRAVELING. CRITICAL engineers like Noyce were leaving, top execs didn't understand the semi business, and science was being replaced by politics. Noyce phoned Arthur Rock, now the éminence grise of Silicon Valley investing, and told him that he and Moore wanted to start their own semiconductor company. Rock (who holds nearly $500 million of Intel stock today) raised the money nearly overnight. Moore told Grove of the plan, and he decided to join his bosses, Grove says, "almost instantly." Someone suggested the name Integrated Electronics, which was quickly shrunk to Intel.

Intel did not enjoy an uninterrupted march to greatness. The problem wasn't any lack of candlepower, but the business itself. It kept changing. Just as Intel's leaders decided the future was in, say, selling dynamic RAM (a kind of short-term computer memory), messages started trickling back that sales were tanking, customers were evaporating and, ahem, top management had better pick a new strategy. It was a miserable way to run a company, but the years of anguish produced rich rewards made possible by some neck-snapping breakthroughs. The key to the company's

CLASS ACT At Stanford, Grove teaches survival in the digital age. It's "like learning from God," says one pupil

success dated back to 1965, when Moore calculated that chip power doubled roughly every 24 months, even as costs fell by half. The rule (amended to 18 months) became known as Moore's law. Though it frustrates consumers—it's the reason that $2,500 PC you bought will be obsolete in a year—the law has given Intel a road map, enabling the company to shift resources ahead of demand.

Moore is a shy, methodical man who early on saw something special in the young Hungarian and decided to nurture it. In 1970, as the two were strolling through the zoo in Washington, D.C., Moore told Grove, "One day you'll run Intel." For the next two decades Moore shaped and polished Grove's thinking about everything from plastic packaging to Japanese trade. "He was," says Grove, "a father figure." In 1979 Grove became president, and when Moore stepped down as CEO of Intel in 1987, Grove stepped up.

For all the fear it inspires in competitors, Intel looks harmless enough. The firm's Santa Clara headquarters is an off-blue Dilbert maze, a land of cubicles, coffee cups and security badges. Inside, Grove and Moore work from 8-ft. by 9-ft. cubicles accessible to anyone bold enough to wander by for a chat. There are no special privileges. If Grove rolls in late, he has to prowl Intel's jammed lot looking for a space just like any shavetail engineer.

But do not confuse casual with unchallenging. Grove sets the tone, and it is always demanding. The people (mostly men) who work for him have inherited (and enforce) an engineer's creed that brings a bloodless "just fix it" intensity to everything from human relations to fabrication. For years Grove enforced discipline with a quick, violent temper. (In 1984 FORTUNE named him one of America's tough-

MICHAEL
MULLANY

GEORI
HUNGER

est bosses.) Later, Grove recognized that he sometimes had gone too far, and would apologize.

But the merits of that no-b.s. culture became clear as the world around Intel began to crack. Beginning in 1976, the firm sailed into one iceberg after another: weak demand for memory chips, factory problems, ruthless Japanese "dumping." In 1981, when Intel steamed into yet another exhausting chip slowdown, Grove decided that instead of laying off employees he would order Intel's staff to work 25% harder—two hours a day, every day, for free. The "125% solution" turned Santa Clara into a sweatshop, but Grove's message was clear: Intel would do whatever it took.

The biggest iceberg came in 1994, when Intel released millions of flawed Pentium chips. The problem was a small, internal routing glitch that caused a mathematical error, and it occurred infrequently. Thus Intel's hyperrational, Grove-trained engineers told concerned callers not to worry. The callers hung up and dialed the newspapers. Grove, who was on a Christmas ski trip, was floored, and at first retreated into himself. Then, after a weekend conferring with his top advisers, he decided to switch courses, By the middle of the next week, Intel had agreed to spend $475 million to replace the Pentiums. As a result, Intel's name became better known than ever, and customers began to appreciate its commitment to getting things right. Confronted with another disaster, Grove had saved the chip. Next it was time to save himself.

IN LATE 1994, GROVE WAS TOLD HE HAD A TUMOR
growing on the side of his prostate gland. He was 58 years old. It wasn't immediately life threatening, but the doctors couldn't seem to agree on a course of action. Grove the scientist pursued one on his own: he hit the library. "I hadn't done that much research since I got my Ph.D.," he recalls. At night Grove would paw through research looking for something new. One doctor suggested surgery. Grove continued reading. A second doctor offered another opinion: radiation-seed therapy. Grove kept reading. A third doctor, a third opinion: just watch and wait. Grove listened to them all and then picked the course he's chosen for years: "I bet on my own charts." He decided on a "smart bomb" of high-dose radiation, a new procedure that he felt offered the best chances. It seems to have put the cancer away for now. Grove won't say he's "recovered," just that levels of the telltale prostate-specific antigen in his blood have sunk.

His marriage to Eva—the daughters call her "Eva the Saint"—has been the essential constant in Grove's life. He is clearly still nuts about her, and there is a world-worn gentleness in their touch. She takes care of him: lays out his breakfast, orders the small details of his life, helps him find whatever he needs. (Grove's parents moved to the U.S. in 1965. His father died in 1987; his mother lives in California.) Grove and Eva are still trying to figure out what to do with all their money. Grove could almost not care less. He doesn't spend his money on planes, giant homes or fast cars, living on a relatively modest scale. He and Eva plan to leave their daughters "comfortable," but the bulk of his fortune will go to charity.

Mostly, though, he continues to fret about Intel's future. The firm faces dozens of challenges—from cheap PCs to antitrust investigations—and Grove is engaged in the metamovements of the technology world more deeply than ever. If Grove is tough on people inside Intel, he is brutal with competition. Advanced Micro Devices CEO Jerry Sanders, whose company was a recent victim of Grove's tactics, says Intel makes it nearly impossible for competitors to get access to the big customers—Compaq, Dell, Gateway—that make for economies of scale. "In my view," Sanders says, "Intel goes right to the edge—and sometimes over it."

Grove has so effectively squashed the competition that his biggest worry isn't the rumblings of AMD but the strategic risk of a slowing PC market. The hottest-selling PCs in 1997 were dirt-cheap, sub-$1,000 models. Growth there could wreck Intel's business model. As a result, though cheap PCs are a tiny part of the overall market—businesses generally buy pricier PCs—Intel may be heading into a sea change. Grove, of course, sees that as an opportunity. He is in the midst of rejiggering Intel's operating model so the firm can make money on sub-$1,000 PCs. That means taking more risks and finding new applications for Intel chips. As Von Clausewitz craved the decisive battle, Grove hungers for the decisive risk, the bet that will guarantee Intel's future.

There are other worries. The Federal Trade Commission launched a second probe of Intel last fall. Though the firm escaped with a clean bill of health in the past, its dominant market share may look like a fat bull's-eye to trustbusters. Intel's close relationship with Microsoft does seem to make competition more difficult. Grove, for one, isn't slowing any plans because of the government. "We're very careful," he says, "and clean."

Grove has no intention of resigning any time soon. Though he is building a management legacy by bringing along a chain of bright, driven engineers, he remains as engaged as anyone else at Intel. That Grove could remain so in the midst of such a turbulent business is perhaps the best explanation for his success. Others chased fads or indulged their arrogance. Grove remained constant.

"Lucky or good?" is one of the questions Grove likes to ponder. Grove, who believes he's good, also suspects he's been amazingly lucky. He was lucky enough to escape Hungary; good enough to make it to the U.S. Lucky enough to find CCNY; good enough to graduate first in his class. Lucky enough to join Intel; good enough to lead it to the top. Lucky enough to marry Eva and have two healthy daughters; good enough to raise them into beautiful American women. That's the kind of life it's been. Andrew Steven Grove, TIME's Man of the Year 1997: lucky, good, paranoid. ■

How the Chip

■ The microprocessor acts as **the brain of the computer,** and it doles out instructions for every component

A **computer** consists of hundreds of parts, including a monitor, mouse, disk drives and keyboard

Inside the computer is a **circuit board.** It houses all sorts of microchips, including those for ROM (read-only memory) and RAM (random-access memory)

Mounted on the circuit board is a **microprocessor,** which is housed in a protective container and connected to rows of gold-plated pins

Inside the micro-processor package is **the chip** itself. This tiny square of silicon is packed with transistors that process data and instructions for the computer

---

■ Scientists have managed to squeeze **millions of transistors** onto each chip

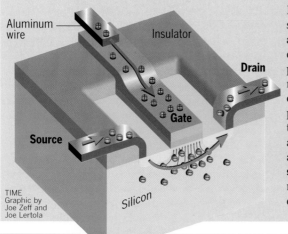

Aluminum wire
Insulator
Drain
Gate
Source
Silicon

TIME
Graphic by
Joe Zeff and
Joe Lertola

Each transistor on the surface of a silicon chip acts as a switch that can open or close a **gate.** Computers process information by manipulating sequences of opened and closed gates. A positive charge applied to the gate attracts electrons, allowing current to flow across the gap from **the source** to **the drain.** A negative charge stops the current and closes the gate.

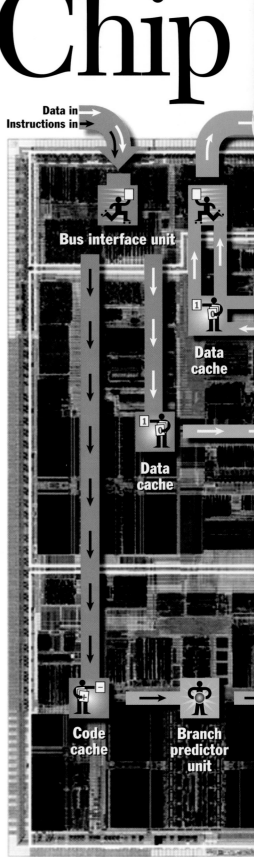

Data in
Instructions in

Bus interface unit

Data cache

Data cache

Code cache

Branch predictor unit

Works

Data out

Floating point unit

Execution units

Reservation station and reorder buffer

Instruction fetch and decode unit

■ A Pentium II chip can process **500 million instructions** every second. Here's how:

Information flows into the chip ...

The **bus interface unit** retrieves data and instructions from the computer's main memory (RAM)

Information goes either to a **code cache,** which stores the instructions that tell the processor what to do ...

... or to a **data cache,** where the data to be processed are stored until needed by other parts of the microprocessor

... where it's processed ...

The **branch predictor unit** anticipates the most likely path the instructions will take, thus getting a head start on the work

The **instruction fetch and decode unit** translate instructions into simple operations that the execution units can perform

The **reservation station and reorder buffer** determine the most efficient order for instructions to be processed

The heart of the chip is its **execution units.** They perform various operations and send results back to the data cache

The **floating point unit** handles mathematical operations on the largest and smallest numbers

... then sent out into the computer

The data cache ferries the processed information to the **bus interface unit,** which in turn sends the results to RAM

Peace breaks out
in cyberspace as
ancient enemies
Microsoft and
Apple pull off a
shotgun wedding

THE GREAT DIGITAL
DETENTE

T HE DUO HAD BEEN DUELING
for more than a decade, the binary wonders of the computer age: Steve Jobs, the flower-child dreamer whose
Apple Computer brought the world the cheerful desktop
icons of the Macintosh, and Bill Gates, the brilliant and
ruthless competitor whose Microsoft tamed the world
with Windows after sneaking in behind those scary
columns of DOS code. Their battle for control of the home
computer suggested '60s barricades re-erected for the corporate '80s and bullish '90s: yin vs. yang. Luke Skywalker
vs. Darth Vader. Jeans vs. pinstripes. Art vs. Commerce.

**MEET THE NEW
BOSS: Apple
fans in Boston
booed Gates'
digital visage**

And the winner? We're so conditioned to Hollywood's underdog victories that it came as a shock in August when Commerce whipped Art, hands down and forevermore. The end came at the annual confab of the Apple faithful, the MacWorld Expo in Boston, with what will surely go down as one of our era's iconic images: Gates' tousled-haired grin looming from a giant video screen over the tiny figure of Apple "adviser" Jobs, who stood on the podium watching his strange bedfellow confirm Microsoft's decision to bail out the seminal Silicon Valley start-up.

THE LESSON? ART MAY CAST A BRIGHTER LIGHT IN the short term, but Commerce generally wins big in the final tally. The high-tech world had spent the previous month wondering which Apple-preserving rabbit Jobs would pull from his hat during his MacWorld speech, his first major appearance as Apple's "interim" CEO since Gilbert Amelio was ousted from his ineffective 17-month reign in early July. Jobs, who helped launch the personal-computer revolution with his partner Steve Wozniak when they released the first Apple computer in 1977, had been booted out of Apple in 1985. He returned to a failing company: Apple had sales of $9.8 billion in 1996, but revenues dropped significantly in the first half of 1997, and the company seemed rudderless and adrift.

Still, no one had expected Jobs to attempt to revive Apple by embracing the company's old enemy. "The era of competition between Apple and Microsoft is over," Jobs told the stunned conclave. He then outlined a deal that included a $150 million investment in Apple by Microsoft, and the payment of an undisclosed onetime fee by Microsoft to settle previous disputes that its Windows software was based on Apple technology. In addition, Microsoft propped up the tottering Macintosh platform by pledging it would produce Mac versions of its office software for three years and cooperate with Apple on upcoming products.

Suddenly, Gates' smug smile blossomed on a vast Orwellian screen, and the wizard of Microsoft regaled the Apple masses with his boundless love for the operating system whose commercial viability he had spent much of his adult life undermining. The message: All operating systems are equal—even if some are more equal than others.

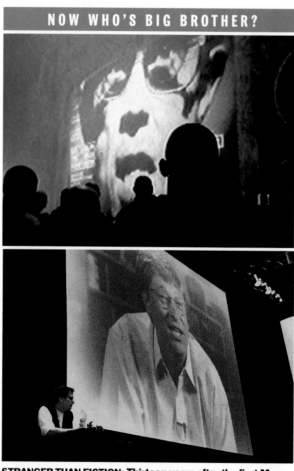

NOW WHO'S BIG BROTHER?

STRANGER THAN FICTION: Thirteen years after the first Mac ad, top, cast IBM as Big Brother, Gates played the role for real

"We think Apple makes a huge contribution to the computer industry," Gates assured the room, respectfully observing the taboo against speaking ill of the dead—or, at least, the gravely ailing. Observers recalled that Gates was not heard extolling the wonders of Apple in the late 1980s, before Microsoft vanquished Apple in their bitter duel to dominate the innards of the personal computer. Bill Gates celebrating Apple in 1997 was like the Department of the Interior celebrating the spotted owl by fencing in its nesting grounds and trying not to let the last ones die.

The faithful's reaction to the Gates-Jobs deal was pretty much what anyone conversant with the fanatical Apple cult might have expected. "Mass suicide planned tonight in Silicon Valley," read a typical posting to the newsgroup *alt.destroy.microsoft*. And the MacWorld crowd booed Gates' image even more than Jobs' turncoat words.

Wall Street, by contrast, cheered: within hours of the announcement, Apple stock soared 33%, to $26.31. Apple's richest boon, though, may have been psychological: by promising to publish Mac software into the next century, Microsoft lets Mac customers and developers alike trust the platform to exist that long. And Apple cultists don't need much encouragement to stay psyched. Sales of the 1997 release of a new operating system, Mac OS 8, the first major Mac update in a decade, have been four times Apple's expectations. And the company can still point to considerable leads in the education and graphics arenas.

But the wide-angle view is grim. A decade of bungled opportunities and misguided investments has left Apple in an intractable negative spiral: lower market share means fewer developers, which means less software, which means fewer customers, which means still lower market share. Not pretty. Even the belated decision to license the Mac OS to clonemakers only drained Apple of hardware revenue—a fact Jobs tacitly acknowledged shortly after the MacWorld convention when he announced Mac would not license its new OS 8 operating system, and would buy the chief maker of Mac clones, Power Computing Corp.

Microsoft's bear hug bought Apple a few months' breathing room, and, in another necessary piece of housekeeping, most of Apple's reviled board of directors were replaced with bold-faced techies like Oracle's Larry Ellison and Intuit's Bill Campbell. But regaining traction will require what Jobs called "a new paradigm." Just what this might consist of, though, is unclear. Build low-cost networked computers? Split up into hardware and software siblings? Or just rely on the expected 1998 release of Apple's new operating system, Rhapsody, based on new technology developed at Jobs' post-Apple company, NeXT (which Apple shelled out $424 million for in 1997)? True believers call Rhapsody the greatest operating system ever—and Apple's savior; skeptics call NeXT a marketplace failure and an albatross Apple should have left around Jobs' neck. Regardless, it's hard to see any operating system other than Windows flourishing under digital networks' natural tendency toward monopoly.

Above all, the Apple-Microsoft détente underlined Gates' unequaled strategic genius. His $150 million investment in Apple maintains Microsoft's $300 million annual income from selling software to the 20 million-strong Mac users, even as it increases Apple's reliance on Microsoft software to keep the public hooked on its computers. The deal, said Mike Homer, a Netscape executive, "puts the whole application base in Microsoft's hands. And if they control that, they control the Macintosh."

And there's still a good deal about Macintosh that's worth controlling. Gates' richest prize may be Apple's intellectual property, whether silicon- or carbon-based. The graphic designers, software gurus and other artsy types who constitute the Mac's most fervent cadres are a disproportionately influential market niche. Some two-thirds of all Websites are thought to have been created on Macs. "It's very attractive to Microsoft to have access to cutting-edge Mac developers," says Kurt King, an analyst with San Francisco–based Montgomery Securities, "particularly in areas like video streaming and other graphics technologies that represent the likely future of Internet content."

Ditto Apple's technology patents. Under the new cross-licensing agreement, they will no longer cause endless litigation (those among the Mac faithful will surely consider Microsoft's undisclosed payment to Apple to settle infringement claims de facto proof that Gates stole their operating system). For the first time, the patents will be weapons for Microsoft coders to wield.

And the time is now; the turf is the Web; and Gates' enemy is Netscape, whose browser market share still dwarfs Microsoft's. The Apple deal makes Microsoft's Internet Explorer the default browser for all future Macs. That's yet another coup for Gates, who is painfully aware that the Web poses a threat to the operating-system standards whose implacable rigidity led to Microsoft's rise in the first place. Gates spent the Web's first two years pretending it didn't matter, and the next two frantically refocusing his company on the Net, battling Netscape for supremacy in a battle of internet browsers,

SALAD DAYS: Despite their battle to dominate the desktop, Jobs and Gates strike a friendly pose for the camera in 1991

and snapping up any company that might further that goal.

The most dire threat to Windows' hegemony may be Java, the Web-minded programming language created at Sun Microsystems in the early 1990s. Java's greatest strength is its "portability"; in a Java-centric future, developers would be able to write programs not for one operating system at a time, but for the Java Virtual Machine, a single software that could run numerous next-wave computers: PCs, smart cell phones, personal digital assistants, stripped-down network computers and so on.

The deal between Apple and Microsoft, which commits them to creating a joint Java platform, was an attack on the triple alliance among Sun, Netscape and Apple that hoped to use Java to fight Microsoft for control of the Web. Bill Gates wants a proprietary Java platform specially designed for Windows. The Apple deal moves him closer to that goal, while nudging his rivals further from their own.

"Netscape could have shored up the Macintosh situation," says Dave Winer, an early Mac developer. "Same with Sun. They could have given Apple $150 million. They just weren't playing strategically. Microsoft was."

Microsoft always is, and that's why Microsoft always wins. Whether Jobs can flourish by bargaining with the master is open to question. Can Apple survive? Sure, and the spotted owl will probably hang in there too. The Mac remains the most usable, intuitive operating system around, and it will never disappear entirely. Still, it must be tough for Jobs and his old pals at Apple. Ten years ago, they were visionary champions of the future. Now they are fringy advocates of an endangered technology. ■

All operating systems are equal— but some are more equal than others

CHECKMATE, DEEPER BLUE

One year after world chess champ Garry Kasparov whipped IBM's computer, the tables are turned

DEEP BLUE IS THINKING. OR RATHER, ON move 16, the supercomputer's 512 processors are reviewing 200 million chess positions per second in order to create the illusion that Deep Blue is thinking. And it isn't really Deep Blue either. It's what the folks at IBM's Thomas J. Watson Research Center in Yorktown Heights, N.Y., call Deeper Blue: the second generation of the original Deep Blue, the chess program that threw a stunning uppercut to human self-esteem in 1996 by winning the first game of its six-game match against world champion Garry Kasparov. Kasparov, of course, went on to score three victories and two draws to win the match and save mankind; the 33-year-old Russian isn't considered the best player in history for nothing.

The Deep Blue team, led by senior manager C.J. Tan, has been plotting revenge ever since; now it is prepping for the rematch, scheduled for Manhattan in May, 1997. Today, in February, in this cramped lab at T.J. Watson, Deep and Deeper are playing their first father-son game, a silicon Oedipal struggle.

The first 15 moves are what chess types yawn at as "standard"—established openings. Very safe. No surprises. Move 16 is when Deeper Blue pauses to "think." Finally, its human monitor announces, "f4." f4? An excited buzz sweeps the room. f4! Deeper Blue has advanced the king's bishop's pawn two squares, loosening its kingside defense with an assumption of the superiority of its position that would surely be considered arrogant if a carbon-based life-form were making it. "This move was special," murmurs Joel Benjamin, a former U.S. champion and current Deep Blue consultant. The room nods in agreement. Deeper Blue is thinking.

Pretty soon, Deeper Blue is kicking butt. From f4 onward, its inexorable kingside march swallows one pawn after an-

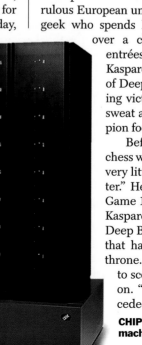

other, and Deep Blue resigns 18 moves later. The room erupts in applause. The same thought is on everyone's mind: the new program is better. The new program is a lot better. We're gonna crush Kasparov like a bug.

The bug in question wasn't nervous, though—at least not yet. "I'll have to play well and have a couple of surprises, but I feel that my chances are still superior," Kasparov says over lunch in Manhattan the next day to an audience of six, including Tan. "I know quite a lot, and I'll control my temper and my psychology." Kasparov is handsome and burly; he has a temperament more befitting a garrulous European uncle than a genius geek who spends his life hunched over a chessboard. Over entrées a smug Tan hits Kasparov with the news of Deeper Blue's smashing victory over the program that made him sweat a year before, and suddenly the champion focuses, laserlike, on his favorite subject.

Before the 1996 match, he admits, the chess world believed "a computer would have very little chance of beating a top grand master." He soon knew better. Halfway through Game 1, faced with daunting circumstances, Kasparov undertook a blitzkrieg aimed at Deep Blue's king, the sort of hell-bent gambit that had devastated every pretender to his throne. But Deep Blue didn't flinch: it went on to score the first win over a world champion. "Then I realized," Kasparov now conceded, "that this would be tough."

CHIP OFF THE OLD BLOCK: IBM's Deeper Blue machine also beat its "forefather," Deep Blue

But so is Kasparov, and in the ensuing games he mercilessly exposed his opponent's weaknesses. The computer was a data-crunching engine of staggering proportions: a 1.5-ton behemoth able to sort 40 billion combinations in an average three-minute move, shining its searchlight far into a game's future to find a winning strategy. But Kasparov prevailed to win the match.

In 1997 Deeper Blue—and IBM—had the last laugh. Kasparov triumphed in the first game of the six-game match, which was highlighted by an exchange of queens. But in the second game, Kasparov yielded to a relentless end-game attack by the computer and resigned on the 45th move. Three draws followed, with real fireworks erupting in the fifth game. With most experts rating Kasparov clearly ahead, and perhaps only a few moves from victory, the computer managed to force a perpetual check and thus a draw. Kasparov became visibly angry and seemed to lose heart. The next day, the champion lost his queen early on; more important, he later admitted, "I lost my fighting spirit." He resigned the final game after only 19 moves, conceding the match. The final tally: Deeper Blue 2, Kasparov 1, and three draws.

EEKS AFTER THE DEFEAT, WRITING IN TIME, Kasparov said, "The decisive game of the match was Game 2 . . . in Deeper Blue's Game 2 we saw something that went well beyond our wildest expectations of how well a computer would be able to foresee the long-term positional consequences of its decisions. My opponent was psychologically stable, undisturbed and unconcerned about anything going on around it, and it made almost none of the typical computer-chess errors." But his spirits were back: "IBM owes mankind a rematch," he demanded. Or, as they say in low-tech sports: "Wait till next year!" ∎

FOR THE BEST PART OF 15 YEARS NOW, STEVE CASE has nurtured a vision. Back in the days when computer modems creaked along at 300 bits a second, when it took half an hour to download a small black-and-white photo, and when most Americans were obsessing over CB radios, the future chief of America Online imagined a world where ordinary folk, like the ones he grew up with in Hawaii, would find utility and entertainment in connecting their computers. Almost everyone considered that a ridiculous idea.

Since 1985, when he founded the company that would eventually become AOL, Case has jousted continually with the doubters. Even his loyal board members lost faith: in 1987, after a particularly rough patch, they were ready to fire him—until someone argued that surely Case had learned something while spending millions without a penny of profit. Whatever that was didn't seem apparent as his online service hit rock bottom in the early winter of 1997, suffering through one gaffe after another, leaving Case exhausted and his critics smirking. "Look," he snapped to a reporter at the time, "what I've figured out is that I *can* predict the future! I just can't predict when."

It arrived in the fall of 1997. On Monday, Sept. 8, AOL astonished the computer and media world with the news that it would swallow CompuServe, the nation's oldest online service, and its 2.6 million members. As part of the deal, AOL sealed a long-term pact with WorldCom, Bernard Ebbers' upstart telephone company based in Jackson, Miss. WorldCom's scads of capacity will help AOL lock in access to phone lines at low rates for the next five years—and probably boost profits. In the convoluted three-way agreement, WorldCom bought CompuServe and then handed AOL the online company's subscribers in exchange for AOL's networking and Internet-access division, called ANS. When the deal is concluded, AOL will probably number some 12 million members, almost six times as many as its nearest competitor, the Microsoft Network (MSN). Only in the digital age can an outfit go from worst to first so quickly.

In the 24 months before the WorldCom deal, AOL had dodged everything from a Bill Gates bull rush (his Microsoft Network spent millions to compete with AOL) to a tussle with the Internet, whose wide-open spaces threatened to make AOL's narrow "gated community" irrelevant. Case, 39, had been famously (if inadvertently) self-destructive, infuriating AOL members by offering too little capacity and too many headaches. Overeager users had crashed parts of the service twice in the previous year by bombarding it with more calls than computers could handle. And as "America On Hold" angered customers, it perplexed Wall Street. Accountants demanded that AOL refigure its books, erasing every dollar of profit the company ever made. It faced potential lawsuits from the attorneys general of 36 states over billing practices. William Razzouk, a hotshot executive from FedEx, split after just five flabbergasted months as president of the service. The company endured the inevitable collapse of its too-rich stock price. Twice.

Even in the wake of the WorldCom deal, many of the same problems remain. AOL, which has always had a high turnover of subscribers, still serves for many as training

HOW AOL
LOST THE BATTLE BUT
WON
THE WAR

In a roller-coaster 1997, Steve Case took America Online from the depths to the heights

wheels from which they eventually graduate by getting directly onto the Internet. Retaining customers will become even harder as phone companies, cable companies, Microsoft and Netscape make it ever easier to use the Internet's open standards for browsing the Web, chatting and sending mail. AOL hopes the WorldCom deal will eventually allow it to offer higher-speed access through phone lines, but cable and wireless technologies could lure impatient users away from cumbersome dial-up services. Customers could also become turned off by the increasingly intrusive ads, upon which AOL's flat-price business model depends.

And while Microsoft has yet to perfect its own MSN service, even Case observes that Gates' behemoth usually gets things right on the third or fourth try. When Microsoft finally gets its browser, mail, Internet access and content fully integrated into its Windows operating system, users may find it easier to get to the rich content of the Web that way, rather than through the suburban environment of AOL. But despite all those challenges and the predictions of doomsayers over the years, Case's company showed in 1997 that it has at least the potential to thrive.

In a world of tech-heavy computers, Case hewed to one truism: easy is better

Indeed, the WorldCom-CompuServe deal certified AOL as cyberspace's first true empire, a global online service that's adding 6,000 members a day and will soon be available in more than 100 countries. Revenues have pumped up with impressive speed, from $53 million in fiscal 1993 to nearly $2 billion in 1997. And, slowly, profits are emerging. The stock price, which traded at $23 in the fall of 1996, hit a high above $91 in October 1997. "AOL has won the battle to become the No. 1 brand in home online access," says Keith Benjamin, a Wall Street analyst.

The anchor for this success is a truism as relaxed as Case's laconic charm: easy is better. In a world of over-featured, tech-heavy computers and Internet gadgets, Case built a business on the simple idea that the electronic world should be easy to use. "The geeks don't like us," Case said. "They want as much technology as possible, while AOL's entire objective is to simplify." It was Case, for instance, who introduced the first graphical interface to the online world in 1985, allowing users to point their mouse arrows at whatever they wanted, and click to get it.

Simplicity has let AOL build an electronic community that includes not only the geek next door but the geek's parent and grandparents as well. It's a place where a generation of Florida retirees has found that the keyword JEWISH links to the "Ask a Rabbi" feature, where teens can buy MTV clothes and where *Business Week* and the New York *Times* come free with a subscription to AOL. Case hopes for a service that is as clean, organized and trouble free as the manicured suburbs that surround AOL's Dulles, Va., headquarters. Internal research suggests that AOL could reach 25 million members by 1999. Says Case, once a PepsiCo marketer: "We want to be the Coca-Cola of the online world."

Case, a Williams College graduate, began his professional career working for corporate giants like PepsiCo and Procter & Gamble, where he learned that listening to

I WANT MY AOL: Pittman brought MTV's style—and an emphasis on branding—to cyberspace

consumers is the key to marketing. But even as he worked on the Pizza Hut business at PepsiCo, his own tastes were going digital. He bought a Kaypro, a clunky home computer connected to a snail-paced modem. Even for a hobbyist, the machine was a nightmare—hard to set up, impossible to maintain, boring to use. But the modem was a revelation. As he connected to early online services such as Compu-Serve and the Source, Case felt the electronic rapture that would one day seduce millions of AOL users: "There was something magical about the notion of sitting in Wichita and talking to the world," he recalls.

The convergence of Case's entrepreneurial spirit and his hobby came in 1983, when his brother Dan helped him land a job at Control Video, a Virginia-based company with the premature idea of shipping Atari video games to home computers over telephone lines. Two weeks after Case arrived, the firm's capital dried up. Out of the ashes, Case crafted Quantum Computer Services. His idea was to create an online bulletin board for owners of Commodore 64 computers. It wasn't a sexy niche, but he thought it might have potential.

From 1985 onward, Case nurtured Quantum from a few thousand members to more than 100,000, while refining his ideas about how computers should communicate and what his audience needed. In 1991 Quantum became America Online. Boasting a mere 150,000 members, Case prepared to battle both CompuServe, which had 800,000 members, and Prodigy, an IBM-Sears joint venture with 1.1 million subscribers.

This seemed nutty. Compete with IBM? Sears? But Case was operating with a bit of screwy good luck and the market savvy that comes from hard knocks. He looked at American consumers and somehow understood what it

> **Pittman built MTV from a low-budget channel to an empire of hair and attitude**

would take to get them online. IBM and CompuServe bet that the real lure would be lots of fancy computer features. Case, who had seen dozens of sophisticated pizza recipes fail in his Pizza Hut days, knew better. What America wanted was cheese, tomato sauce and a touch of pepperoni. AOL would reek with simplicity.

The online experience wasn't an easy sell at first, but when the business began to pick up in the early 1990s, it picked up fast. From 200,000 members in 1992, AOL surged to 1 million by 1994, 4 million by late 1995 and 8 million in January 1997. As America Online shot up, it passed CompuServe and Prodigy on the way down. The cyberspace marketplace changed almost overnight, and forever. Millions of Americans began to recognize the value of getting their computers online, and AOL was their first, best hope.

Case and Robert Pittman, the chief executive of AOL Networks, are working to make AOL even easier to use. Their goal is to capture the mindless simplicity of a television: on, off, a channel tuner. In Case's marketing terms, simplicity is what puts the fingers on the mice. A new generation of AOL software that was being tested in the fall of '97 offered a seamless link between the Web and AOL. Everything was as neatly organized as a small-town library: AOL had put a frame around the chaotic tumble of the Internet. The frame, Case hoped, would make the Net easier to use, simpler to understand, and more carefully edited to keep young kids from seeing things they shouldn't see.

ROBERT PITTMAN, WHO HELPED BUILD MTV FROM A low-budget cable channel into an empire of hair and attitude, believes in the consumerist approach. The veteran media executive, 43, has an intense charm that makes him a natural for AOL's dichotomous culture, where V.P.s brag alternately about late nights and mountain-biking exploits. "I've spent my whole life building brands," Pittman says. "And we're focusing more on brand building than others. My experience tells me that's a good thing."

As AOL's audience grows to approach those of such cable-TV networks as MTV, CNN and a few others, advertisers are shelling out to reach its affluent members. In 1998 analysts expect the company to sell close to $150 million in ads. As Case sees it, that's just a start. The hidden victory of the WorldCom deal is that it gives AOL a technological leg up. WorldCom is building bigger pipes—broadband, in the parlance—over which AOL can push a richer service. If AOL can attract 12 million users just with snappy graphics and chat, imagine what it will be able to do with full-motion video and stereo sound. That's the kind of pepperoni even Steve Case would enjoy. ■

Will Reno Brake Windows?

The Justice Department levels antitrust charges at Bill Gates' mighty Microsoft

JANET RENO STOOD STEELY-EYED BEFORE THE MICROphone on Oct. 20, the Attorney General Like She Oughtta Be, bringing bad guys to heel on behalf of the American populace. The bad guy in question was the software titan Microsoft Corp. The Justice Department's antitrust division, led by new chief Joel Klein, claimed that Microsoft had violated the terms of a 1995 agreement that sought to bar the company from using its operating-system dominance to strong-arm PC makers such as Compaq Computer Corp. and Micron Technology into installing additional Microsoft software on their machines, thus squeezing out competitors' products.

It is Microsoft's practice to require its hardware partners to plant the company's Web browser, Internet Explorer, on the desktop of every PC they make—or lose the right to sell Windows 95 computers. Since Windows operating systems now run some 85% of PCs in the U.S., that loss would be tantamount to going out of business. Microsoft, Reno said, "is unlawfully taking advantage of its Windows monopoly to protect and extend that monopoly and undermine consumer choice." She asked the federal district court to order Gates to drop the Explorer demand or pay the startling fine of $1 million a day.

Microsoft's Windows hegemony gives Gates an often insuperable lever that he has never been shy about using to elbow his way into the market for the countless applications that live within today's PCs. In testimony heard by Justice officials, one PC executive after another described how Microsoft's absolutist licensing agreements had forced them to feature Explorer in their machines.

The Justice Department, declared Reno, "won't tolerate any coercion by dominant companies in any way that distorts competition." When it comes to Microsoft, however, her department has often talked tough, then caved. Gates bailed out of his proposed acquisition of financial software giant Intuit after the Justice Department objected, but for the most part the agency has spent recent years trying to slap Microsoft down—only to cut easy deals that left the software giant even more deeply ensconced.

In November a phalanx of Microsoft executives flew into Washington to face various strains of nasty music: delivering the company's response to the contempt action and girding for assaults by both the House and Senate judiciary committees. Washington influence peddling is that rare arena in which Gates is a legitimate underdog. In the past Microsoft had seemed to regard the Federal Government as an industrial-era irrelevancy. Gates has donated startlingly little political money by CEO standards, and he opened an official lobbying office only in 1995.

Microsoft's disdain for D.C. was written between every line of its response to the Justice complaint, which Microsoft labeled "perverse." The tactic backfired: on Dec. 11, Federal Judge Thomas Jackson issued a temporary ruling that Microsoft must indeed "unbundle" its Explorer browser from its Windows 95 operating system. However, the judge denied the requested $1 million-a-day fine, calling the terms of the 1995 agreement "ambiguous." The ruling threw the company's plans into turmoil: it had scheduled the release of Windows 98, its new operating system that is closely bundled with the Explorer browser, for spring 1998.

Microsoft quickly announced it would appeal the temporary order, calling Judge Jackson's ruling an "error" and "inappropriate." It then announced it would seek to comply with the order by offering PC makers two choices of its operating system: the current version, bundled with the browser—or the original version of Windows 95, a two-year-old program that was badly out of date and that would not even allow purchasers access to America Online and other applications. Furious Justice Department officials said that Microsoft was mocking the temporary order and renewed their request for the daily $1 million fine. In addition, they asked that the judge grant them the unusual power to review any new operating systems or browsers made by Microsoft prior to their commercial release. In the battle between Janet Reno and Bill Gates, round one had clearly gone to Reno. ■

SQUARING OFF: Reno challenged— and Gates refused to retreat

At Last, a ROM of Their Own

Smart, socially oriented software gives girls new ways to play with computers

YOUR NAME IS ROCKETT. IT'S YOUR FIRST DAY AT A NEW junior high school, and you're pretty nervous, but outside the building you meet this girl named Jessie who gives you the lay of the land ("Watch out for Nicole." "Who's Nicole?" "Don't worry, you'll find out sooner than you'd want to"). Now, do you walk into homeroom by Jessie's side or go it alone? She's nice, but is it smart to commit to a best friend already? What do you do?

If this doesn't strike you as hot gaming action, you're probably not a girl between eight and 13, which is to say a member of Brenda Laurel's favorite demographic group. Laurel, a veteran of computer-game wars going back to Atari, has taken on the mystery of why there aren't better games for girls. The result, backed by the deep pockets of Interval Research, the high-tech think tank of Microsoft cofounder Paul Allen, is a start-up company called Purple Moon, whose CD-ROMs debuted in 1997.

Purple Moon's games weren't alone. Nearly two dozen CD-ROMs aimed at preteen girls were released in the fall by companies with names like Her Interactive and Girl Games. It's a market that had been all but ignored in favor of the seemingly bottomless appetite of boys and young men for so-called twitch games, like the bloody shoot-'em-ups Quake and Doom. Why the sudden interest in what young women may want? In a word: Barbie. In the fall of 1996 Mattel released a disc called Barbie Fashion Designer that was a runaway best seller, proving that if the pitch is right, the girls will sit down at their keyboards and play.

"There's always been an interest in marketing for girls," says Suzanne Groatman, children's software buyer for the retail giant CompUSA. "Barbie just exploded the market. People are looking at this year as the time to launch on the coattails of that traffic." The iffier question is how much traffic there will be for games that aren't as retrograde as,

MAKE PALS, NOT WAR: Purple Moon's Brenda Laurel

Is there a market for girls' games—beyond Barbie Magic Hair Styler?

say, Barbie Magic Hair Styler, the 1997 fall offering from Mattel. Some of the new titles come linked to popular books like the American Girl and Babysitters' Club series or Hollywood franchises such as *Clueless* and *Sabrina, the Teenage Witch*. But a few hardy souls sailed unlicensed into waters that, given the hit-or-miss track record of CD-ROMs, are most kindly described as uncharted.

Laurel and her Purple Moon CEO Nancy Deyo are among the pioneers. They hope to give girls what they don't get enough of: a chance to use play to deal with the issues in their increasingly complex emotional lives. Purple Moon's market testing found that girls prefer games that feature covert competition, intricate narratives and group efforts based on complex social hierarchies. "We call the age between childhood and adolescence the Two-Headed Girl," says Laurel. "On the one hand you're constructing your social persona, and on the other hand you're constructing your inner self, finding out what it is you value and how your emotions work. Those two sides don't talk to each other very well."

So Purple Moon built two new games that do. In Rockett's New School (the first of a promised series), carrot-topped Rockett has to steer through the dangerous shoals of junior high. Players decide how to interact with other characters, guiding and shaping the story based on how they think Rockett is feeling about a given situation. The debut title of Purple Moon's second line of games, Secret Paths in the Forest, is a gorgeously illustrated adventure game whose players take soul-baring journeys that are essentially preteen female versions of Robert Bly.

Will such diversions capture the hearts—and leisure time—of nine-year-old girls? The question involves more than toy sales: three-quarters of today's working women regard computer proficiency as essential to professional advancement, a 1997 survey by Avon Products reported. For years, boys have been using video games as entry points into the world of serious computing. If girls are going to compete, it's high time they got their share of the action. ∎

Cellular Phones Go Digital

The cellular phone industry needed an answering machine—not one that took messages but one that gave answers. The wireless market was growing faster than the market for video recorders or fax machines had at a comparable stage of development. By 1997, deregulation had

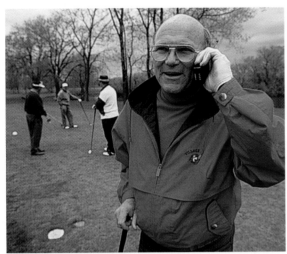

BEEP! There's no escaping the cellular craze

created a free-for-all that was bringing real competition, not to mention utter confusion, to the burgeoning market for wireless phones (1996 sales: $25 billion). Cities across the U.S. were suddenly finding themselves with as many as half a dozen wireless-phone companies to choose from. That was good news for callers: the average price of a wireless minute fell from $1 in 1987 to 50¢ in 1997. But it also brought breathless ad wars and numbingly complex price plans. Driving the demand was a new digital service called PCS (for personal communications system), created by the Federal Communications Commission. Unlike many older systems, which turn voices into analog waves, PCS uses digital signals that break sound into discrete bits— the 1s and 0s that run computers—enabling PCS to offer such features as E-mail, caller ID and paging as well as compact-disc-quality sound and greater security.

The Market's Sag Gives Online Investing a Lift

The New York Stock Exchange recovered quickly from its momentarily frightening "correction" in October 1997. But the scare was also a watershed—the moment when online money management finally came of age as an everyday tool for investors. Which isn't to say everything went smoothly. On Monday, Oct. 27, elec-

GETTING PERSONAL More than 200 subjects in a case study published in January in the journal *Science and Engineering Ethics* claimed they had been discriminated against as a result of genetic testing of their DNA.

BANDWIDTH BOON The FCC handed $70 billion in space on public airwaves to the nation's TV broadcasters—for free—supposedly to ease their transition to HDTV, the high-definition digital TV format. Critics called the boon a boondoggle.

tronic shops such as Schwab, E*Trade and Waterhouse bogged down when calls from anxious investors doubled their normal traffic. But by the end of Tuesday, hundreds of thousands got through and acted as their own online traders. They swore by the experience of maneuvering their funds minute by minute as they followed the hectic market's jagged path.

The Web's Own Winchell

Drudge is the name. Matt Drudge. And gossip is his game. Online gossip. Drudge is the brains behind the *Drudge Report*, the Internet's favorite celebrity scandal sheet. Drudge has power, see? One press of a key and—bang!—an item is broadcast to the 60,000 Internet subscribers who receive his breathless E-mail bulletins (and

DRUDGE: Is he a journalist—or a jester?

to tens of thousands more who visit his Website): tomorrow's Washington *Post* headlines, what Paula Jones saw, who's up and who's down in Hollywood. Drudge boasted that his items were "80% accurate." But victims like White House aide Sidney Blumenthal weren't laughing. When Drudge printed a claim that Blumenthal had beaten his wife, the presidential aide—a former journalist—filed a libel suit.

At Long Last, DVD Debuts

After years of hype, two dozen models of digital videodisc players reached the market in 1997, at prices ranging from less than $500 to more than $1,000. All offered DVD's stunning sound and vision, along with such bells and whistles as PG- and R-rated versions of a given movie on one disc, multiple languages, no rewinding, instant searches—in short, enough custom setup and picture adjustments to keep early adopting cinephiles hot and bothered.

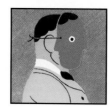

The Promise Keepers march their men-only crusade into the nation's capital. Is their movement just—or just plain intolerant?

IN GOD THEY TRUST

Lawton, Okla., is a spit-and-shine military town, where real men aren't supposed to cry. This is the home of Fort Sill, a U.S. Army post, where soldiers learn to kill with gun, mortar and missile, where the big boys belly up to the bar at Gertlestone's pub and down stiff shots of Jaegermeister, where the measure of a man lies partly in his ability to tuck his pain away in a place where nobody—nobody—can see it. Yet a few miles away, in the dimly lighted sanctuary of the First Assembly of God church on a humid Thursday night, dozens of men are weeping openly in the

A Coach Heeds the Call

Bill McCartney, the founder of the Promise Keepers, was named head football coach at the University of Colorado in 1982. By 1989 he had turned a struggling program into one of the nation's best. Yet McCartney's family life suffered. His wife Lyndi drifted into depression as her four children grew up, and her husband was often on the road. In 1989 the coach's only daughter, 20-year-old Kristyn, gave birth to an illegitimate child; the father was Colorado football star Sal Aunese, a notorious campus playboy. Bill McCartney stayed close to Aunese, helping him accept Jesus nine weeks before he died of cancer in 1989. The following year, McCartney was struck by a vision of stadiums filled with men committing themselves to Christ: the result was Promise Keepers. In 1994 McCartney gave up his football career, not to give more time to evangelism, but to make up for the time he lost with Lyndi.

pews, men who have come from the base, men who aren't supposed to cry unless their team has won the Super Bowl, if at all. But here they are, middle-aged guys sobbing and hugging and professing love for one another. They admit to having broken promises, they beg forgiveness—for insensitivity, for infidelity, for abandoning their children, for racial hatred, for sins as petty as reading pornography or transgressions as heinous as abusing their wives—and they swear to be Promise Keepers.

The scene is repeated in similar small, regularly held fellowship groups around the U.S. (about 20,000 at last count) and has been displayed in spectacular proportions in stadiums across the country. In 1996 an average of 50,000 men congregated at each of 22 sites for a total of 1.1 million souls. Male souls always, for the Promise Keepers are intent on carving God's masculine face back onto the spiritual tableau where they believe the model of divine fatherhood has eroded. The seven-year-old organization boasts annual revenues of $87 million, a two-story brick headquarters in Denver and 360 paid staff members. It is out to retake male responsibility—and re-establish male leadership—in a country that it sees as badly detoured from a godly and natural course, having fallen into the snares of poverty, illegitimacy, drug abuse and juvenile delinquency because American men have forsaken Christian values.

Such patriarchal fervor sets off political alarms. As proof of its arrival on the national scene, the Promise Keepers has attracted a group of watchdogs wary of any threat to civil liberty posed by these men who have found a very male god. On Saturday, Oct. 4, the group's critics got a lot to watch. Hundreds of thousands of Promise Keepers brought their tears-and-revival extravaganza to Washington in a six-hour program of worship, repentance and prayer, titled "Stand in the Gap," at the National Mall.

Was their cause, as critics claimed, a dangerous movement toward Christian-male domination? In *Promise Keepers: The Third Wave of the American Religious Right*, co-authors Alfred Ross and Lee Cokorinos of the Center for Democracy Studies accused Promise Keepers of using outwardly benign teachings on prayer and social responsibility to create a grass-roots network designed to buttress the religious right. In May, 59 religious liberals, including Joseph Hough, the dean of Vanderbilt University, and William Howard, the president of New York Theological Seminary, warned the nation's churches of the potential dangers of Promise Keepers. The National Organization for Women passed a resolution declaring Promise Keepers "the greatest danger to women's rights" and staged a press conference in Washington to voice their opposition to the gathering.

Promise Keepers declared it had no political agenda. Nevertheless, it made no attempt to hide such allies on the religious right as supporter James Dobson, a psychologist and Christian activist who produces the most widely heard Christian daily radio program, and Pat Robertson, the former presidential candidate and Christian Coalition head.

Promise Keepers founder Bill McCartney, 57, is without a doubt deeply conservative. As head football coach for the University of Colorado, McCartney held mandatory pregame prayers, for which he was attacked by the American Civil Liberties Union. In 1989 he caused an uproar at the university when he addressed a pro-life rally. The school was infuriated again in 1992 when McCartney supported Amendment 2, which banned some gay-rights laws in Colorado. He has also said, "The only way God can be worshipped is through Jesus Christ. There is no other way."

AT THE HELM OF PROMISE KEEPERS, MCCARTNEY has toned down some of his rhetoric. But part of what concerns NOW and other opponents is not what Promise Keepers leaders say but what they fail to say. The group's mission is vague and unsettling regarding its relationships with women. It calls for men to take "spiritual leadership" over their wives, for example, and suggests that women follow. Feminists say this is a throwback to the days of women's servitude and oppression. Says NOW president Patricia Ireland: "Two adults standing as equals and peers, taking responsibility for their family, is a much different image than the man being the head and master, and women being back in an old role that historically was very detrimental."

Promise Keepers believe a man's spiritual makeup differs from a woman's. Men need something McCartney calls a "masculine context that allows them to come clean." The organization seeks to lead men to Christ by creating a climate in which men are more likely to view themselves and their lives more honestly. Indeed, women are seen as an impediment to a man's inmost soul searching and are not invited into Promise Keepers rallies or other activities.

The group makes a strong case for single-sex worship. While generic Evangelical appeals open Promise Keepers rallies, the sermons can quickly get down to male nitty-gritty. At a 1997 gathering at the Pontiac Silverdome, in a Detroit suburb, the second speaker spent half an hour hitting hard at details of sexual sins, not just inner lust and the use of pornography but adultery and abuse as well.

Why? Promise Keepers surveys indicate that 62% of stadiumgoers struggle with sexual sin in their lives. No other issue comes close. At the end of his sermon, the second speaker at the Silverdome asked men who had committed sexual impurities to come to the front and confess. At first nothing happened. Then a few came forward. Suddenly, thousands jammed the front, falling to their knees, weeping. "When a man sees a stadium full of other men crying, he figures it's all right to cry too," says Donald Burwell, a Promise Keepers organizer in Detroit. "With women there, he might not get that honest."

McCartney insists that a man's "leadership" at home actually translates into "servanthood" rather than domination. In fact, many women, including many members' wives, support the group. Hillary Clinton, while cautious about its leadership, praised the Promise Keepers in her book *It Takes a Village.* And at a press conference before the Washington event, a group of conservative women from mainline Protestant and Roman Catholic churches denounced NOW for its attack on the Promise Keepers.

Outside the home, Promise Keepers also preaches a rather amorphous message of "racial reconciliation," constantly pointing out that 11 a.m. Sunday is the beginning of the most segregated hour of the week. Promise Keepers president Randy Phillips admits the organization is still paying a price for failing to reach out to minorities during its inception. "We started off with white leaders," so men of color were "the add-on, not the DNA. That was wrong, and we got hurt." The organization has made major progress since then: today minorities constitute 38% of its staff and a growing share of the attendance at its rallies.

Promise Keepers seems intent on framing the issues of gender and race in the most biblical of contexts. But the sonorities of Scripture, which can work miracles in individual souls, can also alienate non-Christians. Even so, liberal watchdogs were probably overstating their case when they argued that the movement was part of a Trojan-horse strategy of the religious right. For Promise Keepers at the grass roots see only their own souls at stake—to a man. ∎

Women need not apply: they are seen as a barrier to male soul searching

Big Tobacco cuts a deal with the states to 'fess up and pay up—if Washington approves

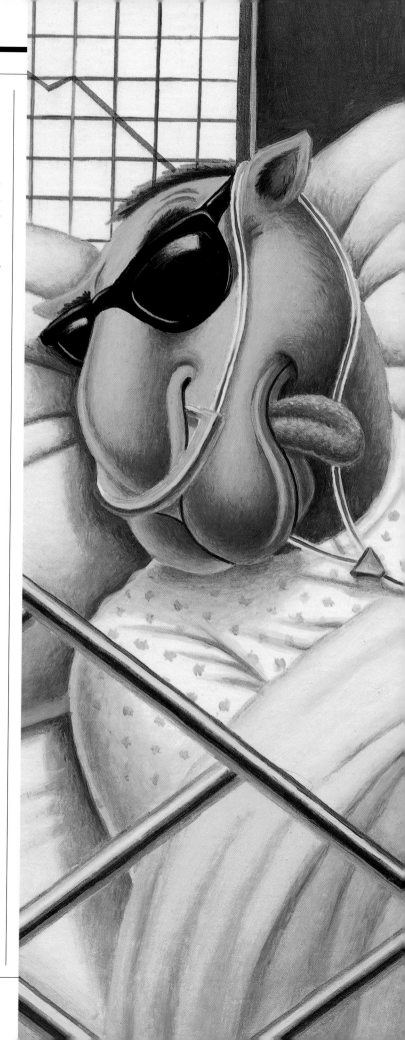

FOR FIVE DAYS THE NEGOTIATORS, EXHAUSTED and increasingly needing fresh shirts, darted between Washington's Park Hyatt and ANA hotels, from conference room to mezzanine, hallway to bedroom conference call. Every so often, rumpled lawyers would emerge with wildly divergent claims about the progress of the fractious tobacco talks: a settlement was imminent, negotiators had hit the worst impasse since the start of deliberations on April 3, and so on. Finally, at 3:30 p.m. on June 30, a chorus of state attorneys general gathered around a microphone in the ANA's ballroom to congratulate themselves on what Mississippi Attorney General Michael Moore called "the most historic public-health achievement in history."

Although the attorneys general talked as though they had just cured cancer, in truth they may have done the next best thing. They forced the tobacco industry to concede, in so many grudging words and so many, many more dollars, that cigarettes are a deadly regimen. The companies—Philip Morris, RJR Nabisco Holdings Corp., B.A.T. Industries, PLC's Brown & Williamson and Loews Corp.'s Lorillard—reached a resolution with the attorneys general of nearly 40 states in which the industry will pay out $368.5 billion in compensation over the next quarter-century, will drastically alter marketing programs and will submit to the regulatory heel of the FDA.

Tobacco's retreat began in March, with the obvious but startling admission by one of the smallest tobacco companies, Liggett Group, that cigarettes are addictive and have been pointedly marketed at kids for years. The confession signaled the first real break from the industry's see-no-evil posture. Under the June agreement, the tobacco company money, divvied out in annual payments starting at $10 billion and rising eventually to $15 billion, would be used to compensate states for health-care costs related to treating smokers, pay individuals who sue successfully, finance health research and promote education programs aimed at deterring youths from taking up the evil weed. To that end, Joe Camel was finally put to death (humanely) on July 10, and the Marlboro Man will eventually be put out to pasture, because the industry also agreed to sweeping reforms that proscribe the use of human or cartoon forms in advertising. Billboards, stadium signs, T-shirt giveaways and other promotional freebies will also be forbidden, as will product placements in films.

The linchpin of the deal was the effort by the attorneys general—and such groups as the American Heart Association and the American Cancer Society—to cut the rising rate of smoking among youngsters. According to the Centers for Disease Control and Prevention, each day in America 6,000 teenagers risk their first cigarette; 3,000 teens enter the ranks of "regular smokers," (those who smoke at least one cigarette a day for a month); and 1,000

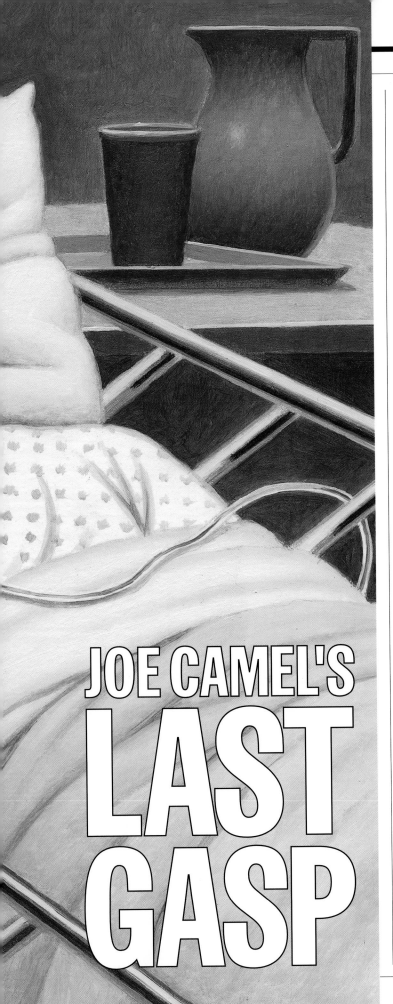

JOE CAMEL'S LAST GASP

adults die prematurely as a result of a youthful decision to take up smoking. All told, 400,000 Americans die each year from smoking-related illnesses.

The settlement was greeted euphorically, but when advocates of both sides began probing its fine print, the wrangling began all over again. Critics complained that the tobacco companies got off too easily. The proposed settlement, the argument went, would buy them freedom from future class actions and would cap the portion of the annual payout allotted for past wrongdoing at $5 billion. It also ensured predictability for stockholders, a prospect that had sent the stocks of the two largest companies, Philip Morris and RJR, soaring in the weeks before the settlement.

STILL, FOR THE $50 BILLION-A-YEAR INDUSTRY, the settlement plainly had the sour taste of a bad cigar. Under the terms of the 68-page, single-spaced proposal, any portion of the $368.5 billion not used to settle lawsuits—including those brought by 40 states to recover Medicaid expenses incurred for smoking-related illnesses and 17 class actions—would be applied to antismoking campaigns targeted at youths, to health research and to rigorous federal oversight of the tobacco industry.

In addition, cigarette companies would pay $60 billion in punitive damages. Of that, $25 billion would be placed in a trust fund to be used for public-health programs, with some of the remainder applied to providing health coverage for uninsured children. This agreement amounts to an admission of moral wrongdoing, a stunning development for an industry that for 40 years has steadfastly refused to admit any culpability or accept any responsibility for the health consequences of smoking. "Nobody's ever gotten a dime from them yet," reminds John Coale of the Castano Plaintiffs' Legal Committee, a group of 60 personal-injury law firms that made the first serious legal moves against Big Tobacco back in March 1994.

In the waning days of Congress's fall term, Republicans and Democrats began to stake out their turf, as they looked to hammering out a final national agreement in 1998. But no matter what shape the final agreement takes, one fact remains inarguable. The anemic revolt that began quietly 30 years ago—with a handful of scientists who were concerned about the potential health consequences of smoke and a handful of nonsmokers who were bothered by the constant haze of smoke in their eyes—has finally achieved enough muscle to bring the tobacco industry to its knees. The long-lasting cultural parade of Joe Camel, the Marlboro Man and cigarette-waving screen stars is headed for history. ∎

MOST GOLFERS KNOW THE FEELING. You're just about to hit your second shot after a decent enough drive when suddenly another ball comes whistling past, rolling much farther down the fairway. You turn to look back at the foursome behind you with mixed emotions: annoyance for the impertinence and admiration for the prowess.

Welcome to the 1997 P.G.A. Tour. It began as the Year of the Tiger, what with Eldrick ("Tiger") Woods winning the Masters by an incredible 12 strokes just four months after his 21st birthday. But it went on to become the Year of the Young Lions: the only time in history when the first three major tournaments were won by players under age 30: Woods got the famous green jacket of the Masters champion; South African Ernie Els, 27, collected his second U.S. Open trophy; and Texan Justin Leonard, 25, took home the claret jug of the British Open. It took Davis Love III—at 33 years old, a geezer by comparison—to break youth's grip on the big prizes by winning the P.G.A. championship at Winged Foot in Mamaroneck, N.Y., in August.

The twentysomething brigade started off with a bang, firing enough 60-something rounds to win 15 of the first 30 events on the tour. In a sport that usually demands 10 or so years of servitude, the upstarts were clearly playing through. Why the sudden blossoming of talent? Tour veteran Tom Kite, 47, who captained the American Ryder Cup team that lost to an inspired gang of Europeans under Seve Ballesteros in Spain in September, chalked it up to the cyclical nature of the game.

"When I won the U.S. Open at Pebble Beach in '92," said Kite, "it was, 'Oh, no, another 40-year-old wins a major.' There just weren't a lot of 20-year-olds out there at the time." Indeed, golf history seems as well ordered as Sunday-afternoon groupings: Hogan, Nelson and Snead, all born in 1912; Palmer, Player and Nicklaus, winning 10 of 16 majors from 1960 to 1963; Watson, Kite and Crenshaw, turning pro one right after the other.

The next threesome up on the tee remains to be seen, but clearly Woods will be one of them. After his big Masters win, overheated journalists likened him to Jesus, Mozart and Gandhi. His father Earl Woods once predicted, "Tiger will do more than any other man in history to change the course of humanity." A tall order for a 21-year-old—so instead think Palmer, Jordan and Ashe.

As Arnold Palmer did in the early 1960s, Tiger Woods electrified the sport of golf. He is, in the parlance of the gallery, "the Man." Tournaments in which he is playing sell twice as many tickets as those in which he is not. His gallery at the Masters dwarfed every other golfer's. Spectators are drawn to him both because of his unusual racial heritage (Asian, African, Caucasian, American Indian) and the ice water in his veins. Like Palmer, Woods invariably goes for the pin, but Palmer

YOUTH COMES TO THE FORE

A threesome of fine young players grabs golf's biggest prizes

never had Tiger's swing: a breathtakingly sweet release that routinely drives a ball twice as many yards as Tiger has pounds (155). Amazingly, he has birdied or eagled more than 50% of the par fives he has played as a pro. Tiger is like Palmer in another way as well: he plays his best in the biggest tournaments. His mastery of the Masters was complete. Not content to outplay the 1997 field, he outplayed every other Masters competitor in history, setting a new tournament record for the venerable Augusta, Ga., course.

Such feats put Woods in an endorsement league with only one other man, basketball's Michael Jordan. Nike pays Woods $8 million a year to wear its trademark swoosh.

> Forget the years of preparation—these fresh-faced pros are playing through

PIONEER: Tiger put golf on the map for kids—and minorities

Titleist gives Woods $4 million a year to endorse its line of golf products. Much to his credit, Woods doesn't simply take the money and play. He conducts clinics for inner-city kids, and he is planning to form a Tiger Woods Foundation that will create opportunities for youngsters who would otherwise never get a chance to pick up a club. Golf is still the most restrictive of America's major sports, and Woods has already confronted that discrimination, in much the same way that Arthur Ashe challenged tennis. "Golf has shied away from [facing racism] for too long," says Woods. "Some clubs have brought in tokens, but nothing has really changed. I hope what I'm doing can change that."

But an appearance on *The Oprah Winfrey Show* after winning the Masters taught Woods how tough the role of racial pioneer can be. When asked if it bothered him—the only child of a black American father and a Thai-American mother—to be called an African American, he replied, "It does. Growing up, I came up with this name: 'I'm a Cablinasian.'" Woods explained this self-crafted acronym reflected his one-eighth Caucasian, one-fourth black, one-eighth American Indian, one-fourth Thai and one-fourth Chinese roots with a precision that a racial-classifications expert under South African apartheid might have admired. He said when he was asked to check a box for racial background, he couldn't settle on only one. "I checked off 'African American' and 'Asian.' Those are the two I was raised under, the only two I know."

Kerboom! A small racial fire storm erupted. Woods' remarks infuriated many African Americans, who had hailed his triumph at the Masters as a symbol of racial progress, but now saw him as a traitor. To them Woods appeared to be running away from being an African American—a condition, they were quick to point out, that he himself had acknowledged when he paid tribute to black golf pioneers Teddy Rhoades, Charlie Sifford and Lee Elder in his graceful Masters victory speech.

But if Woods needed some coaching as a talk-show guest, there was no doubting his leadership of golf's kiddie corps. "There's definitely a Tiger effect," said CBS golf announcer Jim Nantz. "Once the other young golfers saw Tiger bypass the customary apprenticeship, they thought, 'Hey, I can do that too.'" Justin Leonard said as much after his British Open victory: "Having seen Tiger do so well, having seen Ernie do so well, maybe I thought it was O.K. to go out and win a tournament like this, being the age I am."

Growing up in Dallas, Leonard was heir to a Texas golf tradition that includes Ben Hogan, Lee Trevino and Ben Crenshaw. He was so golf-mad that he wrote school

YOUNG LIONS: Long-hitting South African Ernie Els, top,and dedicated Texan Justin Leonard, above, are two of the brightest stars in golf's swarm of twentysomething champs

1994 NCAA championship. In 1996 he earned nearly $1 million, won the Buick Open and found himself in *Cosmopolitan* as one of the magazine's most eligible bachelors.

There is another theory to explain the sweet birdies of youth. As with most sports, the athletes are simply better than they once were, and that has enabled them to make a quicker impact. Woods is, of course, Exhibit A, the longest hitter on the tour despite his tender age and slender build. But Els is also a prime example of the new athleticism. When President Clinton saw the 6-ft. 3-in. Els at the U.S. Open, he commented, "Big, strong kid, isn't he? Looks like a linebacker."

Growing up in Johannesburg, Els showed promise in tennis, rugby and cricket, as well as golf. When at 14 he beat Phil Mickelson (now 27) for the Junior World Golf Championship, Els' father, who owned a trucking company, decided to scrap the tennis court in the backyard and build a putting green. Following high school, Els spent two years in the army, then turned pro. But it wasn't until after a postparty car accident that Els decided to take golf seriously. "I wasn't living right and just felt like it was time to get focused, stop the bull and go for it,"he said.

After Els introduced himself to the world with his victory in the 1994 U.S. Open at Oakmont, Pa., playing partner

papers on Nicklaus, Player and Palmer and practiced his short game inside the house. He recalled one hole as "up the stairs, around the dining room table and over the dog."

THE ENORMITY OF LEONARD'S DESIRE WAS SOMEwhat mitigated by his small stature, but he delighted in beating opponents who far outdrove him. Because Leonard rarely loses his composure, tour friend Brad Faxon calls him a flat-liner. That trait is, in one way, a gift from his father and his golfing buddies—they routinely threw tees and taunts at the kid just as he would swing. While at the University of Texas, Leonard won both the 1992 U.S. Amateur and the

Curtis Strange said, "I think I just played with the next god." Eschewing that elevation, Els said he thought he might win another Open some day. That day came in June, when he outlasted Tom Lehman, Colin Montgomerie and Jeff Maggert to win America's toughest tournament.

"This youth thing is definitely catching on," said Kite. "The youngsters are really bringing new excitement to golf. The galleries are larger, younger, more exuberant." One consolation for the golfers being chased off the course is that yet another generation is waiting a few holes back. One day this summer, an eight-year-old in Franklin, Tenn., made his second hole-in-one of the summer. His name is Patrick Wood. Guess what his nickname is. ∎

Make Way for the Women!

With a league (or two) of their own, they bring fun—and fans—back to the game

An hour and a half before the tip-off, the doors of the Charlotte Coliseum swing open, and America comes pouring in. Families, senior citizens, teenage girls and boys enter the arena popularly known as the Hive and begin buzzing around the souvenir stands and the floor on which the players practice. Charlotte is about to play New York, and the excitement is as palpable as it would be before any game between the Hornets and the Knicks.

But … time out! This was July 1997, the two teams were called the Sting and the Liberty, and the players the fans were beseeching for autographs were not Ewing and Rice but Lobo and Bullett. One of the hottest items at the souvenir stands was a T shirt that read INVENTED BY MAN, PERFECTED BY WOMAN. Soon the announcer thundered, "O.K., Charlotte, we got next!"

Welcome to the WNBA, the Women's National Basketball Association. Think of it as the National Basketball Association's baby sister. Supported by the powerful existing infrastructure and marketing savvy of the NBA, the WNBA exceeded all expectations for its inaugural season. The new women's league not only averaged 9,669 in attendance, well above its projection of 4,500 a game, it also occasionally eclipsed both Major League Soccer and PGA golf in the television ratings.

GO, GIRL! The WNBA's Comets and Sparks square off

The league's slogan, "We Got Next," is a phrase commonly used on playgrounds to reserve the next game, but by late August, after the Houston Comets beat the New York Liberty to win the league's first championship title, the phrase took on a new meaning. The age of women's basketball had definitely arrived in America.

Indeed, the launch of two new magazines (SPORTS ILLUSTRATED'S WOMEN/SPORT and Condé Nast's *Sports for Women*) made 1997 a watershed year for all women's athletics. The WNBA even had competition for fans: the all-female American Basketball League. The ABL, which launched in the fall of 1996, operates in smaller markets during the fall and winter and is known as a players' league. It pays more—the average salary is $80,000 a year—and boasts of having the best players (Olympians Dawn Staley, Teresa Edwards and Katrina McClain). The ABL, playing in cities like San Jose, Calif., Richmond, Va., and Columbus, Ohio, averaged 3,500 fans a game with very little TV exposure. Two leagues, two strategies: by one estimate, the ABL spent $6 million on salaries in its first year and $1.5 million on marketing. The WNBA, on the other hand, spent $15 million on marketing and $3 million on salaries.

There was no doubting the marketing acumen of the WNBA, which used regular NBA staff members; team merchandise just flew off the shelves. But women's basketball had more going for it than hype. Affordability was one. Unlike those of the high-priced NBA, women's tickets cost no more than seats for a major league baseball game.

Another attraction was the competition itself. Older fans and purists such as UCLA's legendary coach John Wooden think women's basketball is more watchable than men's basketball; it's more structured and team-oriented than the typically helter-skelter play in the NBA. Then there were the athletes: New York had Olympian Rebecca Lobo, the biggest star in the WNBA. Phoenix fans called Australian guard Michele Timms "Tank Girl" for her spiked blond hair and aggressive play. Lisa Leslie, the Wilhelmina model, played center for the Sparks. Sheryl Swoopes joined the Houston Comets near the end of the season, after giving birth to a son named Jordan—after youknowwho.

But there's another quality that the WNBA has and the NBA hasn't: accessibility for the fans. During one Liberty game, Rhonda Blades, a guard for New York, was kneeling next to the scorer's table, waiting to enter the fray, when she noticed two little girls sitting courtside. Just before Blades went into the game, she gave one of the girls a high-five. The awestruck girl turned around and showed her hand to her friend, as if she had been given a wonderful present. She had—and she's got next. ■

> Unlike the helter-skelter men's game, WNBA play emphasizes teamwork first

A Nanny's Deliverance

A trial that riveted Britain and America ends in a stunning overturned verdict

THE TWO WOMEN SAT IN A COURTROOM IN CAMBRIDGE, Mass., refusing to look at each other. But both would have to listen. Deborah Eappen, 31, read her victim's statement, repeating the horror that had engulfed her family since Feb. 4, 1997. "Our Matty had been hurt," she said, referring to her eight-month-old son. "We soon learned our baby Matthew was dying ... because someone we trusted had hurt him." She recalled in stark detail the decision she and her husband Sunil, both physicians, had reached on Feb. 9: to remove life support from their brain-dead son and let him die.

And then it was Louise Woodward's turn to speak. The night before, a jury of nine women and three men had found the 19-year-old British au pair guilty of second-degree murder in the death of Matthew Eappen. She too repeated her story of the past nine months: "I would never hurt Matty, and I never did hurt Matty, and I don't know what happened to him. I didn't kill Matthew Eappen." And then, as she did on first hearing the verdict, she collapsed in sobs.

The verdict surprised the public, which had been swayed by televised images of a cherubic, well-groomed Woodward calmly testifying from the stand. Her defense team, which included Barry Scheck, formerly of O.J. Simpson's "dream team," had been so confident that it turned down an offer by the prosecution to include man-

WOODWARD: Was her defense team the culprit?

slaughter as an option to present to the jury. Instead the defense forced the jurors to choose between murder or acquittal—and the gamble went wrong. The verdict brought a mandatory sentence of life imprisonment, with no possibility of parole for 15 years.

The case had swung dramatically in and out of Woodward's favor ever since she dialed 911 from the Eappens' home in the affluent Boston suburb of Newton and said to the dispatcher, "Help! There's a baby. He's barely breathing." Officers on the scene later said the

au pair told them that she may have been "a little rough" with the baby, tossed him on a bed and "dropped" him on some towels on the bathroom floor—statements she later denied. Over the summer, as the defense team re-examined the infant's medical records, it put forward a new hypothesis: that the baby had been suffering from a fractured skull for weeks, and a jolt was enough to restart the bleeding that killed him. The team decided to fight for Woodward's innocence.

The case was more than a private tragedy. For one thing, many Britons seized on the story and watched the trial on TV. When the guilty verdict was read, viewers in a pub in Woodward's home village of Elton were silenced in shock: for a time all that could be heard was the amplified sound of their onetime neighbor sobbing in a courtroom 3,000 miles away.

Moreover, two women seemed to be on trial. Deborah Eappen was demonized, stereotyped as a "do-it-all, want-it-all" working woman and part-time mother. Many saw the Eappens as rich doctors selfishly pursuing their careers while leaving their son with second-rate child care. Au pairs—young women who come to the U.S. under a cultural-exchange program—are typically undertrained in caring for infants but work much more cheaply than trained nannies. In fact, both Eappens were still in debt for medical school; their house was modest by Newton standards. And Deborah Eappen worked only three days a week, coming home at lunchtime to breast-feed her baby when she could, otherwise preparing her milk for Woodward to bottle-feed him.

Days after the decision, Judge Hiller Zobel set aside the jury's verdict. He reduced the charge from murder to involuntary manslaughter and set Woodward free, declaring the 279 days she had already spent in jail to be sufficient punishment for an act he declared to be "characterized by ... immaturity and some anger, but not malice." While many cheered, Deborah Eappen asked TIME, "How did Louise become the hero and I become the villain?" She knew that verdict would not soon be set aside. ■

> "How did Louise become the hero and I become the victim?" the mother asked

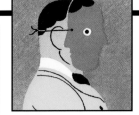

Farewell, Gray Lady!

What's black and white and read all over? Well, the answer is no longer America's self-styled "newspaper of record," the New York *Times.* Media-savvy Gothamites, who had long referred to the *Times* as "the good gray lady," rolled out of bed one day in September to discover a *Times* newly arrayed in four-color hues. The color offensive (traditionalists preferred to reverse the term) was the product of boyishly ebullient publisher Arthur Sulzberger Jr., 46, the latest scion of the *Times's* ruling family to run the paper. The consensus of veteran readers: the *Times* benefited from color—but its new format, featuring a gaggle of sections, was bloated and user-unfriendly. And the darn ink still comes off on your hands.

THE *TIMES:* Now it offers all the blues fit to print

The Great HMO Backlash

America's health-insurance revolution has reached adolescence. After more than a decade, managed-care plans—with their incentives for doctors to hold down treatment costs—covered about half the population. Fee-for-service plans—with their equally problematic incentives, for doctors to provide too much costly treatment—continued to shrink. But the backlash of angry consumers was growing, as enrollees in health maintenance organizations recited a litany of horror stories: nitpicking "utilization reviews" of doctors' bills by insurance companies; patients hustled out of a hospital within hours, even after surgery as traumatic as breast removal; gag orders forbidding doctors to tell a patient about an expensive treatment. Doctors felt pressured, employers fielded rafts of complaints from workers, and patients and consumer advocates demanded a crackdown. President Clinton appointed an advisory committee to draft a patients' bill of rights and study what kind of legislation may be needed to enforce it.

X-CELLENT! Once scorned as a passel of slackers, the 45 million "Generation Xers" born between 1965 and 1977 were found in a new survey to be savvy and ambitious and materialistic and ... whatever.

GO FIGURE: In the year's strangest religious trend, Hollywood stars and fellow hipsters were grooving on the Kabbalah, the long-secret system of mysticism and numerology first followed by medieval Jews.

THE ZOHAR: Kabbalah's esoteric medieval text

"Special K" Hits the Street

In a year that saw drug use among teenagers rising again, more kids were trying "Special K," an anesthetic most commonly administered to cats and monkeys. Generically called ketamine, "street K" is most often diverted in liquid form from vets' offices, then dried by cooking, ground into powder and snorted. "K" causes hallucinations because it blocks chemical messengers in the brain that carry sensory input; the brain fills the resulting void with a whirl of visions, dreams and memories.

The Supreme Court: No Prescriptions for Suicide

Late in June the Supreme Court delivered a much anticipated judgment on one of the era's most wrenching dilemmas. In a unanimous decision, the Justices

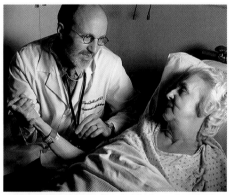

THE COURT: Assisted suicide is not a right

sustained Washington and New York state laws forbidding the terminally ill to enlist a doctor's help in committing suicide. At first hearing, the court's decisions seemed immutable. Wrote Chief Justice William Rehnquist (whose wife died in 1991 after battling ovarian cancer): "The asserted 'right' to assistance in committing suicide is not a fundamental liberty interest ..." The Justices also rejected the parallel between assisted suicide and the request of someone on life support to have the plug pulled, a right upheld by the court in the past. In reality the court's deliberations were more nuanced. Although the 35 states with outright bans on doctor-assisted suicide may now enforce them with greater assurance, the court's decision did not preclude states from voting to allow assisted suicide, as Oregon did in 1994. The right Rehnquist denied was so broadly stated that more modest constitutional claims may someday be affirmed. And five Justices, a majority, wrote concurring opinions that further qualified the Chief Justice's opinion.

READY TO ROLL—ALMOST: Before the six-wheeled Sojourner could roam, the airbag at right had to be moved aside

Pathfinder and the tiny
Sojourner rover hit
a bull's-eye on Mars on
the Fourth of July,
opening a new era in
planetary exploration

RETURN TO THE RED PLANET

F ROM THE SURFACE OF MARS—WHERE THE SKY is salmon and Earth is a blue morning star—you probably would have noticed the spaceship coming. It may have been the noise the thing made that caught your attention; although the Martian atmosphere is spent and shredded, it's not too tenuous to carry sound. And it's certainly not too tenuous to make anything that tries to punch through it pay the price, causing the interloper to glow like a meteor as it plunged toward a touchdown somewhere on the ancient world. That you couldn't have missed.

There was, of course, no one in Mars' Ares Vallis floodplain to mark the moment when NASA's 3-ft.-tall Pathfinder spacecraft dropped onto the soil

THE SEVEN-MONTH VOYAGE

Every 26 months, Mars and Earth are close enough to make travel between the two practical. In December 1996 Pathfinder was launched on an arcing course that took it to its landing in July. Though the two planets were 119 million miles apart when Pathfinder landed, the spacecraft's looping trajectory covered 310 million miles

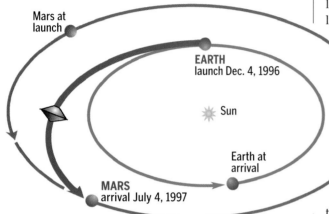

Mars at launch

EARTH
launch Dec. 4, 1996

Sun

Earth at arrival

MARS
arrival July 4, 1997

THE FINAL SECONDS BEFORE IMPACT

2 MINUTES
A 40-ft. parachute deployed less than seven miles above the surface.

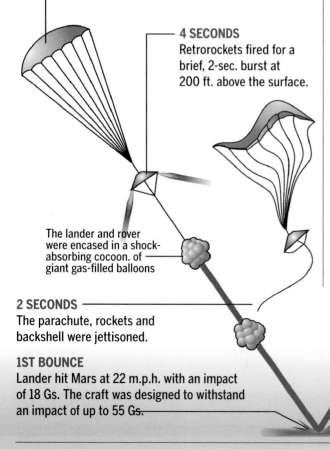

4 SECONDS
Retrorockets fired for a brief, 2-sec. burst at 200 ft. above the surface.

The lander and rover were encased in a shock-absorbing cocoon. of giant gas-filled balloons

2 SECONDS
The parachute, rockets and backshell were jettisoned.

1ST BOUNCE
Lander hit Mars at 22 m.p.h. with an impact of 18 Gs. The craft was designed to withstand an impact of up to 55 Gs.

50 ft.

23 ft.

2ND BOUNCE
Impact of 9 Gs.

of the long-dry valley. But there was a planet more than 100 million miles away filled with people who were paying heed when it landed, appropriately enough, on July 4.

For the first time in 21 years, a machine shot from Earth once again stirred up the Martian dust. More important, for the first time ever, it was going to be able to keep stirring it up well after it landed. Curled up inside Pathfinder like a mechanical kangaroo joey was Sojourner, a 1-ft.-tall, 2-ft.-long robot car, or rover, designed to trundle away from the lander and investigate rocks all over the desert-like site. The touchdown was not without problems. Early pictures revealed that one of the airbags that cushioned the craft during its descent had bunched up in a way that hindered the rover from leaving the lander. In addition, the computer aboard Sojourner and the one aboard Pathfinder were having trouble talking to each other, preventing the rover from getting the data it needed to move beyond the immediate vicinity of the lander. But these glitches, which engineers promptly fixed, did little to dampen the excitement when Pathfinder sent back the stunning panoramas of its eerie orange landing site.

Across the U.S. and much of the world, the ship's successful arrival was greeted with the most attention accorded to an otherworldly landing since, perhaps, *Apollo 11* touched down on the moon 28 years earlier. At the Pasadena, Calif., convention center, near NASA's Jet Propulsion Laboratory, where the mission was being run, a standing-room-only crowd of more than 2,000 people whooped as the pictures from Pathfinder streamed onto a 25-ft. screen.

J UST GETTING PATHFINDER FROM CAPE CANAVERAL to Ares Vallis required a remarkable bit of cosmic sharpshooting. Mars is only 4,200 miles across (about half as big as Earth), and the area NASA aimed for is only 60 miles wide. The barest flutter in Pathfinder's trajectory could have caused it to swing far wide of its destination. When the spacecraft actually reached the upper limits of Mars' wispy atmosphere, the 1,256-lb. polyhedron-shaped pod was screaming toward the planet at 16,600 m.p.h., experiencing deceleration forces nearly 20 times as great as Earth's gravity.

When Pathfinder was closer than seven miles above the red planet and two minutes from landing, a 40-ft. parachute opened. Less than 1,000 ft. up, a swaddling of shock-absorbing airbags inflated. Then a cluster of retrorockets fired for a 2-sec. burst, applying a final brake. The almost comically balloon-like ship hit the surface of the planet, bounced as high as 50 ft. and finally came to rest in the 4.6 billion-year-old dust.

Preliminary information from the ship indicated that Pathfinder was tilted at an angle of less than 3 degrees, plenty flat enough to allow the rover to disembark. The solar arrays were bathed by the sun and were producing all the power the spacecraft needed. (The sun, however, was providing little heat: the temperature at Ares Vallis

COLLISION COURSE: Rover encounters a rock named Yogi

was a crisp −64°F.) In the next stage of the operation, the landing airbags had to deflate completely, and actuator motors, strong enough to pull a small boulder, had to draw them under the ship. Then Pathfinder itself had to open up, exposing the Sojourner rover inside and sending back the first black-and-white pictures.

The images that appeared on mission control monitors were, by any measure, astounding: scrub plains without the scrub, prairie land without the prairie grass. A few hours later the Pathfinder team convened a press conference to unveil the panoramic color images the ship had beamed home. They revealed the Marsscape with a richness and resolution the black-and-white shots couldn't—and they also revealed the problem of the obstructing airbag. A prerehearsed maneuver successfully retracted the bag, and after the communications glitch between the Sojourner and the lander was resolved, the rover was off and crawling.

For all its anthropomorphic sweetness, the plucky rover was a rather dimwitted machine. Its route from rock to rock was programmed at J.P.L. and relayed through the Pathfinder lander. The skateboard-size car thus moved excruciatingly slowly—just 2 ft. per minute. Built-in gyroscopes served as a sort of onboard vestibular system, helping the rover feel for bumps and potholes, while a tracery of five laser beams helped detect obstructions.

Over the next few days, Earthlings watched in amusement as the gritty Sojourner explored the terrain surrounding the landing site. In what NASA termed a "rock festival," the rover investigated a number of nearby boulders, which were given such whimsical names as Barnacle Bill, Yogi, Casper, Flat Top and Boo-Boo. The rover made major discoveries, confirming the idea that floods of water poured over the Martian surface in earlier times, and finding that Mars, like Earth, has an inner metallic core. In all, Pathfinder transmitted some 16,000 pictures of the rocky landscape

of Ares Vallis, while Sojourner conducted 20 detailed chemical analyses of the soil.

As one final achievement, the two planetary explorers lasted three times their design lifetime of 30 days. The craft continued their communication with Earth until Oct. 1, when their signals finally faded out, two months after they were expected to quit. By that time, though, there was additional good news from Mars: in September, NASA's Mars Global Surveyor settled easily into orbit around the planet and began a two-year program of photographing the Martian geology and atmosphere with a special camera.

The scientists at NASA reveled in their double play. In the past few years, under the direction of Daniel Goldin, the space agency has been reinventing itself. The organization that grew so fat in the post-Apollo years has been downsizing itself to resemble the NASA of the late 1950s: a crew of garage engineers cobbling spacecraft from simple parts and getting the job done both on budget and on deadline.

The results are starting to show. Indeed, what was perhaps most remarkable about the spacecraft that set up shop in Ares Vallis was how unremarkable they were. NASA's early interplanetary spacecraft were limousine ships packed with scientific instruments and backup systems. When Goldin took over NASA in 1992, he decreed that the luxury ships would be replaced by stripped-down spacecraft built mainly from available, off-the-shelf parts. Thus, Pathfinder cost $171 million to build, and Sojourner only $25 million.

But the returns have been enormous. Pathfinder not only revived Americans' interest in exploring space; it continued the only known cultural-exchange program anywhere in the cosmos. In the summer of 1996 an ancient Martian meteorite gave the creatures of Earth the first compelling evidence of life beyond our own. In the summer of 1997 the creatures on Earth answered back, sending our sister-planet evidence that terrestrial life not only exists, but that it is—when it tries to be—wonderfully intelligent. ■

The rover rolled to a stop and into an upright position. The airbags slowly deflated, and the lander unfolded its three petal-shaped solar panels.

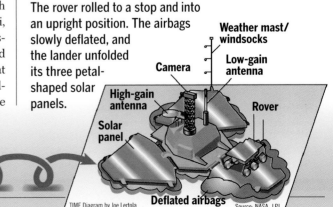

Weather mast/ windsocks
Low-gain antenna
Camera
High-gain antenna
Rover
Solar panel
Deflated airbags

The craft rolled over Mars' rocky terrain for 92 sec.

TIME Diagram by Joe Lertola   Source: NASA, J.P.L.

COMET
OF THE DECADE

All hail, Hale-Bopp! A starry visitor
from beyond Jupiter sketches a
glimmering scrawl across the skies

ALL THAT GLITTERS:
Hale-Bopp's
sparkling trail is
merely sunlight
reflecting off ice

WHAT A SHOW! THEIR HEADS CRANING, THEIR necks straining, people around the globe peered into the nighttime sky in the spring of 1997 to view a celestial fireworks display unrivaled in decades. Without a telescope or even binoculars, from such light-polluted vantage points as midtown Manhattan and downtown Chicago, millions viewed the bright visitor from the fringes of the solar system, Comet Hale-Bopp.

"This could be the most viewed comet in all of human history," said Daniel Green, an astronomer at the Harvard-Smithsonian Center for Astrophysics in Cambridge, Mass. Hale-Bopp may have come as news to most earthlings, but astronomers, amateur and professional alike, had been buzzing about it ever since its discovery nearly two years earlier. At that point the comet was more than half a billion miles from the sun, well beyond the orbit of Jupiter, and invisible without a telescope. But not necessarily a huge telescope: like most comets, this one was found by a pair of amateurs as familiar with their favorite regions of the sky as most people are with their own neighborhoods.

On July 23, 1995, Alan Hale, who has a Ph.D. in as-

tronomy and makes his living running a research and educational company, was scanning the skies above his home in Cloudcroft, N.M. He was waiting for an already discovered comet to rise over his house when he trained his telescope on M70, a well-known cluster of stars in the constellation Sagittarius. "As soon as I looked," he said, "I saw a fuzzy object nearby. It was strange, because I'd looked at M70 a couple of weeks earlier and the object hadn't been there."

Hale checked his sky atlas, then logged on to the computer at the quaintly named Central Bureau for Astronomical Telegrams, located at the Harvard-Smithsonian Observatory. Maybe this would turn out to be a known object. It didn't. "Now I felt I had a pretty live suspect," he says. He fired off an E-mail message to Daniel Green and Brian Marsden, who run the Bureau for the International Astronomical Union, reporting a possible new comet. A few hours later, he looked again, and the object had moved. It was a comet for sure.

A few hundred miles away, in Stanfield, Ariz., Thomas Bopp was going through a similar exercise at almost precisely the same time. Bopp is a supervisor at a construction-materials company and, like Hale, a longtime amateur astronomer. He too saw the intruder and sent his own E-mail to the bureau. Thanks to their nearly simultaneous discoveries, Hale and Bopp shared the honor of giving the comet their names. Within a few days, Green and Marsden had calculated that Hale-Bopp was incredibly far away and must therefore be unusually bright.

But comets are not especially well behaved. All too often they show great promise early in their career but turn out—like the infamous Kohoutek in the early 1970s—to be celestial duds. The uncertainty has to do with the way comets are put together. They're basically chunks of ice—chiefly water with a fair amount of carbon dioxide and other frozen gases mixed in, plus a lot of sooty dust. Billions upon billions of comets orbit lazily out beyond Neptune. When one happens to fall in toward the sun, the ice begins to vaporize, surrounding the solid core with a hazy cloud of dusty gas.

This cloud, which can grow to thousands of miles across, is the comet's head, the light-reflecting shroud that turns an otherwise insignificant iceberg into a brilliant object. Just how brilliant depends on many factors. The solid comet's size is one, and Hale-Bopp, an estimated 20 miles across, is bigger than most. (Halley's was less than half as large.)

The comet's history is another factor. Out in deep space, a comet can get encrusted with a layer of gummy dust. This layer can seal in most of the ice and prevent it from vaporizing. Some gas may spurt out through cracks in the crust, giving a comet a premature air of greatness that amounts to not much at all. Admitted Hale: "It's been kind of nerve-racking to sit through all those months wondering if the comet would fizzle."

NOT TO WORRY. HALE-BOPP STEADILY GREW IN brightness, giving amateur astronomers an increasingly satisfying show. Professional astronomers too watched Hale-Bopp, and not always with detachment. "We're delirious," said Tobias Owen of the University of Hawaii. "It's been 20 years since a really bright comet came by, and now, within just a year, we've had Hyakutake and Hale-Bopp."

In the intervening two decades, astronomical hardware has improved markedly, giving scientists the chance to study comets in unprecedented detail. They want to know precisely what these bodies are made of, since comets are believed to be the only objects that have remained unaltered since the solar system was born 4.5 billion years ago. The planets and the asteroids have been heated and cooled, smashed apart and re-formed, but the comets, lingering on the solar system's periphery, have stayed relatively pristine. So goes the theory, at least, and early studies of Hale-Bopp's gases bore this out. "We've found a type of hydrogen cyanide that's otherwise seen only in interstellar space," says Owen.

Astronomers also believe a comet's impact on the Earth is probably what did in the dinosaurs 65 million years ago. That object was perhaps 10 miles across. At double the size, Hale-Bopp packs a lot more potential energy. Luckily for civilization, Hale-Bopp missed the earth by 120 million miles. "If Hale-Bopp [had come] as close as Hyakutake did," said Harvard's Green, wistfully, "it would have been incredible. You'd have been able to see it easily in the daytime." But along with the rest of us, Green gladly settled for the best heavenly light show in decades. ∎

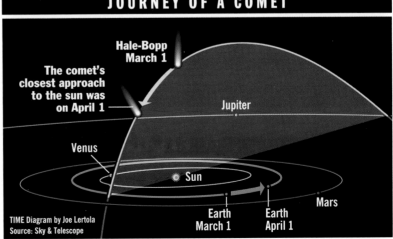

JOURNEY OF A COMET

Hale-Bopp
March 1

The comet's closest approach to the sun was on April 1

Jupiter

Venus

Sun

Mars

Earth
March 1

Earth
April 1

TIME Diagram by Joe Lertola
Source: Sky & Telescope

THE DAY THE BLUEBIRD BEGAN TO CHIRP aboard the Mir space station, American astronaut Michael Foale didn't notice. Ordinarily, anyone in the station's core module could not have missed the sudden trilling. But at the moment, Foale was elsewhere. And the 40-year-old British-born astrophysicist had other things on his mind besides a singing bird. Of course, the Mir bird was not a real bird. It was a small plastic model that broke into song when its switch was thrown. Lately it had begun singing whenever it was jostled, and on this day, June 25, it got jostled hard.

Just moments earlier, the station's commander, Vasili Tsibliyev, had tried to bring an unmanned cargo vessel in for a remote-control docking. When the ship was just a few yards from the station, it suddenly flew wide of the docking port, sideswiped one of the station's solar panels and slammed broadside into its Spektr science module.

Seconds before the impact, Tsibliyev had ordered Foale to move into the Soyuz spacecraft that is permanently attached to Mir as an escape vessel for re-entry to Earth. But just as Foale entered the spherical transfer node that connects the main module to Soyuz and the four other modules, he felt and heard a sudden, sickening thud. That's when the bluebird began singing in the main cabin. The cargo ship had hit Spektr fast and hard. The collision punctured the science module's hull, releasing its atmosphere, and sent the entire station into a slow roll. For several days the lives of the crew members—as well as the future of the Russian space program—were in grave jeopardy.

provide nearly 40% of Mir's power. To ration electricity, the crew shut off Mir's stabilizers for several days and kept the ship from spinning out of control by firing its thrusters manually. Meanwhile, the Russian space controllers on the ground concocted a risky scheme to try to revive the moribund section of the station: a four-hour "internal" spacewalk in the frigid, airless and possibly contaminated lab.

Then, shortly before the fix-up attempt, Tsibliyev announced he was having heart problems; he couldn't perform the more extensive repairs the ship needed. If NASA was willing, the Russian space agency wanted Foale to put on a space suit and try to help put Mir back together. But even as NASA was giving the go-ahead for Foale to start his training for this unanticipated job, another disaster struck. Someone pulled the wrong plug on an onboard computer, sending Mir into a spin and robbing it of power once again. The crew had to retreat to the Soyuz space capsule and use the smaller craft's rockets to aim the tumbling space station's solar panels back toward the sun. The mishap pushed back the repairs to early August, when two fresh cosmonauts, Commander Anatoli Solovyev, 49, and engineer Pavel Vinogradov, 43, would relieve Tsibliyev and his fellow cosmonaut, Alexander Lazutkin.

On Aug. 7 the two Russians arrived, in true Mir-style: as they approached the beleaguered station, the automatic docking system failed, forcing the cosmonauts to complete the linkup manually. But on Aug. 22, in a superbly executed internal spacewalk, Solovyev and Vinogradov floated into the airless Spektr lab and installed a new cable system that would provide electricity to Spektr and the rest of the power-thirsty station.

Bad Year for Mir

Moscow, we have a problem: balky computers, midair crashes and narrow escapes imperil Russia's 11-year-old space station

The mishap was the most troubling incident in a troubled year for the geriatric Mir. Already the 11-year-old station had experienced a breakdown in its oxygen system, a series of leaks in its cooling system and an onboard fire. In the months after the collision, there would be power blackouts, repeated failures in the ship's flickering computer and even an alarming irregularity in Tsibliyev's heartbeat. The foul-ups brought new scrutiny to America's role in Mir, for which it pays the cash-strapped Russian space agency $472 million a year. But NASA officials pointed out that Mir enables American astronauts to conduct zero-G science experiments that are invaluable to further space research.

After the smash-up, the crew hurriedly sealed off Spektr, site of Foale's racks of experiments and his living quarters, disconnecting the cables from solar panels that

When the cosmonauts entered the crippled Spektr module, they had no idea what they would find. In the wake of the accident, officials feared the lab would be filled with waving wires, glass debris and even globules of blood collected from the crew for medical tests. But when Vinogradov popped his head inside and peered around with a flashlight, he found that the place was surprisingly undisturbed. The darkened instrument panels were covered with a layer of sparkly frost, and a cloud of white crystals floated about like fireflies—possibly droplets from a shampoo bottle that had ruptured in the vacuum. Reassured, Vinogradov connected power cables from outlets in the wall to a new hatch. Before he finished, the space station's solar panels caught a shaft of sunlight, and power began flowing to the blacked-out lab, causing it to stir to life.

THE BIG CRASH

Cosmonauts Tsibliyev and Lazutkin are in the core module trying to dock a Progress supply vessel by remote control when the craft overshoots its target, smashes into a solar panel and punches a hole in the Spektr science module.

Astronaut Foale, who has been manning a laser beacon in the Kvant 1 module, rushes toward the Soyuz spacecraft to prepare for possible evacuation, but only makes it as far as the transfer node when he hears the thud of the collision.

The crew seals off the leaking Spektr, in the process disconnecting cables that supply half the space station's electrical power. At the end of the day, Mir and its crew are drifting helpless in space.

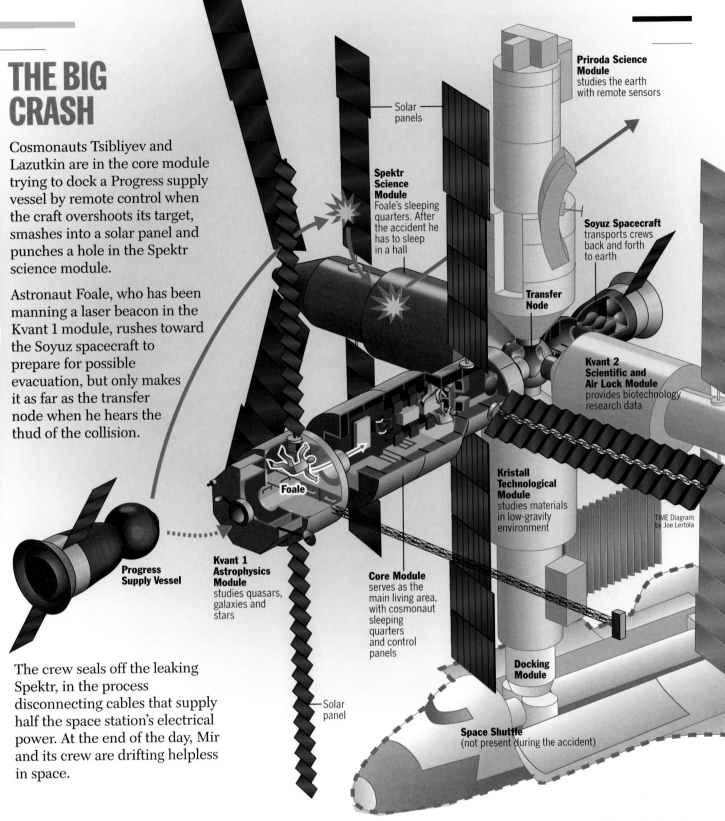

Solar panels

Priroda Science Module studies the earth with remote sensors

Spektr Science Module Foale's sleeping quarters. After the accident he has to sleep in a hall

Soyuz Spacecraft transports crews back and forth to earth

Transfer Node

Kvant 2 Scientific and Air Lock Module provides biotechnology research data

Foale

Kristall Technological Module studies materials in low-gravity environment

TIME Diagram by Joe Lertola

Progress Supply Vessel

Kvant 1 Astrophysics Module studies quasars, galaxies and stars

Core Module serves as the main living area, with cosmonaut sleeping quarters and control panels

Solar panel

Docking Module

Space Shuttle (not present during the accident)

Even the triumphant repair job followed a week of too-familiar problems for the pratfall-prone station. Four days before, the onboard computer had failed—again. Shortly after, there had been a touch-and-go moment as a cargo ship approached the station—again. Foale returned to Earth in mid-October, when the shuttle *Atlantis* ferried up astronaut David Wolf to replace him. In early November, Solovyev and Vinogradov successfully installed a new solar panel during a six-hour spacewalk, finally concluding the months of repairs on Mir's damaged power system.

Mir was shipshape—for now. Still, many critics called on America to stop sending people and money to the shaky station. They included one veteran of outer-space calamities, NASA astronaut Jim Lovell. Said the hero commander of *Apollo 13*: "Mir has done an exceptionally fine job. Now it's time to give it a very respectful retirement." ∎

Researchers in Scotland clone an adult mammal—leaving a surprised world to ponder the ethics of biotechnology

d R. FRANKENSTEIN WORE A WOOL SWEATER and a baggy parka. He spoke in a soft British accent and had the face of a bank clerk. Yet there he stood, in all his banal benignity, a creator in chinos: Dr. Ian Wilmut, the first man to conceive fully formed life from adult body parts since Mary Shelley's fictional mad scientist. Wilmut may not look the part of Frankenstein—or God the Father—but he played it.

In late February a landmark paper published in the scientific journal *Nature* confirmed what the headlines had been screaming for days: researchers at the Roslin Institute near Edinburgh, Scotland, had indeed pulled off what many experts thought might be a scientific impossibility. From a cell in an adult ewe's mammary gland, embryologist Wilmut and his colleagues managed to create a frisky lamb named Dolly (with apologies to Ms. Parton), scoring an advance in reproductive technology as unsettling as it was startling. Unlike offspring produced in the usual fashion, Dolly does not merely take after her biological mother. She is a carbon copy, a laboratory counterfeit so exact that she is in essence her mother's identical twin.

What enabled the Scottish team to succeed where so many others have failed was a trick so ingenious, yet so simple, that any skilled laboratory technician should be able to master it—and therein lies both the beauty and the danger: once Wilmut and his colleagues figured out how to cross that biological barrier, they ensured that others would follow. And although the Roslin researchers had to struggle for more than 10 years to achieve their breakthrough, it took political and religious leaders around the world no time at all to grasp its import: if scientists can clone sheep, they can probably clone people too.

Without question, this exotic form of reproductive engineering could become an extremely useful tool. The ability to clone adult mammals, in particular, opens up myriad exciting possibilities, from propagating endangered animal species to producing replacement organs for human patients in need of transplants. The world of agriculture might be revolutionized. Dairy farmers, for example, could clone their champion cows, making it possible to produce more milk from smaller herds. Sheep ranchers could do the same with their top lamb and wool producers.

But it's also easy to imagine the cloning technology being misused and, as the news from Roslin spread, apocalyptic scenarios proliferated. Journalists wrote about the possibility of virgin births, resurrecting the dead and women giving birth to themselves. In the New York *Times*, a cell biologist from Washington University in St. Louis, Mo., named Ursula Goodenough quipped that if human cloning were perfected, "there'd be no need for men."

little lamb, who made thee?

MY MOTHER, MYSELF: Dolly is an exact double of her mother

Scientists have long dreamed of doing what the Roslin team did. After all, if starfish and other invertebrates can practice asexual reproduction, why can't it be extended to the rest of the animal kingdom? In the 1980s developmental biologists at what is now Allegheny University of the Health Sciences came tantalizingly close. From the red blood cells of an adult frog, they raised a crop of lively tadpoles. These tadpoles were impressive creatures, remembered University of Minnesota cell biologist Robert McKinnell, who followed the work closely. "They swam and ate and developed beautiful eyes and hind limbs," he says. But then, halfway through metamorphosis, they died.

Scientists who have focused their cloning efforts on more forgiving embryonic tissue have met with greater success. A simple approach, called embryo twinning (literally splitting embryos in half), is commonly practiced in the cattle industry. Coaxing surrogate cells to accept foreign DNA is a bit trickier. In 1952 researchers in Pennsylvania successfully cloned a live frog from an embryonic cell. Three decades later, researchers were learning to do the same with such mammals as sheep and calves. "What's new," observed University of Wisconsin animal scientist Neal First, "is not cloning mammals. It's cloning mammals from cells that are not embryonic."

Embryonic cells are infinitely easier to work with because they are, in the jargon of cell biologists, largely "undifferentiated." That is, they have not yet undergone the progressive changes that turn cells into skin, muscles, hair, brain and so on. An undifferentiated cell can give rise to all the other cells in the body, say scientists, because it is capable of activating any gene on any chromosome. But as development progresses, differentiation alters the way DNA—the double-stranded molecule that makes up genes—folds up inside the nucleus of a cell. Along with other structural changes, folding helps make vast stretches of DNA inaccessible, ensuring that genes in adult cells do not turn on at the wrong time or in the wrong tissue.

THE DISADVANTAGE OF EMBRYONIC CLONING IS THAT you don't know what you are getting. With adult-cell cloning, you can wait to see how well an individual turns out before deciding whether to clone it. Cloning also has the potential to make genetic engineering more efficient. Once you produce an animal with a desired trait—a pig with a human immune system, perhaps—you could make as many copies as you want. In recent years, some scientists have speculated that the changes wrought by differentiation might be irreversible, in which case cloning an adult mammal would be biologically impossible. The birth of Dolly not only proves them wrong but also suggests that the difficulty scientists have had cloning adult cells may have less to do with biology than with technique.

To create Dolly, the Roslin team concentrated on halting the cell cycle—the series of choreographed steps all cells go through as they divide. In Dolly's case, the cells the scientists wanted to clone came from the udder of a pregnant sheep. To stop the cells from dividing, the researchers starved them of nutrients for a week, and the cells fell into a slumbering state that resembled deep hibernation.

At this point, Wilmut and his colleagues switched to a mainstream cloning technique known as nuclear transfer. First they removed the nucleus of an unfertilized egg, or oocyte, while leaving the surrounding cytoplasm intact. Then they placed the egg next to the nucleus of a quiescent donor cell and applied gentle pulses of electricity. These pulses prompted the egg to accept the new nucleus—and all the DNA it contained—as though it were its own. They also triggered a burst of biochemical activity, jump-starting the process of cell division. A week later, the embryo that had already started growing into Dolly was implanted in the uterus of a surrogate ewe.

An inkling that this sort of approach might work, says Wilmut, came from the success his team experienced in producing live lambs from embryonic clones. "Could we do it again with an adult cell?" wondered Wilmut, a reserved, self-deprecating man who likes gardening, hiking in the highlands and the occasional dram of venerable single-malt Scotch (but who was practical enough to file for a patent before he went public).

It was a high-risk project, and at first Wilmut proceeded in great secrecy, limiting his core team to four scientists. His caution was justified, for the scientists failed far more often than they succeeded. Out of 277 tries, the researchers eventually produced only 29 embryos that survived longer than six days. Of these, all died before birth except Dolly, whose historic entry into the world was witnessed by a handful of researchers and a veterinarian.

Rumors that something had happened in Roslin, a small village in the green, rolling hills just south of Edinburgh, started circulating in scientific circles in early February. It was only late in the month, when the rumors were confirmed and the details of the experiment revealed, that the real excitement erupted. Cell biologists, like everybody else, were struck by the simple boldness of the experiment. But what intrigued them even more was what it suggested about how cells work.

CREATOR AND CLONE: Dr. Ian Wilmut with Dolly, whose fatherless conception sparked global debate

Many scientists had suspected that the key to getting a donor cell and egg to dance together was synchronicity—getting them started on the same foot. Normal eggs and sperm don't have that problem; they come predivided, ready to combine. An adult cell, though, with its full complement of genes, has to be coaxed into entering an embryonic state. That is probably what Wilmut did by putting the donor cell to sleep, says Colin Stewart, an embryologist at the National Cancer Institute. Somehow, in a manner scientists have yet to understand, this procedure seems to have reprogrammed the DNA of the donor cell. Thus when reawakened by the Roslin team, it was able to orchestrate the production of all the cells needed to make up Dolly's body.

But Wilmut's breakthrough raised more questions than it answered. Among the most pressing were questions about Dolly's health. At the time, she was seven months old and appeared to be perfectly fine, but no one knew if she would develop problems later on. For one thing, it is possible that Dolly may not live as long as other sheep. After all, observed NCI's Stewart, "she came from a six-year-old cell. Will she exhibit signs of aging prematurely?" In addition, as the high rate of spontaneous failure suggests, cloning can sometimes damage DNA. As a result, Dolly could develop all sorts of diseases that could shorten her life.

Indeed, cloning an adult mammal is still a cumbersome, difficult undertaking—so much so that even agricultural and biomedical applications of the technology could be years away. PPL Therapeutics, the small biotechnology firm based in Edinburgh that provided a third of the funding to create Dolly, has its eye on the pharmaceutical market. Cloning, said PPL's managing director, Ron James, could provide an efficient way of creating flocks of sheep that have been genetically engineered to produce milk laced with valuable enzymes and drugs. Among the pharmaceutical applications the PPL team is looking at is a potential treatment for cystic fibrosis.

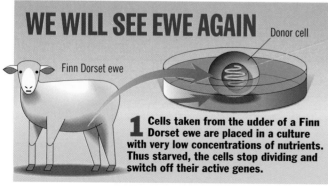

WE WILL SEE EWE AGAIN

Finn Dorset ewe

Donor cell

1 Cells taken from the udder of a Finn Dorset ewe are placed in a culture with very low concentrations of nutrients. Thus starved, the cells stop dividing and switch off their active genes.

2 Meanwhile an unfertilized egg cell is taken from a Scottish Blackface ewe. The nucleus (with its DNA) is sucked out, leaving an empty egg cell containing all the cellular machinery necessary to produce an embryo.

Blackface ewe

Egg cell

DNA

Only a week after the news of Dolly's birth surfaced, there was another flap: researchers at the Oregon Regional Primate Research Center let it be known that they had cloned a pair of rhesus monkeys, named Neti (for nuclear embryo transfer infant) and Ditto, that squinted in the glare of TV lights and clung to each other for dear life.

It was two clones too many—or, more to the point, clones too close to human for comfort. Politicians wasted no time in expressing their concern. The President, proclaiming that "each human life is unique, born of a miracle that reaches beyond laboratory science," banned the use of federal funds for human cloning. He charged a federal commission with the task of investigating the legal and ethical implications of the new technology and reporting back to him with their findings within 90 days. Meanwhile Republican Representative Vernon Ehlers of Michigan introduced not one but two anticloning measures.

Dr. Harold Varmus, director of the National Institutes of Health, told a congressional subcommittee that cloning a person is "repugnant to the American public." And a TIME/CNN survey found that 3 out of 4 Americans believed such research is "against the will of God."

Lost in the rush of legislative activity was the fact that Neti and Ditto were not so much a step toward a brave new world as a diversion. Unlike Dolly, they were produced by dividing embryos, which made them clones only in the way that identical twins or triplets are clones. The same technique had already been used with sheep, cattle, rabbits, pigs and even humans—although in the last case the embryonic clones were destroyed. What made Dolly special is that she was cloned from an adult sheep, not from an embryo. She is the only mammal ever born that is identical to her biological mother.

bUT THE ODD TRIO OF DOLLY, NETI AND DITTO TRIGgered wide-ranging social and philosophical temblors. The questions on the ethics of cloning proliferated. How—and by whom—would the new technology be regulated? What would the ability to make genetic stencils of ourselves say about the concept of individuality? Do the ants and bees and Maoist Chinese have it right? Is a species no more than an *über*-organism, a collection of multicellular parts to be die-cast as needed? Or is there something about the individual that is lost when the mystical act of conceiving a person becomes standardized into a mere act of photocopying one?

"This is not going to end in 90 days," said Princeton University president Harold Shapiro, chairman of President Clinton's committee. "Now that we have this technology, we have some hard thinking ahead of us." Bioethicist Daniel Callahan of the Hastings Center in Briarcliff, N.Y., agreed. "We are at the mercy of these technological developments. Once they're here, it's hard to turn back," he said.

Hard, perhaps, but not impossible. If anything will prevent human cloning from becoming a reality, it's that science may not be able to clear the ethical high bar that would allow basic research to get under way in the first place. Cutting, coring and electrically jolting a sheep embryo is a huge moral distance from doing the same to a human embryo. It took 277 trials and errors to produce Dolly the sheep, creating a cellular body count that would look like sheer carnage if the cells were human. "Human beings ought never to be used as experimental subjects," said Shapiro.

Whether they will or not is impossible to say. Even if governments ban human cloning outright, it will not be so easy to police what goes on in private laboratories that don't receive public money—or in pirate ones offshore. Years ago, Scottish scientists studying in vitro fertilization were subjected to such intense criticism that they took their work underground, continuing it in seclusion until they had the technology perfected. Presumably, human-cloning researchers could also do their work on the sly, emerging only when they succeed.

Scientists don't pretend to know when that will happen, but some science observers fear it will be soon. The first infant clone could come squalling into the world within seven years, according to Arthur Caplan, director of the Center for Bioethics at the University of Pennsylvania. If he's right, science had better get its ethical house in order quickly. In calendar terms, seven years from now is a good way off; in scientific terms, it's tomorrow afternoon. ∎

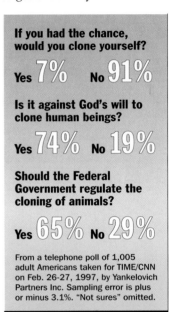

If you had the chance, would you clone yourself?

Yes **7%** No **91%**

Is it against God's will to clone human beings?

Yes **74%** No **19%**

Should the Federal Government regulate the cloning of animals?

Yes **65%** No **29%**

From a telephone poll of 1,005 adult Americans taken for TIME/CNN on Feb. 26-27, 1997, by Yankelovich Partners Inc. Sampling error is plus or minus 3.1%. "Not sures" omitted.

3 The two cells are placed next to each other, and an electric pulse causes them to fuse together like soap bubbles. A second pulse mimics the burst of energy at natural fertilization, jump-starting cell division.

Fused cells

4 About six days later, the resulting embryo is implanted in the uterus of another Blackface ewe.

Embryo

5 After a gestation period, the pregnant Blackface ewe gives birth to a baby Finn Dorset lamb, named Dolly, that is genetically identical to the original donor.

Baby Finn Dorset

TIME Diagram by Joe Lertola

El Niño's Fury

From the smog-fouled skies of Southeast Asia to the battered coast of Mexico, a pesky current skews the world's weather

OR THE FIRST SIX MONTHS OF 1997, A SPLOTCH of tropical warmth spread across the Pacific Ocean, from the international dateline to the South American coast. Climatologists traced the progress of the phenomenon with concern, for it wasn't simply the Pacific that was in hot water; it was the entire planet. El Niño, that mischievous gremlin of the atmosphere and oceans, had once again grabbed control of the world's weather machine and was preparing to unleash meteorological havoc.

Soon enough, it came. In late summer and fall, the skies of six Southeast Asian nations filled up with a heavy smog produced by raging fires in the tropical forest. The haze blanketed the region, triggering the worst environmental crisis in memory. Hundreds of children and old people were hospitalized, and the smog played a role in the crash of an Indonesian airliner that killed 234. Behind the smog lurked El Niño, which had spread drought throughout the area, delaying the September rains that usually drown the region's normal July and August fires.

Across the Pacific, Hurricane Pauline slammed into the coastal states of Oaxaca and Guerrero, Mexico, in October,

devastating the tourist city of Acapulco. Muddy torrents of debris flowed through the streets, and huge boulders tumbled down slippery hillsides as winds raged up to 124 m.p.h. While tourists huddled in the oceanfront hotels, thousands of poor residents of the surrounding hills watched helplessly as their shanties collapsed into flash-flood waters and were swept away. By the storm's end, some 300 were dead, and more than 50,000 were homeless.

In midsummer, temperatures on the Pacific's surface were rising so rapidly that they seemed likely to equal those of the notorious El Niño of 1982-83, which left 2,000 people dead and $13 billion in economic losses. Alarmed scientists issued dire warnings that the 1997-98 El Niño might dwarf any other seen in this century. By year's end, despite the damage in Southeast Asia, Mexico and elsewhere, the new El Niño had proved less calamitous—but there was plenty of time in 1998 for this "child" to tear up its playpen.

El Niño generally peaks around December, which is why Peruvian fishermen long ago gave the Christmastime weather visitor a name that in Spanish represents "Christ Child." The term is a misnomer, for among the "gifts" previous El Niños have bestowed on the world are landslides, flash floods, droughts and crop failures.

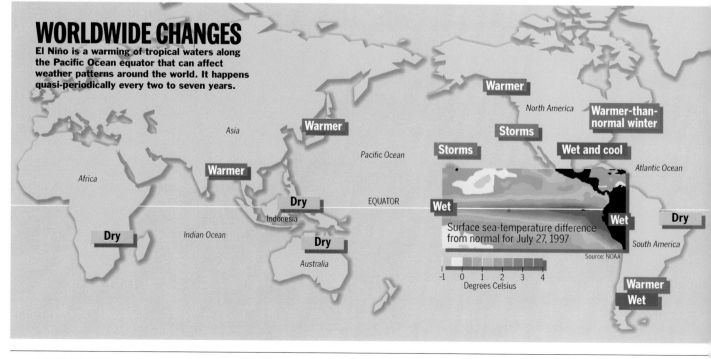

WORLDWIDE CHANGES

El Niño is a warming of tropical waters along the Pacific Ocean equator that can affect weather patterns around the world. It happens quasi-periodically every two to seven years.

Asia — Warmer

Africa

Warmer

Dry — Indonesia

Dry

Dry — Indian Ocean

Australia — Dry

Pacific Ocean

EQUATOR

Storms

Storms

Wet

Surface sea-temperature difference from normal for July 27, 1997

-1 0 1 2 3 4
Degrees Celsius

Warmer — North America

Storms

Warmer-than-normal winter

Wet and cool

Atlantic Ocean

Wet

Dry

South America

Warmer
Wet

Source: NOAA

STORMY PERILS: Beetles get a mudbath in Acapulco

But El Niño can also bestow a patchwork of benefits. Off Chile, fishermen caught anchovies normally found much farther north. Peruvians enjoyed balmy beaches in the middle of their winter. And residents of the U.S. anticipated an earlier spring in the Northeast in 1998, along with a blessed lull in tornadoes throughout the Midwest. All things considered, said Florida State University oceanographer James O'Brien, Americans should think of El Niño as a "good dude." Deep-sea fishermen in California who reeled in species normally seen only in latitudes much farther south no doubt agreed with him.

Until recently, most weather scientists paid scant attention to the periodic episodes of warm water that for countless centuries have appeared off the coast of Peru. Not until the early 1970s, when the collapse of Peru's lucrative anchovy fishery was accompanied by drought and crop failures around the world, did the global reach of El Niño become clear. However, it took the disastrous weather of 1982-83 to convince scientists and policymakers that weather patterns in the tropical Pacific merited close watching.

In terms of the earth's climate machine, El Niño is more than just a sudden warm current off Peru. It refers to a rise in sea-surface temperatures over much of the equatorial Pacific as well as a change in winds and ocean currents. Indeed, there is a kind of climatic flip-flop, with a reversal of conditions across a wide stretch of ocean. Consequently, climate experts no longer refer to El Niño alone but speak of the El Niño Southern Oscillation. Rather like a pendulum, the ENSO cycle swings between an El Niño state and its opposite, a cold-water state known as La Niña (the girl) or El Viejo (the old man). Taken as a whole, ENSO is a powerful driver of global weather patterns. In fact, say scientists, besides seasonal variations caused by the earth's travels around the sun, it is the major cause of month-to-month variation in climate.

WHY DOES A REGIONAL PHENOMENON AFFECT weather around the world? The reason, scientists claim, is the extra heat. Like fresh coal tossed on a fire, it creates more and larger storms. And as the warm water spreads into the central and eastern Pacific, these storms inevitably follow in its path, moving the tropical storm belt from one part of the Pacific to another. The rearrangement has reverberations throughout the atmosphere, causing droughts in places as far-flung as northeastern Brazil, southern Africa and Australia, while other regions, from California to Cuba, can be hit by torrential rains.

These effects are variable. El Niño may weaken the Indian monsoon—or barely affect it at all. But that didn't stop El Niño from stealing the honors from Comet Hale-Bopp as the year's all-purpose whipping boy. As TIME essayist Charles Krauthammer noted, "[El Niño has] been blamed for an invasion of Argentine ants in Southern California, for starving seabirds off Oregon, for albatrosses abandoning their nests in the Galápagos Islands ... But if you are selling umbrellas in Los Angeles, where a 500% increase in rainfall was predicted ... business is good." Who said an ill wind isn't appreciated now and then? ■

WHAT NORMALLY HAPPENS

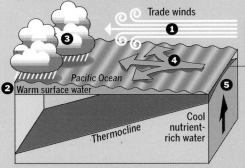

Trade winds

Pacific Ocean
Warm surface water
Thermocline
Cool nutrient-rich water

❶ Tropical trade winds blow from east to west across the equatorial Pacific Ocean.

❷ The winds drag the surface water along with them, causing the ocean in Asia to be about 2 ft. (60 cm) higher than the ocean along the coast of South America.

❸ The winds pick up moisture as they blow across the ocean, then release it as monsoon rains over Indonesia.

❹ The surface water moves westward, and near the equator is diverted poleward by the effect of the earth's rotation.

❺ The divergent flow causes an upwelling of deep water that is cooler, especially in the eastern Pacific, where the transition layer between warmer, shallower water and cooler, bottom water (known as the thermocline) is close to the surface.

❻ As the cool water comes up into the sunlight, plankton feed on the nutrients. These creatures support vast amounts of marine life in the waters off Peru and Chile.

THE EL NIÑO PHENOMENON

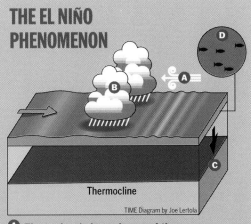

Thermocline
TIME Diagram by Joe Lertola

🅐 The trade winds weaken, and the warm water stays in the eastern Pacific.

🅑 The monsoon rains fall over the middle of the Pacific instead of over Southeast Asia.

🅒 The thermocline flattens.

🅓 Marine-life population drops as the nutrients that support it are withdrawn.

Forecast: Cosmic Showers

A physicist discovers Earth is bombarded by 40,000 watery comets each day

HARDLY ANYBODY TOOK LOUIS FRANK SERIOUSLY WHEN he first proposed, more than 10 years ago, that Earth was being bombarded by cosmic snowballs at the rate of as many as 30 a minute. Part of the problem was how preposterous his theory sounded: every day, he suggested, tens of thousands of icy comets, each the size of a small house and containing 40 tons of water, were vaporizing in the upper atmosphere and raining down on Earth. It didn't help that the University of Iowa physicist happened to release his findings on April 1, 1986. "Newspapers phoned to ask if this was an April Fool's joke," he recalls with amusement.

Frank is unlikely to hear that kind of question again. In May, at the American Geophysical Union's annual convention in Baltimore, Md., he backed up his theory with evidence that was not only fresh, but convincing: satellite images that captured his unearthly hail in midflight. After Frank's presentation, it began to seem entirely possible to his fellow scientists that the source of much of the water on Earth—and even of life itself—might be his "cosmic rain."

Did a gentle "cosmic rain" fill the oceans and bring life to Earth from outer space?

Frank first began formulating his theories in the 1980s when he was analyzing satellite pictures and found the atmosphere in the images flyspecked with thousands of spots. The altitude of the flecks and the wavelength of light they absorbed led him to conclude that they were clouds of extraterrestrial water that had somehow been carried to Earth. But the images, taken from NASA's Dynamics Explorer 1 spacecraft, were grainy, and few other scientists were convinced.

So Frank came to the Geophysical Union meeting in May armed with better photos from a new NASA satellite, the Polar, and this time his pictures carried the day. Frank is principal scientist for the visible-imaging system of the satellite, which circles in an elliptical orbit anywhere from 3,200 to 32,000 miles above Earth. "We have a large population of objects that have not been detected before," he now says confi-

dently. Extrapolating from the number of the objects he saw in his pictures, he estimated that as many as 43,000 of these celestial snowballs arrive on Earth every day.

Using a special filter that detects a particular signature of visible light emitted by water molecules, Frank was able to prove that that the snowballs consisted mainly of water. Robert Hoffman, project scientist for the Polar satellite, called the images "remarkable" and said they gave scientists "a fascinating, new and important phenomenon" to consider in theorizing about the evolution of solar systems.

How could so many comets stay hidden so long? For one thing, they are not true comets. Big-name comets like Hale-Bopp may measure 20 miles across—giants compared with Frank's 40-ft. pellets. The large comets are studded with rock and metal, while Frank's are almost all water.

It's a good thing for us that so much of what rains down on Earth amounts to cosmic bird shot. A collision with a full-scale comet would be a global calamity; the minicomets, by contrast, are remarkably fragile. Well before they hit the planet—between 600 miles and 15,000 miles up—they begin to disintegrate. Sunlight then breaks them down further, transforming them into ordinary clouds that produce ordinary rain. Over the course of 20,000 years, this cosmic sprinkling can add an inch of water to the planet; multiplied by Earth's 4.5 billion-year history, that could help account for the oceans themselves.

But it is not just water the comets import. In order to remain intact in space, they must be held together by a supporting shell. Frank believes this shell is made of carbon, created as cosmic rays break down traces of methane. Carbon, of course, is one of the essential building blocks of biology. It may be, Frank says, that his comets carried the very stuff of life to Earth, helping give rise to all the planet's creatures. "This relatively gentle cosmic rain—which possibly contains simple organic compounds—may well have nurtured the development of life on our planet," he claims. That hypothesis may still sound preposterous to some Earthlings, but in the scientific community, nobody was saying April Fool. ■

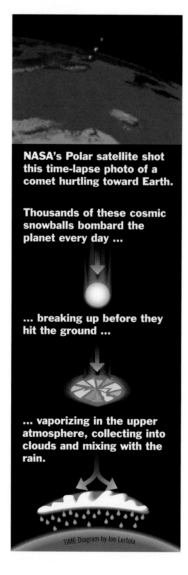

NASA's Polar satellite shot this time-lapse photo of a comet hurtling toward Earth.

Thousands of these cosmic snowballs bombard the planet every day ...

... breaking up before they hit the ground ...

... vaporizing in the upper atmosphere, collecting into clouds and mixing with the rain.

TIME Diagram by Joe Lertola

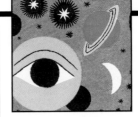

Climate of Concern

Global warming, a strong majority of scientists now believe, threatens the planet with climatic upheaval: melting glaciers, rising sea levels and more frequent and vicious storms. In December some 160 nations met in Kyoto to forge a treaty to combat climate change. After tough talks that pitted environmentalists against industries and economically developed countries against the underdeveloped, the attendees

SMOG: China will soon be the top polluter

reached agreement on the "Kyoto Protocol," which mandated a cut in average emissions of carbon dioxide and other "greenhouse" gases to 5% below 1990 levels during the period 2008 through 2012. A compromise that would allow industrial nations to buy or trade emission credits from countries whose limits are within acceptable levels was included in the agreement, but details will not be resolved until 1998. A tough fight for approval of the treaty loomed in the Senate.

A New Species of Early Man?

Spanish scientists announced that fossil remains they found in 1994 in northern Spain belong to a new, possibly cannibalistic species of early man that roamed Europe nearly 800,000 years ago. Called *Homo antecessor,* this creature may be the last common ancestor shared by modern humans and Neanderthals. It showed a mix of modern and Neanderthal facial traits.

Storms on the Sun

Solar physicists were beaming over the results from a new generation of solar observatories: a NASA–European Space Agency satellite known as SOHO (for Solar and Heliospheric Observatory), which has

GALACTIC PUZZLE Astrophysicists were startled by William Purcell's observation of **a colossal fountain of antimatter** spewing from the center of the Milky Way trillions of miles into space.

LIFE ON EUROPA? New images from the Galileo space probe captured

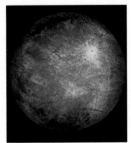

EUROPA: Could its oceans harbor life?

Jupiter's moon in new detail, showing that Europa's frosty rind is a **planet-wide ice cap** floating atop an ocean of ordinary water. Brown stains now revealed on the ice could possibly be a mix of hydrogen cyanide and other chemicals that one NASA scientist termed **"a recipe for life."**

been circling the sun since December 1995, and the National Science Foundation's global network of ground-based solar stations. The new glimpses of the sun's workings included discovery of an astonishing doughnut-shaped jet stream of hot gases circling the sun's "Arctic" region, like the earth's own circumpolar winds. The scientists also got a close-up look at the sun's lower-latitude trade winds, whose existence they had only suspected. These winds—actually, great bands of plasma slightly warmer than neighboring solar gases—dive deep into the sun's interior, itself a mass of gases, then flow back toward the equator, creating a circular gyre resembling the earth's great ocean currents.

Building Good Brains Earlier

An explosion of research into the brains of embryos and infants infused new passion into the political debate over early education and day care. Among the findings: the brain during the first years of life is so malleable that very young children who suffer strokes or injuries that wipe out an entire hemisphere can still mature into highly functional adults. Moreover, children who don't play much or are rarely touched develop brains 20% to 30% smaller than normal for their age; thus, rich experiences produce rich brains. A White House conference tackled the controversial policy options arising from the new research, including preschool programs designed to boost the brain power of youngsters born into poorer families.

LEARNING: The first three years are critical

Redux, Prozac and other mood-altering substances can make people happier or thinner— but at what cost?

DRUGS THAT MASTER THE MIND

BRIAN GOODMAN, 20, IS OBSESSED WITH THE IDEA THAT DISASTER and death are about to strike his family. The only way to stave off catastrophe, his mind tells him, is to follow self-imposed rituals to the absolute letter: making coffee in a way that never varies, driving around Los Angeles along the same route every day. A classic victim of obsessive-compulsive disorder, Goodman has been in treatment since he was seven, without much change. Now he is on Zoloft. "Before the medicine," he says, "it was like living in hell."

For Chicago journalist Susan Schwendener, the symptoms were as familiar as the runny nose of a cold or the scratchiness of a strep throat. "You can't sleep, you

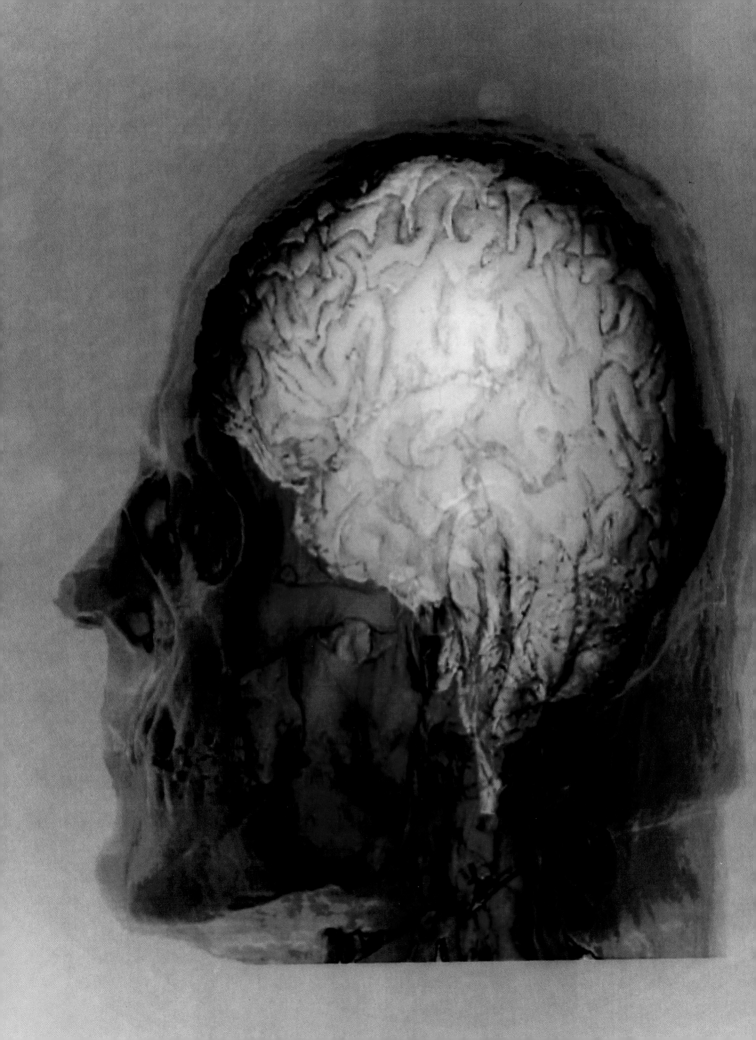

Antidepressants

▼PROZAC, ZOLOFT, PAXIL, ELAVIL

These drugs work by making serotonin and in some cases another neurotransmitter, norepinephrine, available in the brain for longer than usual, thus boosting their mood-enhancing effects.

can't eat, you lose weight because your mood's so blue." Schwendener, 33, suffered her first bout of depression as a teenager. She started taking Prozac 10 years ago. "The pain," she says, "sort of evaporated over time."

By age 21, Beth Herwig, now an executive assistant in St. Louis, Mo., weighed more than 500 lbs.; she couldn't resist treats. At 29, after years of yo-yo dieting, she was carrying 545 lbs. on her 5-ft. 4-in. frame. Then Herwig went on a combination of fenfluramine and phentermine, popularly known as fen/phen. Today she weighs just 265 lbs.

At first glance, these stories seem completely unrelated—three profoundly different disorders treated with three different drugs. Yet all three medications have one crucial element in common: they target the brain chemical serotonin. Though serotonin has been known to science for nearly a half-century, only in recent years have neuro-

Eating-Disorder Drugs

▼PROZAC, ZOLOFT

Antidepressants can help bulimics stop binging; the starved brains of anorexics respond only after they've been renourished. But scientists have not yet discovered why these drugs are effective, or located the area of the brain they affect.

chemists begun to understand how important this one substance is to the functioning of the human psyche. Serotonin, or the lack of it, has been implicated not only in depression, uncontrollable appetite and obsessive-compulsive disorders but also in autism, bulimia, social phobias, premenstrual syndrome, migraines, anxiety and panic, schizophrenia and even in tendencies to violence.

The growing awareness of serotonin's central role in mood and emotion has been paralleled—and in some cases driven—by a boom in drugs that target serotonin more or less specifically. Among them are such popular antidepressants as Elavil, Prozac, Zoloft and the hot new herbal medication St. John's wort; appetite suppressants, including Redux and fenfluramine; and antipsychotics such as clozapine. Like every other drug, the ones that zero in on serotonin have side effects. Elavil makes people sleepy. Zoloft can trigger headache and nausea. Zoloft and Prozac may cause sexual dysfunction. Even so, many sufferers have willingly paid these steep prices to relieve deeper problems.

But in September it became startlingly clear that monkeying with the chemistry of the human mind can trigger problems much more serious than a dull sex life. Just 1½ years after it approved Redux for treatment of obesity, the FDA issued a warning advising patients to stop taking it and its close chemical cousin fenfluramine immediately. At the same time, the drugs' chief manufacturer and distributor, Wyeth-Ayerst Laboratories, told physicians to stop prescribing them and took the dramatic step of pulling both medications from the market. Reason: new evidence had revealed that as many as 30% of Redux and fen/phen users could develop abnormalities in the shape of their heart valves—changes that could eventually lead to serious cardiac weakness and perhaps even death.

Natural Antidepressants

▼ST. JOHN'S WORT

Used in Europe over many centuries, this wild-growing plant contains substances that enhance the effects of serotonin, norepinephrine and another neurotransmitter, dopamine. St. John's wort has yet another benefit: it has few known side effects.

These were not the first lethal side effects associated with Redux and fenfluramine. When Redux was approved, both Wyeth-Ayerst and the FDA knew that the medication could lead to a potentially fatal lung condition known as primary pulmonary hypertension. But this problem seemed to affect only a small minority of users, and morbid obesity carries significant risks of its own: heart disease, diabetes, high blood pressure and stroke. On balance, the benefits seemed to outweigh the risks.

Why did the equation suddenly seesaw the other way? In part because clinical trials reveal only the most obvious side effects; the heart-valve changes discovered over the summer do not initially cause significant symptoms in most patients. Also, many doctors went overboard, giving Redux and fen/phen to patients who were merely overweight, not obese, a violation of the FDA and drug-company prescription criteria that skewed the risk-benefit ratio.

The entire history of serotonin and of drugs that affect it has been largely a process of trial and error marked by chance discoveries, surprise connections and unanticipated therapeutic effects. The chemical was not even first dis-

Drugs for Obsessive-Compulsive Disorder

▼PROZAC, ZOLOFT

Science has yet to explain why these drugs help alleviate obsessive-compulsive behavior, but it may be that they replace a natural serotonin boost triggered by repetitive motions like compulsive hand washing.

Diet Drugs
▼REDUX, PONDIMIN
These medications do what Prozac does, but they also stimulate nerve cells into pumping out extra serotonin. This helps overeaters feel full more easily, but also may explain the dangerous side effects that led to the recall of Redux.

covered in the brain. It was stumbled on in the late 1940s by U.S. and Italian scientists, working independently, in the blood and intestines, respectively.

At first the connection between serotonin and moods was not clear. But experiments at the National Institutes of Health in the 1950s revealed that compounds that depressed serotonin levels depressed patients as well. The research seemed to point to serotonin as the most important mood-enhancing chemical, though not the only one, and so neurochemists set about looking for a drug that would boost the influence of serotonin alone. In 1974 chemists at Eli Lilly came up with Prozac, first of the so-called selective serotonin reuptake inhibitors, and it was finally approved by the FDA in 1987. Later studies showed that serotonin might play a role in helping people sleep—or act out aggression. The development of Prozac led to the discovery that the drug was effective in treating obsessive-compulsive disorder as well as panic disorder and social phobias. And, intriguingly, patients on Prozac also tended to lose weight.

This fact led Richard Wurtman, an M.I.T. neurologist and Lilly consultant, to begin working to develop a drug to suppress appetite. Instead of using Prozac as a starting point, he turned to fenfluramine, a well-known European weight-loss drug. Because fenfluramine acts on both serotonin and dopamine, it has the unfortunate side effect of putting its users to sleep. That is why doctors came up with fen/phen; the "phen" (phentermine) is an amphetamine-like drug that wakes the patient up and boosts the metabolism to burn calories faster.

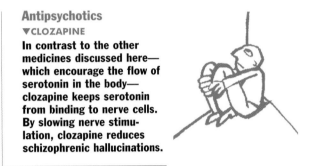

Wurtman separated fenfluramine into its two component chemicals, levofenfluramine and dexfenfluramine. The latter has revealed itself to be a powerful weight-loss medication. Wurtman patented the drug for M.I.T., founded a company to manufacture it under license to Wyeth-Ayerst and began moving the drug, dubbed Redux, through the FDA-approval process.

From the start, it was clear that Redux has serious potential side effects. One is primary pulmonary hypertension, a rare form of high blood pressure that strikes the blood vessels of the lungs. Another, considered even more serious by some of Redux's critics, was the possibility of brain damage. When fed to monkeys, dexfenfluramine can destroy neurons. But until 1997 nobody considered the

Antipsychotics
▼CLOZAPINE
In contrast to the other medicines discussed here— which encourage the flow of serotonin in the body— clozapine keeps serotonin from binding to nerve cells. By slowing nerve stimulation, clozapine reduces schizophrenic hallucinations.

possibility that either Redux or its parent compound fenfluramine might damage heart valves.

But if Redux and fenfluramine are too powerful for the body to handle—a proposition not fully accepted by some doctors, despite the FDA and its manufacturers' action— research into serotonin-boosting drugs is hardly slowing down. If anything, the discovery of a new set of side effects will spur researchers to hone their pharmacological handiwork even more, to create medicines that will not just fine-tune the way serotonin is used in the brain but also might target specific serotonin receptors or act on only specific parts of the brain and nervous system.

A serotonin drug could target chronic pain more directly than today's antidepressants do—or help us sleep, fight jet-lag, even suppress our appetites without Redux's dangerous side effects. Advanced mood-enhancing medicines may eventually revolutionize psychiatry, self-improvement and health care in general. But in the wake of the Redux-fenfluramine debacle, it could be many years before the FDA is ready to approve the new drugs. Or before the rest of us are ready to swallow them. ■

Hallucinogens
▼LSD, MESCALINE, PSILOCYBIN, ECSTASY
Basically anti-antipsychotics, these recreational drugs plug directly into serotonin receptors in the brain. Scientists believe this may cause brain neurons to rev up into a kind of overdrive state.

MR. NATURAL

Meet Dr. Andrew Weil, New Age medicine man. Is he selling health—or snake oil?

ANDREW WEIL LIKES TO TELL THE STORY of Oliver, the man who was cured by a bumblebee. There was a time when nobody believed Oliver, but when Weil heard the story, he didn't doubt it for a minute. At the time of his cure, Oliver was 64 years old and had been suffering from rheumatoid arthritis since he was in his 30s. His hands were so swollen that he had given up trying to find gloves to fit them. His feet were two sizes larger than they used to be and seemed to be growing each year. He took up to a dozen different pain relievers every day, though few actually relieved his pain.

One evening Oliver was putting on a pair of pajamas that had been dried on the backyard line when he felt a sharp pain in his left knee. He slapped at the spot, shook his pajama leg and out tumbled a bee. The next day Oliver's knee was tender, swollen and hot with venom. After another day or two, a curious thing happened: as the pain from the sting subsided, the ache from the arthritis in that knee began to diminish as well. A few weeks later, the swelling in all of Oliver's joints was gone. A short while after that, the chronic body-wide pain vanished too. In 1997 Oliver was a limber 86 years old; he hadn't been bothered by arthritis for 22 years.

"There's a long history of studies documenting the benefits of animal venom," Weil says today. "Bee venom in particular contains some very powerful anti-inflammatory compounds. Oliver was the lucky beneficiary of that." Weil, 55, a Harvard-educated physician, ought to know better than to tell stories like this. But he has a thousand of them. To hear the medical establishment tell it, Weil's stories are the worst kind of hooey—or, in the far more clinical but equally damning phrasing of the scientist, "merely anecdotal." Yet Weil, best-selling author, TV personality, Internet columnist and medical school instructor, intends to keep telling them. And Americans, to all appearances, are buying much of what he has to say.

As recently as 1995, few people had even heard of Weil. Since then, few people haven't. Weil's 1997 book, *8 Weeks to Optimum Health*, a familiar mix of herbal medicine and nutrition and life-style tips, spent 22 weeks on the best-seller lists, with more than 800,000 copies in print. An earlier book, *Spontaneous Healing*, spent more than two years on the lists, with a press run of more than

1 million. His site on the World Wide Web—cozily titled "Ask Dr. Weil"—recorded 1 million hits in April 1997 alone. His appearances on PBS stations around the country drew record audiences; his audio CD of music and meditations was selling briskly. He was, in short, the man of the moment in America's eternal search for an alternative to the conventional, interventionist, pharmaceutical medicine most of us grew up with.

The appeal of alternative healers and their uncommon cures is hardly new. Nationwide, health-care consumers spend nearly $14 billion a year for medical treatments rarely offered by the family doctor. Deepak Chopra, Dr. Bernie Siegel and Marianne Williamson are among those

duces them to herbalism, acupuncture, naturopathy, osteopathy, chiropractic and hypnotism. But he gets into trouble when he wanders farther still, uncritically endorsing treatments such as cranial manipulation that seem like folly even to many alternative-medicine believers.

Where Weil wins many of his critics back, however, is when he avoids straying from the medical fold at all. He concedes that for all the promise of alternative cures, often the best answer is the high-tech medicine of the industrialized West. "If I'm in a car accident," says Weil, "don't take me to an herbalist. But when it comes to maximizing the body's natural healing potential, a mix of conventional and alternative procedures seems like the only answer."

Weil makes his home in the Arizona desert, and in the summer of 1997 he and the University of Arizona medical school launched a fellowship program designed to train M.D.s in various protocols of alternative medicine, or, as Weil prefers to call the eclectic healing he practices, "integrative medicine." In addition to classroom training and research work, physicians in the program will get hands-on experience with patients, working alongside Weil at a new integrative-medicine clinic the university has established. Even before the program had begun, Weil was developing plans to market the curriculum to other medical schools looking to develop similar fellowships.

Dr. Weil's floral pharmacology makes readers happy—and scientists mad

"Ultimately," he says, "we'd like to set up an American College of Integrative Medicine that will establish residency training, set standards, administer exams and do all the other things that lead to accreditation." Whether conventional medicine will ever extend such diplomatic recognition to breakaway practitioners like Weil is an open question. Part of the problem appears to be Weil himself. Many of his mainstream colleagues still remember him mostly for what some saw as a pro-marijuana study he conducted in the late 1960s, and persist in seeing him, at best, as a drug apologist and, at worst, as an advocate.

What disturbs Establishment doctors more about Weil, however, is his science—or lack of it. When you look behind all the miracle testimonials in Weil's books, they insist, the research that supports them looks just plain shabby. "Weil cites a lot of anecdotes," says Dr. James R. Allen, a vice president of the American Medical Association, "and while they can be instructive, that doesn't mean they are necessarily valid in terms of scientific proof."

The debate between alternative and mainstream medicine will not get settled anytime soon. But even if Andrew Weil the scientist does not prevail, it's clear that Andrew Weil the healer-dealer and crusader has already made a lasting impression on millions. What's less clear, at least for now, is whether Weil and other alternative healers are selling real cures or, like the hypnotist, just casting good spells. ■

who have prospered by offering a buffet of alternative approaches that range from meditation and visualization to the curative powers of love and positive thinking.

What distinguishes Weil from the rest is his radical eclecticism. Almost any treatment can have a place in his healing universe, so long as it doesn't cause harm. Indeed, much of what Weil recommends is pretty simple stuff: self-administered, commonsense cures like eating less fat, getting more exercise and reducing stress. He champions olive oil, ginseng, ginger and garlic—and 6,000 mg of vitamin C a day. He leads readers a little farther afield when he intro-

DESERT SAGE: From his hideaway in Arizona, Weil ministers to the nation, takes on his critics—and counts up his cash

Aching Head? Cures Are Afoot

Science moves on several fronts toward relieving the pain just above the neck

THE INCAS USED TO TREAT HEADACHES BY DRILLING A hole in the skull. The French favored cold compresses. Today we use shelffuls of heavily advertised over-the-counter remedies: aspirin, Advil, Tylenol, Aleve. But how much do scientists really know about headaches and what causes them? Quite a bit, as attested by doctors who gathered in New York City in June for a meeting of the American Association for the Study of Headache.

Researchers have known since the 1960s that not all headaches are the same, medically speaking. Tension headaches, which are the easiest to treat, are triggered by clenched muscles in the head and neck. Migraines, which generate a throbbing pain that is sometimes preceded by an "aura" and can last 12 to 24 hours, are produced by blood vessels that alternately constrict and expand. Cluster headaches are even worse than migraines—if you can imagine such a thing—and scientists suspect that overactive blood vessels play a role in them too. One of the hallmarks of cluster headaches is that they strike in cycles: three or more a day for several weeks, then nothing for a year.

The meeting in New York didn't produce an all-purpose cure for the headache, but it did mark progress on several fronts:

BETTER SCREENING. Treating headaches is difficult because doctors don't know in advance what they are dealing with. Most physicians use trial and error: they prescribe a treatment, and if it doesn't work, they try another. Now scientists at Ohio University are fashioning a simple 15-min. screening test that requires patients to enter yes and no responses to a series of questions posed on a computer screen. If successful, the test will tell doctors where the pain occurs, how debilitating it is and whether other emotional and social factors may be contributing to it. The hope is that physicians will be able to determine in advance whether their patients will respond better to drugs or to, say, a regimen of stress-management therapy, and thus get the treatment right the first time.

What makes you ache? Genes and hormones may bring on the pain.

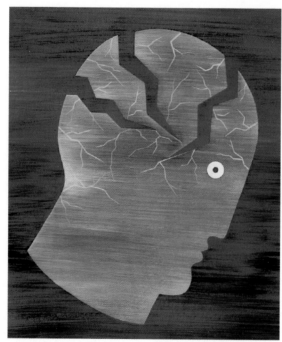

OUCH! Cluster headaches are the most painful of all

BETTER DRUGS. Researchers have long known that the brain chemical called serotonin [*see earlier story*] plays an important role in triggering migraine headaches. For reasons that are still unclear, serotonin sometimes floods the blood vessels of the brain, causing them to constrict. The body then overreacts, sending serotonin levels plummeting and forcing the blood vessels to expand to several times their normal size. This cycle of contraction and expansion results in the headache's characteristic throbbing pain. In 1993 Glaxo introduced a drug called Imitrex that allowed doctors for the first time to prescribe something that was specifically designed to interrupt the cycle of pain.

A GENE FOR MIGRAINES. Migraines, more than any other form of headache, seem to run in families. Neurologists from Leiden University in the Netherlands have for the first time isolated a gene that is linked to some types of migraines. The team, led by Dr. Michel Ferrari, studied 60 subjects from five families with a history of migraines. Inheriting one copy of the defective gene seems to hamper the ability of cells to use calcium molecules to communicate with one another, a key headache factor.

THE HORMONE LINK. Doctors have long suspected a link between headaches and certain sex hormones, particularly in women. A study of 100 women at the University of Mississippi Medical Center suggests that patients who have gynecological problems (irregular menstrual cycles or ovarian cysts, for example) or who have had hysterectomies are up to twice as likely to develop chronic severe headaches as women who have not. Scientists still don't know why some women get headaches during the hormone surges that accompany their monthly cycles.

Clearly, much work remains to be done, in particular on the mystifying cluster headaches. The pharmaceutical companies have yet to design a pill specifically to protect against these attacks, although some doctors have had success treating them with lithium, a drug usually used to regulate the mood swings of manic depression. Apparently lithium can also interrupt the cycles of cluster headaches, although nobody yet understands why. ■

A Little Bit of Bloomin' Luck

St. John's wort is growing in popularity as a mood enhancer—but how safe is it?

TO DISPEL THE DARK MOODS THAT DOGGED HER THROUGH life, Truen Bergen tried every antidepressant imaginable. But she hated the side effects, which ranged from a sharp prickling sensation to mild hypertension. Then she heard about St. John's wort, a medicinal herb that has been used for centuries in teas and tinctures. "I figured it couldn't be any worse than the medication I was already taking," says Bergen, 49, an airline purser from San Diego. "Then after two or three weeks, it dawned on me. I felt balanced and good. I felt happy."

A folk remedy? You bet. But St. John's wort—or *Hypericum perforatum*, as scientists call it—is not just another weed. It has attracted a huge following in Europe, and is now catching on in the U.S. According to Dr. Harold Bloomfield, author of *Hypericum & Depression* (Prelude Press; $7.95), this pretty yellow-flowered plant is nature's own antidepressant, almost as potent as the prescription drug Prozac but without Prozac's troubling side effects.

An ancient folk remedy reminds us that nature can cure— worts and all

Suddenly St. John's wort is hot. Pills and potions containing extracts of hypericum are selling briskly in supermarkets, pharmacies and health-store chains across America. "We are stunned and pleased," says Karl-Heinz Siewert, managing director of Lichtwer Pharma, a Berlin-based company marketing hypericum under the brands Kira and Jarsin.

The hoopla over hypericum began in Germany, where Jarsin, not Prozac, is the No. 1 antidepressant. This isn't as surprising as it may sound. German physicians are far more willing than their American counterparts to recommend herbal medications to patients. And a string of studies by German scientists, many of them sponsored by Lichtwer, have built a tantalizing if tentative case for hypericum's effectiveness as a treatment for mild and moderate depression. As a result, sales of hypericum preparations in Germany have soared from $23 million in 1994 to $66 million in 1996.

But does the evidence of hypericum's efficacy have scientific validity? Over the coming years, nagging questions about its effectiveness and safety may finally be settled. The National Institutes of Health is laying plans for a large clinical trial that will compare hypericum with the most effective antidepressants. But for now, there is reason to be cautious. Like all plants, hypericum contains a wide variety of compounds, including one that is known to cause sun sensitivity. The effects of hypericum in combination with other drugs are also cause for concern. Psychiatrists are worried about the so-called serotonin syndrome [*see earlier story*], a kind of biochemical overload brought on by combining antidepressants. Among the symptoms: nausea and muscle spasms.

Still, the German experience suggests that St. John's wort is relatively harmless. Indeed, just as aspirin (whose active ingredient was first isolated from the bark of the willow tree) has spurred the creation of a new generation of anti-inflammatories, so hypericum may eventually stimulate the creation of safer, more powerful antidepressant drugs.

Hypericum appears to affect the brain much as Prozac does, by prolonging the activity of the mood-enhancing brain chemical serotonin. But in rats and mice, at least, it also extends the action of at least two other powerful brain chemicals—dopamine and norepinephrine—whose deficiency is thought to play a role in depression. In each case, hypericum appears to work not by stimulating the release of the neurotransmitters, but by preventing their reabsorption by nearby nerve fibers and thus prolonging their usefulness.

Despite its promise, experts agree that hypericum should not be viewed as an off-the-shelf solution for depression, especially severe depression that prompts suicidal thoughts. Nor should it be casually ingested in hopes of relieving a milder state of the blues. But, like aspirin, it reminds us that nature itself is a continuing source of pharmacological discovery—worts and all. ∎

**FLOWER POWER:
The plant is very
popular in Europe**

Cholesterol's Co-Conspirator

Homocysteine may be as closely linked to heart disease—and it's easier to treat

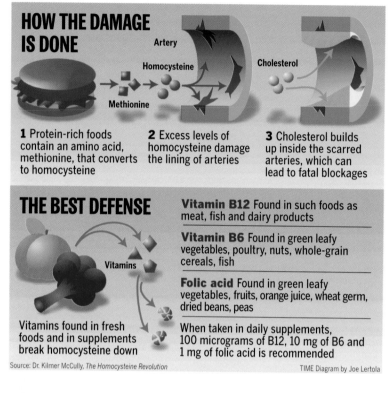

HOW THE DAMAGE IS DONE

Artery

Homocysteine

Cholesterol

Methionine

1 Protein-rich foods contain an amino acid, methionine, that converts to homocysteine

2 Excess levels of homocysteine damage the lining of arteries

3 Cholesterol builds up inside the scarred arteries, which can lead to fatal blockages

THE BEST DEFENSE

Vitamins

Vitamins found in fresh foods and in supplements break homocysteine down

Vitamin B12 Found in such foods as meat, fish and dairy products

Vitamin B6 Found in green leafy vegetables, poultry, nuts, whole-grain cereals, fish

Folic acid Found in green leafy vegetables, fruits, orange juice, wheat germ, dried beans, peas

When taken in daily supplements, 100 micrograms of B12, 10 mg of B6 and 1 mg of folic acid is recommended

Source: Dr. Kilmer McCully, *The Homocysteine Revolution*

TIME Diagram by Joe Lertola

ETWEEN 1992 AND 1996, 64 MEN AND WOMEN IN NORway quietly died, their passing noted by their families but otherwise largely unremarked. All the deceased, after all, suffered from heart disease, and many had undergone bypass surgery. Deaths like these are not the stuff of headlines. In July, however, the dead Norwegians made the news. What all of them had in common, in addition to sickly hearts and premature deaths, was elevated levels of an amino acid called homocysteine. The patients were part of a study, published in the *New England Journal of Medicine*, that shows an almost lockstep correlation between high homocysteine levels and coronary-disease mortality. And that paper followed more than 50 less publicized studies since 1992 with similar findings.

What makes this research so compelling is that unlike cholesterol, which everyone knows is associated with coronary problems but can often be treated only by medication and a rigid diet, homocysteine appears to respond to nothing more demanding than eating enough vegetables and taking the right vitamins. Homocysteine is certainly not the lone gunman of heart disease, but the studies strongly suggest that it's at least a co-conspirator—and one that patients can do something about.

Ordinarily pretty harmless stuff, homocysteine is used by the body to help manufacture proteins and carry out cellular metabolism. Too much of it, however, appears to cause blood platelets to clump together and vascular walls to begin to break down. In older patients, a lifetime of this damage may give arteries the scarred texture that provides circulating cholesterol with a place to stick and accumulate.

The new study, conducted at Haukeland University Hospital in Bergen, Norway, surveyed 587 people with a history of heart trouble. The research suggested that people with elevated homocysteine are $4\frac{1}{2}$ times more likely to die of heart disease than those with normal levels.

No one knows for certain what causes some individuals and not others to overproduce homocysteine. But the evidence points to a shortage of vitamin B_6, vitamin B_{12} and folic acid, all of which work to convert the amino acid into a molecular form the body can use. The answer for people concerned about cardiac health would seem to be for them to keep their intake of the protective vitamins high. The *Harvard Health Letter* has recommended increasing consumption of a range of specific foods—including leafy green vegetables, beans, peas, grains and certain meats and dairy foods—to keep homocysteine in check.

Not everyone is sold on such a simple prescription. Even if homocysteine is behind some cases of heart disease, it's unlikely to be behind them all. Cardiologist Roger Blumenthal of Johns Hopkins University estimates the share of all cardiac cases attributable to homocysteine at fewer than 1 in 5. And there's no guarantee that managing the amino acid will decrease the risk of cardiac trouble. Regardless of circulating homocysteine levels, smoking and obesity will still ravage the cardiovascular system, and a poor diet will still choke the blood with fats. "People are jumping the gun if they think they can just take vitamins and skip the traditional health measures, like exercising and eating a low-fat diet," cautions Blumenthal.

What's more, even for patients whose illnesses are caused by elevated amino acids, a better diet may not be the answer. Scientists know cholesterol levels in the blood fluctuate within a limited range; when people eat less fat, the liver simply manufactures more. It's not yet known whether there is a similar set point for homocysteine. Nonetheless, in a field of medicine in which the bad news often surpasses the good, the evidence from Norway was encouraging indeed. ■

Scientists prove what Mom knew all along—so sit down and eat your veggies

Drowning in a Sea of C?

Are we overdosing on vitamins? Americans have more than doubled their spending on vitamins and minerals in the past six years, from $3 billion in 1990 to $6.5 billion in 1996. They have also ratcheted up the dosages they take, gulping down supplements at 10, 50, even 100

STOP! Vitamin spending doubled in six years

times the daily recommended levels. Yet scientists pointed out that there is little definitive research evidence to support the more ambitious claims being made for vitamins. Among those questioning the extent of Americans' pill popping was Jane Brody, the respected health columnist for the New York *Times*, who wrote, "Consumers are, in effect, volunteering for a vast, largely unregulated experiment."

Estrogen: It's Better Later

To take estrogen or not to take estrogen? For millions of women approaching menopause, no other decision stirs up more anxiety. Study after study has shown that replenishing lost stores of this potent hormone can ward off many of the ailments associated with aging—heart disease, osteoporosis, perhaps even Alzheimer's. Yet these same studies also suggest that long-term use of estrogen increases the chances of developing breast cancer. A new study showed that women who took hormone supplements (mainly Premarin, a form of estrogen derived from mare's urine) for up to 10 years lowered their death rate from all diseases by 37%. Estrogen users with family histories of breast cancer scored a 35% drop. Women who stayed on estrogen for more than 10 years derived a more modest benefit: their risk of dying from breast can-

EAT MORE VEGGIES A new study showed that a diet low in saturated fat that combines fruits and vegetables with low-fat dairy products can dramatically reduce the risk of hypertension and high blood pressure. The secret: eight to 10 helpings of fruit and veggies—a day!

WOOF! Acupuncture is now going to the dogs

STICK WITH IT The National Institutes of Health declared acupuncture to be effective in treating painful disorders of the muscle and skeletal systems, such as tennis elbow. The NIH kept mum on a new craze: alternative medicine for pets.

cer rose 43%, offsetting estrogen's positive effects. What should women do? One good option: they should postpone long-term estrogen therapy until they are older.

The Beef with Vegetarianism

There's little doubt that a diet high in meats and saturated fats can boost levels of bad cholesterol. What isn't so clear is whether the obvious alternative—a vegetarian diet—is the best way to keep the stuff to a minimum. A landmark study of East African Bantu people seemed to show that it wasn't: one group lived near a lake, ate huge amounts of fish and almost no meat; the other was completely vegetarian. The vegetarians, it turned out, had higher blood levels of lipoprotein "a," one of whose components is LDL, the bad stuff.

HIV: Down but Not Out

In 1996 Dr. David Ho announced that he thought he might be able to eliminate the AIDS virus completely from the bodies of his patients by hitting it early with a combination of powerful antiviral drugs. But 1997 studies found a hidden reservoir of HIV in the immune system that survives the treatment and seems capable of reactivating the disease. Yet the good news remains: as long as people infected with HIV keep taking the triple-drug cocktail, they have an excellent chance of surviving the infection for a long time.

Yummy! Sprouts and Ginkgo!

Even noted broccoli hater George Bush may have to knuckle under. A new study showed that three-day-old broccoli sprouts (which look something like alfalfa sprouts) contain a powerfully concentrated cancer-fighting chemical. Also winning raves: an extract of leaves from the ancient ginkgo tree that was found to retard and stabilize the progress of Alzheimer's disease in 33% of patients.

GINKGO: An effective way to fight dementia

*20th century design
ends with a bang,
not a whimper—
thanks to a pair of
grandly innovative
museums by two
of America's most
original architects*

THE SHOCK OF THE NEW

A BENEDICTINE CHRONICLER ONCE
wrote of a "white mantle of churches" stretched across
medieval France. In a related way, America in the past
century has mantled itself with museums, as the temple
of art gradually replaced the church as the emblematic
focus of civic self-esteem. Now, two grand projects by
leading American architects, utterly different from each
other in purpose, appearance and design philosophy, may
be said to mark the climax of the age of American museum expansion. One of them is in Los Angeles and opened

BRAVO, BILBAO!
Cloaked in titanium,
Frank Gehry's building
melts before our eyes

TWO CITIES, TWO VISIONS: Meier, left, fuses Modernism and classicism. Gehry, right, follows his own eccentric path

in December 1997. The other, which opened two months earlier, is under American management but is set in Bilbao, in the Basque region of northern Spain. Neither is likely to have any architectural rivals in what is left of the 20th century, or for a good slice of the early 21st.

In Los Angeles, after 14 years, the Leviathan surfaces at last: Moby Museum, a.k.a. the Getty Center, sheathed in light tan aluminum and elegantly rugged honey-colored Italian travertine, nearly 1 million sq. ft. of it, designed by Richard Meier and perched on a 710-acre hilltop above the San Diego Freeway in the Brentwood section of the city. The Getty is the most expensive arts complex and by some calculations the most expensive building in U.S. history. Meanwhile, Frank Gehry's $100 million Guggenheim Museum in Bilbao, built and financed by the Basque regional government, is essentially a franchise, a major step in the effort by Thomas Krens, director of the Solomon R. Guggenheim Foundation in New York City, to parlay his museum into an international network of satellites exhibiting art from a common pool—an innovative idea that is still viewed with a good deal of skepticism by more traditional museum officials.

T HE GETTY IS NOT "A BUILDING." ITS COLLECTION of six separate units on a ridge linked by plazas and terraces often seems to resemble a very honed and buffed Modernist version of an Italian hill town. Architect Meier himself has grown wary of the hill-town analogy. "Think of it," he says, "as a small college campus with different departments, some more visible than others—not a museum but an institution in which art predominates."

Meier, 63, has come up with a superb piece of place-making. When the EPCOT-style tram delivers you from the parking garage at the bottom to the plaza at the top of the ridge, you step out into a space that seems both amiable and Utopian, dignified but, despite its acreage of travertine, not authoritarian: a respite from the visual chaos of Los Angeles, but offering the best views a public could have of the city spread below.

The six units gathered in this stunning setting are devoted to an art collection, ambitious archival facilities, high-tech conservation, broad research and educational programs, all intended to serve as a sort of cultural con-

denser for the humanities in Los Angeles and beyond. But the museum will inevitably be the Getty's main focus of public attention. Its director is John Walsh, 59, formerly of the Boston Museum of Fine Arts, who was hired in 1983. The collection's focus is fairly narrow; it was never, Walsh points out, meant to be a "Western Met," an encyclopedic museum. Its collection of painting and sculpture, entirely European, stops at the threshold of the 20th century.

The collection moves with ease between fine works by major masters—Rembrandt, Rubens, Cézanne, Van Gogh, Turner—and illuminatingly good ones by less famous figures, such as Franz Xavier Winterhalter's coolly sumptuous portrait of a 19th century princess on the terrace of her villa in the Crimea. It is a deeply serious and discriminating collection that may turn into a great one.

Meier's design serves the art very well, with a series

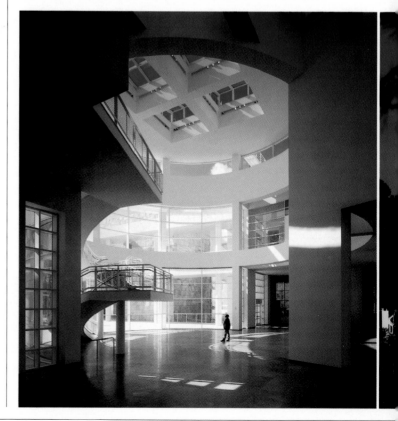

The Placemakers

Richard Meier was chosen to design the Getty Center in 1984, beating out 32 others for the coveted assignment. Meier, America's chief exponent of "late Modernist" classicism, is a noted museum designer whose credits include the Frankfurt Museum for Decorative Arts, 1979-85, and the High Museum in Atlanta, 1980-83.

Meier traveled the world studying museums and monuments before embarking on the design process, which ended up lasting 13 years. The New York City–based architect, who made some 300 round-trip flights to California during this period, claims that over time, "My children grew up, my hair turned whiter, and many friends lost touch with me."

Frank Gehry had an even longer commute: California to Spain. This most original of American architects has had terrible luck on his native ground, as in the delays surrounding the planned Walt Disney Concert Hall in Los Angeles. In contrast, the Basque regional-government authorities in Bilbao provided a free site and more than $170 million in funds to bring Gehry's great new building to their city. Its impetuous confidence is a testament to their vision as well as the architect's.

of generously proportioned, plain, high-ceilinged and top-lighted galleries that don't clamor for attention and do create a feeling of undistracted serenity. The architect has cunningly provided the links between them with unexpected openings, panoramic glimpses of the radiant townscape through glass walls, views of the museum's own light-struck exterior. It is a walker's museum, full of variegated spaces, points of rest, vistas, curves and a continual respiration between inside and outside.

If the Getty is a clear, benign and somewhat remote presence in coastal Los Angeles, the Guggenheim Museum has hit Bilbao with the force of an architectural meteorite. No question that it's there. You are walking through the pleasantly undistinguished, mainly 19th century streets of its quarter; you turn a corner, and—*pow!*—an apparition appears in glass and half-shiny silver (titanium, actually),

massively undulating, something that seems at first glance to have been dropped from another cultural world between the gray townscape and the green hills that rise behind it. Not since Joern Utzon's 1973 design for the Sydney Opera House has a building so dramatically imposed itself on a city. On the river edge of a town planned in terms of axial Beaux Arts order, architect Gehry, 68, has inserted a startlingly irregular building that defies every convention of axiality, including the right angle, of which there doesn't appear to be one, either inside his structure or out.

The structure is huge. But Gehry was astute in framing his design. He didn't want it to defer to the town architecture, but he did want it to chime with other aspects of Bilbao, particularly its industrial landscape: to commemorate the city's former power and presence. All along Bilbao's Nervion River are shipbuilding yards, loading

CITY ON A HILL: Meier's Getty Center is oversize in every way: six buildings, 1 million sq. ft. of space—and a $1 billion price tag

docks, cranes, massive obsolete warehouses—the kind of context that not only Gehry but also some of the artists he is closest to, such as the sculptor Richard Serra, love: disregarded, blue-collar beauty. The rusty pecs of Basque industrial capitalism. Seen from the far side of the river, the museum does indeed evoke a vast metal ship, full of compound curves, run aground—a sort of art-ark. "To be at the bend of a working river intersected by a large bridge," Gehry wrote at an early stage of the design, "and connecting the urban fabric of a fairly dense city to the river's edge with a place for modern art is my idea of heaven."

BUT THERE WAS ANOTHER STRUCTURE GEHRY WANTed to refer to—the mother ship, as it were: Frank Lloyd Wright's original Guggenheim on New York City's Fifth Avenue, with its great empty center wound about by the spiral exhibition ramp. Obviously that couldn't be repeated (it is, in any case, a curator's nightmare), but like the Bilbao industrial metaphor, it could be evoked. One walks down a long flight of steps into the museum, and then the atrium rises—or rather, soars: a large ceremonial space with catwalks and walkways, branching off into galleries at its several levels. In it, the three surface types of the museum's construction can be taken in: white Sheetrock, plate glass hung on steel members with exaggerated joints and flanges, and titanium skin. Their forms swelling and deflating in a strongly rhythmical way, large trunks of glass, plaster and titanium rise to the top of the five-story structure; they house utilities, a stair and an elevator.

The intensity Gehry can give to a vertical space also transfers to the horizontal ones. The biggest gallery,

known as "the Boat," is 1¼ times the length of a football field (450 ft.), but with its curved walls and round ceiling trusses, it hasn't a foot of dull space in it. There are only a few things in the design that seem arbitrary or merely rhetorical: the towering "parasol" that Gehry put over the river entrance is pointless except as a visual element.

This is a building that spells the end of the smarty-boots, smirkingly facile historicism on which so much Postmodernist building was based—a quoted capital here, an ironic reference there. It isn't afraid of metaphor, but it insists that the essence of building is structure and place-making. It confronts the rethinking of structure and the formation of space with an impetuous, eccentric confidence. No "school of Gehry" will come out of it, any more than there could have been a "school" of Barcelona's Antonio Gaudí. His work is imitation-proof, but liberating.

Warts and all, Gehry's Bilbao is the most exciting public building put up in a long time. Unlike Wright's canonical spiral in New York, it shows every sign of working well as a place in which to show works of art, though the size of some of Gehry's galleries and their eccentricity of shape is bound to tell against the smaller paintings. Moreover, as a work of art in its own right, the museum is far more interesting than much of its contents—the dull, inflated conceptual art and late minimalism that appeals to the taste of the Guggenheim's Krens.

The interesting thing, of course, will be to see how, over time, both the Guggenheim and the Getty museums "break in"—how these ambitious projects will be used, how they will function in (and benefit) the social matrices of their cities. And that will be as much up to the public as it ever was to their architects. ∎

OUT OF TIME: Gehry's metal-clad Guggenheim hovers like a time machine from the future amid Bilbao's 19th century streets

From a Cold War, a Hot Novel

Don DeLillo's *Underworld* explores baseball, nuclear war and personal fission

NEARLY EVERYONE WHO CARES ABOUT CONTEMPORARY literary fiction has heard how Don DeLillo got the inspiration for his mammoth novel, *Underworld* (Scribner; 827 pages; $27.50): it all started with a baseball game and a press clipping. Intrigued by the hubbub back in 1991 surrounding the 40th anniversary of Ralph Branca's fateful pitch and Bobby Thomson's subsequent home run—the so-called shot heard 'round the world that gave the New York Giants a playoff victory over the Brooklyn Dodgers and baseball's National League championship—DeLillo went to the library and looked up on microfilm the front page of the New York *Times* for Oct. 4, 1951, the day after the game. He discovered something that produced what he remembers as "a hush in my mind": the Giants' triumph headlined wide on the left and a headline in an identical format on the right announcing the first Soviet nuclear test. "Different kinds of conflict," Delillo recalls musing about the stories. "Two shots heard 'round the world."

The writer's response to this epiphany forms the prologue for *Underworld*. It is an astonishing set piece that captures the sweep and feel of those tumultuous few hours at the Polo Grounds as experienced by, among many others, the radio announcer

DE LILLO: "Observing from the edge," he hits the mark

Russ Hodges ("The Giants win the pennant!"); attendant celebrities Frank Sinatra, Jackie Gleason, Toots Shor and J. Edgar Hoover (yes, DeLillo learned later, they were really present); and a fictional black kid named Cotter Martin, who jumps the turnstiles to get into the stadium and makes off, at the end of the game, with Thomson's home-run ball.

After Thomson's blast, the bulk of *Underworld* jumps forward and then runs in reverse from the early 1990s to the day after the game. DeLillo is offering nothing less than a countdown of a merciful fizzle—of the cold war—from its demise with the collapse of the Soviet Union, back to that moment of infectious, innocent exuberance under an unseen mushroom cloud on a fall afternoon at the Polo Grounds. The subject of *Underworld* is how we got from there to here and what happened to us along the way.

This premise, or promise, is audacious and preposterous. And DeLillo delivers the goods. Several conventional novels, unconventionally told, run through *Underworld*. There is the story of two Bronx-bred brothers, Nick and Matt Shay, plus an account of Klara Sax, a Bronx housewife in 1951 who later becomes a famous artist. DeLillo surrounds them with a host of other characters vociferously trying to make sense out of the times of their lives. Some—many, come to think of it—seem crazy.

But what *is* crazy, the novel insistently inquires, given the context of the past five decades, when people learned how to blow up the world and then, unaccountably, did not, at least not so far? "Everything's connected," the mantra of both paranoiacs and artists, runs throughout DeLillo's pages. Nearly everyone in the novel says or thinks it, including FBI boss Hoover. "It's all linked," Hoover tells his second in command, about the riots against the war in Vietnam. "The war protesters, the garbage thieves, the rock bands, the promiscuity, the drugs, the hair."

They are all in *Underworld*, and more besides. A short history of the Cuban missile crisis of 1962 as traced through DeLillo's imagined creations of Lenny Bruce's monologues. Repeated motifs, as in classical music or jazz: Jayne Mansfield, Greenland, orange juice, the eerie recurrence of the number 13. Amazingly, everything in *Underworld* does connect. Is this novel a vindication of paranoia or a critique of the human hunger for patterns?

DeLillo answers carefully. "I wanted to write a book that would locate itself at the interface of the real world and the searches that people and institutions launch to understand it." He admits that the writer, during our time, has become "a marginal figure," reduced to "observing from the edge." Not this time. *Underworld* thrusts DeLillo into the hot center of a century collapsing on itself. ∎

Goodbye, Grunge— Hello, Hanson!

A new batch of kids is talkin' 'bout their generation. And the message is: "MMMBop"

HANSON: The bro's, above, are endearingly innocent, but more notable for exuberance than talent

FIONA APPLE, right: Her piano-driven songs exorcise demons—and prove that not all the under-20-somethings have to be shallow

I KNOW WHAT YOU DID LAST SUMMER, center: The revival of the slasher genre, not popular since the mid-1980s, was a sign that a new horde of teens was ready to scream

LE ANN RIMES, far right: What a voice! But Dad has a problem: "It changes about every six months."

THE FIRST TIME ZACHARY HANSON saw his own face on MTV, his reaction was a little different from that of most rock stars. "I said, 'Look at the cute girl—no, wait, it's me!'" says Zachary, a cherubic 11-year-old who won't be needing a shave until the next millennium. Zach, one-third of the pop-star siblings known as Hanson, wasn't the only one doing a double take: across a broad spectrum of pop culture, 1997 was the year when a new youthquake rocked the business—on both sides of the stage.

The new faces reflected an enormous new demographic bulge in U.S. society. There were 37 million 10-to-19-year-olds in 1997, and that number will soar to 42 million in the next decade. Think of them as the baby boomers' babies. These youngsters turned their back on the dark anxieties of the last great movement of pop culture, the grunge wave of the early '90s, to revel in brighter, more innocent moods. Out was the old rallying cry, Nirvana's gloomy *Nevermind;* in was the new rallying cry, Hanson's inanely catchy *MMM-Bop.* Yes, the teenyboppers were taking over, from the pop and country charts in music to TV and the movies. And what did they want to see? More teenyboppers, of course. Here are three reports from the front:

HANSON TRIO. "People are coming back to music that's fun and upbeat, and younger artists are filling that gap," says Patti Galluzzi, senior vice president of music and talent at MTV. The potent brother act Hanson led the tot-pop brigade, which also included the groups Radish and Silverchair, as well as guitarist Johnny Lang, 16.

Hanson is composed of Zachary (drums), 13-year-old Taylor (keyboards) and 16-year-old Isaac (guitar). Raised largely in Tulsa, Okla., the brothers are endearingly innocent and spontaneously rambunctious. Their mother schools the three (and three younger siblings) at home, and their father works as a financial exec for an oil-drilling company. Early on, the family traveled a lot, and the brothers passed the time listening to their parents' vintage records—"*Johnny B. Goode, Splish Splash* [and] *Good Golly, Miss Molly,*" remembers Isaac. They began singing at local events, sent tapes to record companies and landed a deal at Mercury. Next stop: Hansonmania, with the single *MMMBop* reaching No. 1 within a month, and the album *Middle of Nowhere*

former to pull that off is veteran megaseller Garth Brooks. At the '97 Grammy Awards, Rimes took the honor for Best Female Country Vocal Performance and beat out several heavily favored rockers to win the highly coveted award for Best New Artist. Her September 1997 release, *You Light Up My Life*, a collection of inspirational songs, did it again, also rocketing to No. 1 on the country charts within a week and selling 3 million copies in only two months.

Rimes is the real thing: the 15-year-old has raw talent and gleaming promise. Born in Mississippi and raised in Texas, she began singing when she was only 18 months old. Her father Wilbur started entering her in local talent contests early on; she had her first session in a recording studio when she was eight. At 11, LeAnn recorded a demo that the family sent to Curb Records, a small company in Nashville that promptly signed her to a recording deal. About a year later, the title song for *Blue* put the youngster on the fast track to stardom. The song was written for Patsy Cline, who died before she could record it, but it seems made for Rimes. The melody is generous, and when Rimes' wild-berry-sweet voice yodels through the chorus—"blooOOooOOoo"—even the country-averse may feel like putting on a cowboy hat and scootin' their boots.

APPLE CRISP. The youth brigade wasn't all sugar and spice. At 23, Alaskan pop-folkie Jewel, whose debut CD, *Pieces of You*, has sold more than 5 million copies, comes across as a wounded veteran of some very hard times—growing up poor, her parents' divorce, life with father in and out of bars, life with mother living out of cars.

But then, why would the baby boomers' babies trust Jewel? She's over 20. They could always listen to Fiona Apple, 19, another old soul in a young body. The victim of a rape at age 12, the Manhattan-bred Apple pours out intense, angry songs that sold more than 500,000 copies of her 1996 CD *Tidal* and garnered her a spot on the summer's hottest tour, the all-female Lilith Fair. As Apple told TIME: "You can be young and know a lot about relationships. I've been in the middle of a couple of marriages, so I've seen a lot about how relationships work."

TV TEENS. Meanwhile, television and movies were ushering in a new crop of stars—and a surprised Hollywood discovered that they were one and the same. In October the teen-scream movie *I Know What You Did Last Summer*, starring a clutch of kids imported from TV-Land, soared to the top of the box office, holding down the No. 1 spot for three weeks and leaving fuddy-duddy films like *The Peacekeeper* gasping in its wake. *Summer's* biggest stars were both imports from teen-themed TV shows: Jennifer Love Hewitt, 18, of *Party of Five*, and Sarah Michelle Gellar, 20, a.k.a. *Buffy the Vampire Slayer.*

> As a tsunami of kids comes of age, today's pop culture smells like teen spirit

Maybe it's a good thing Nirvana's Kurt Cobain wasn't around to see the the latest trend in American life. When it was released in 1991, his biggest hit, *Smells Like Teen Spirit*, was a corrosive assault on conformity. In 1997 its title was a dead-on description of the state of pop culture. ∎

(no doubt a reference to Tulsa, not cosmic anomie) selling more than 3 million copies in its first 3 months of release. Says Taylor: "The alternative thing is fading. People don't hate their parents as much anymore."

COUNTRY CUTIE. LeAnn Rimes' 1996 debut CD, *Blue*, has now sold more than 3 million copies, making it one of the top-selling albums ever by a female country singer. In February 1997 her sophomore album, *Unchained Melody/The Early Years*, a release of archival tapes made in 1993 and '94, beginning when the singer was only 11, debuted at No. 1 on *Billboard's* pop charts. Entering the charts at the top is something the hottest rock and rap acts do on a regular basis, but as far as country acts go, the only other per-

Can Ellen Come Out and Play?

Ready or not, America: Ellen DeGeneres becomes TV's first openly gay star

DIFFERENT MEDIA HAVE DIFFERENT THRESHOLDS FOR scandal. Controversy in the movies might mean making a film that glorifies one of the nation's most repugnant pornographers. Controversy in literature might mean writing a memoir about the affair you had with your father when you were in your 20s. In television, which functions not just as a business and debased art form but also as an increasingly fractured nation's de facto mirror of itself, the threshold is much lower. Controversy could mean starring in a sitcom as a gently scatterbrained former book-store owner who, after years of adult floundering, reluctantly comes to terms that she is homosexual and begins to take a few hesitant baby steps out of the closet and toward getting a life.

"I hate that term 'in the closet,'" maintained Ellen De-Generes, the aforementioned sitcom star, whose all-pants wardrobe and often awkward chemistry with male ingenues was provoking curiosity from fans and reporters long before her sexuality became a minor national obsession. "Until recently I hated the word les-bian too," she continued. "I've said it enough now that it doesn't bother me. But les-bian sounded like somebody with some kind of disease. I didn't like that, so I used the word gay more often."

What she hadn't been able to bring herself to do, until April 1997, was use the word gay along with two other words—"I am"—in public. Indeed, for

> "The word lesbian ... sounded like somebody with a kind of disease."

many men and women whose livelihood depends on the goodwill of millions, those may be the three scariest words in the English language.

"I always thought I could keep my personal life separate from my profession-al life," said DeGeneres. But that hope faded in September 1996, when the news first leaked that DeGeneres wanted to have the character she plays on *Ellen,* her then three-year-old ABC sitcom, discover that she is gay. For DeGeneres, 39, the decision was the cul-mination of a long process of struggling with feelings about

her own sexuality, her fears about being rejected for it, her wish to lead a more honest and open life in public, her weariness at the effort it took her not to. For the public, the news was a sensation: a gay lead on TV—that would be a first, and to those who attach importance to these sorts of things, either a long-overdue breakthrough or another way station on the road to moral abandon.

Through the winter, DeGeneres refused to confirm the rumors. Finally, in March 1997, ABC announced that the char-acter of Ellen Morgan would indeed be coming out in a spe-cial one-hour episode on the last day of April—just in time for network TV's all-important ratings sweeps weeks.

That resolved, DeGeneres decided to come out herself—and promptly did so in a very public forum, the cover of TIME, where she briskly an-nounced, "Yep, I'm gay." To no one's surprise, the coming-out show, featuring the guest star Laura Dern, went on to score *Ellen's* highest ratings ever.

The program earned pre-dictable praise from the Gay & Lesbian Alliance Against Defamation, which built a na-tional "Come Out with Ellen" day around the episode, and equally predictable denuncia-tion from the Rev. Jerry Fal-well, who referred to the star in gentlemanly fashion as "Ellen DeGenerate." The Rev. Don-ald E. Wildmon, leader of the American Family Association, issued barely veiled threats to *Ellen's* advertisers to boycott the show; two sponsors did so. The flap further strained relations between ABC's own-er, the Walt Disney Co., and America's religious right, which already viewed Disney as much too pro-gay.

Yet though the coming-out episode was ABC's top-rated regular program of the year, the problems of featuring a gay character in a leading role on prime-time TV were under-scored in the fall, when ABC ran a parental advisory before an episode in which Ellen Morgan jokingly kissed a straight female friend, and skirmished with the star over a plot that showed Ellen heading for the bedroom with a woman. It was a typically contradictory message from the nation's video mirror: it's fine to come out of the closet on TV—but let's have no hanky-panky once you've emerged. ∎

CRUSH: Pal Laura Dern played Ellen's love interest

NO-STALLONE ZONE: *The Full Monty,* left, and *Soul Food* served notice that in today's theaters, strong scripts can outdraw big stars

The Little Movies That Could

From the Academy Awards to the local multiplex, smaller films are bigger hits

ROLL OVER, HOLLYWOOD, AND TELL *VARIETY* THE NEWS: there's room at the local multiplex not only for the $80 million blockbusters teenagers love but also for smaller movies that dazzle mature audiences with values long missing from the screen: subtlety, characterization, emotional depth. The new era was heralded when the Oscar nominations for 1996 were unveiled in February 1997. Four of the five finalists for Best Picture (*The English Patient, Fargo, Secrets & Lies* and *Shine*) were released by small independent studios; only *Jerry Maguire* came from one of the seven major Hollywood studios. Sure enough, *The English Patient* and *Fargo* snagged the majority of the important statues on Oscar night in March.

The breakthrough for small movies was not so much in their cinematic inventiveness as in their discovery of a new audience. They bypassed the young mass crowd, which prefers broad comedy and spectacular fantasy, to reach older viewers, more sophisticated and more sentimental, liberal in their politics and conservative in their desire for humanist affirmation. This audience wants, as president Ruth Vitale of the independent studio Fine Line put it, "movies that touch your heart, that make you pause, think, maybe pick up the phone and call your dad."

In the wake of the Oscars, small movies continued to register success throughout 1997. Yes, Universal's $80 million *Jurassic Park* sequel *The Lost World*, directed by Steven Spielberg, was a summer smash, as was Sony's *Men in Black*. But the real news was that movies like the $100 million *Batman & Robin* and the $145 million *Speed 2*—both predicted to be box-office winners—fell far short of expectations. Into the vaccum rushed a number of good films that appealed to more mature sensibilities, including *L.A. Confidential, Boogie Nights* and *The Ice Storm.*

The emergence of the small film as an alternative to the blockbuster was evident than in two movies that old-line Hollywood never would have expected to succeed: *The Full Monty*, a British comedy, and *Soul Food*, the stirring, if overwrought, tale of the trials and smiles of a middle-class black family in Chicago. *The Full Monty* told the hilarious story of a clutch of redundant steelworkers in Sheffield, England, who are desperate to get off the dole and redeem their ever mounting debts. After their leader stumbles into a club where male strippers are playing to a packed and howling house of local lasses, he concocts the cockamamie idea that he and his lads—however unqualified—should shed their clothes and garner some pounds.

The actors were a marvelously mixed crew, variously overweight, uptight, overage and ungraceful. And their story was written, directed and acted with an unforced, persuasive ease. Fine—but just imagine the studios' shock when this $3 million film, first released in only six cities, became a major hit, raking in $35 million in the U.S.

Not long after *The Full Monty* got America laughing, *Soul Food*—made for only $7.5 million—began stuffing theaters with a huge middle-class black audience. *Soul Food* was by no means a masterpiece: it pushed emotional buttons with all the subtlety of a poke in the baby-back ribs. Its plot contrivances were predictable and its characters little more than one-dimensional cartoons. But because the movie rejected the stereotypes of black urban life and dealt honestly with the real lives of its target audience, *Soul Food* sizzled. Produced by the highly successful songwriter and record producer Kenneth "Babyface" Edmonds, the film eventually racked up more than $40 million in sales—and raised hopes that the big studios might offer second or even third helpings of the same.

George Tillman Jr., 28, who wrote and directed *Soul Food*, based it on his own family and coming-of-age experiences. "There are sex comedies, 'hood films. We're trying to get away from that," said Tillman. "I wanted to do something that people could appreciate and remember about family." A highly profitable movie about African-American families? In the blockbuster-addicted Hollywood of the '90s, that qualified as a truly special effect. ∎

The New King of Broadway's Jungle

In 1997's musicals, *The Lion King* roars, *The Life* scores with whores—and *Titanic* mans the oars

STAGES OF DELIGHT: Director Julie Taymor brings innocence back to Broadway in *The Lion King*, right. *Titanic*, left, finds a metaphor for social class in its striking three-level design

ABOUT HALF A MINUTE AFTER THE house lights begin to dim, the menagerie of *Lion King* director Julie Taymor appears on the stage and in the aisles. A pair of spindly giraffes (with men on stilts hidden inside) parade regally in front of a golden sun. A cheetah prowls the stage, manipulated by a fully visible actor. Birds "fly" like a kite on the end of a pole, while a huge elephant galumphs down the aisle. As they converge to the strains of *Circle of Life*, it's not just an awe-inspiring sight; it's also a notice to kids and adults alike: the Walt Disney Co. has brought new magic to Broadway.

Disney was taking a risk when it hired Taymor—an avant-garde director who uses puppets, masks and other non-Western theater techniques—to adapt its most popular animated film for the stage. It turns out to have been a masterstroke. *Beauty and the Beast*, which Disney brought to Broadway in 1994, was a by-the-numbers rendering of a film into a play. But Taymor brought the same kind of let's-start-from-scratch inspiration that Walt and his fellow animators must have had when they created Mickey and *Snow White* and virtually invented the art of movie animation.

Taymor's imaginative ideas seem limitless. Actors wear masks atop their heads and manipulate life-size puppets, in bold defiance of conventional stage literalism. Dance numbers brim with vibrant, carnival colors. The action scenes, like a wildebeest stampede conveyed by wheels and masks, dazzle with their originality. Some of the most striking images are the simplest. Women with grass headdresses stand in a row and sway to manifest wind in the savanna. Grieving lionesses pull ribbons of fabric from their eyes to suggest tears. Yes, there are a few longueurs in the show's running time of well over two hours. More important, though, this gorgeous, gasp-inducing spectacle has innocence. It appeals to the audience's primal, childlike excitement in the power of theater to make us see things afresh.

That power was in short supply elsewhere on Broadway: a year after *Rent* was supposed to have revolutionized the form, the Great White Way scarcely seemed to have noticed. Far from showcasing a new generation of talents,

like *Rent's* Jonathan Larson or *Bring in 'Da Noise/Bring in 'Da Funk's* Savion Glover, 1997 could have passed for a Friars Club reunion of old Broadway tunesmiths, with Cy Coleman (*Sweet Charity*), John Kander and Fred Ebb (*Cabaret*), Maury Yeston (*Nine*) and Leslie Bricusse (*Stop the World—I Want to Get Off*) all back on the boards. Stop the recycling; we want to get off!

It even looked as if this season would bring another of those old-fashioned megabudget bombs of Broadway legend. A $10 million musical called *Titanic* seemed to be ill-fated indeed, after its ship had a bit of trouble sinking during previews. But the show wasn't a disaster; it was just an uninspired melodrama with watery songs, a predictable book and a surfeit of clichéd characters, including the ship's craven owner, aristocrats who drown with dignity and some tiresomely idealistic Irish immigrants in steerage.

Titanic's strength was its staging by director Richard Jones and scenic designer Stewart Laing. In their imaginative, haunting production, the stage is divided into a series of horizontal planes that aptly convey the social stratification of the passengers; as the ship lists, the stage tilts omi-nously; faces of the doomed passengers appear at portholes like apparitions. The happy ending? *Titanic* proved unsinkable, outlasting some negative reviews to find an audience and win the Tony Award for the year's best musical.

In a year that also brought two over-the-top follies (*The Scarlet Pimpernel* and *Jekyll & Hyde*) as well as *Side Show*, one of the rare shows to deal with Siamese twins (don't forget *The King & I*), the other standout was *The Life*. This dark, brashly entertaining musical from composer Cy Coleman and lyricist Ira Gasman explored the seedy denizens of Times Square circa 1980. *The Life* was far from perfect. While startlingly raw for Broadway (the hookers are foul-mouthed, grungy and fleshy), its melodrama was heavy-handed. What transformed it was Coleman's vital, jazzy score and Michael Blakemore's crisp staging. The show kicks off with an infectiously cynical ode to self-interest (*Use What You Got*), and the up-tempo number *Why Don't They Leave Us Alone* turns the hookers and pimps into the most inspired chorus line in town. *The Life* may, in truth, be just another kind of Broadway hustle, but when the con men are this slick, you drop your money with a smile. ■

A Roundup of Rauschenbergs

They called it a major retrospective—with the emphasis on the first word. A survey of the work of modern master Robert Rauschenberg filled both the Guggenheim Museum's uptown and SoHo branches in Manhattan and, as if that were

CANYON: A "combine" by Rauschenberg, 1959

not enough, the Ace Gallery in SoHo as well. The result was initially intimidating, but finally invigorating. Featuring some 400 works in all sorts of media, the sprawling show caught Rauschenberg's effusive, uncontained energy, his street smarts, his command of the American vernacular—and his surprising affinity with an equally polymorphous ancestor: poet Walt Whitman, the entranced 19th century celebrator of American variety.

The God Squad Hits TV

Is there room for God on television? For years the networks carefully avoided the subject of religion, but the Top-10 ratings success of 1996's surprise CBS hit, *Touched by an Angel,* prompted a deluge of shows with religious themes. Returning to the nation's tubes in the fall of '97 were three religious-themed shows, including Dan Aykroyd's successful priestly sitcom on ABC, *Soul Man.* Joining them were four newcomers: UPN's jokey sitcom *Good News,* ABC's kid-com *Teen Angel* and Fox's UFO-meets-religion drama *The Visitor.* The most controversial offering was the show with the most on its mind: ABC's *Nothing Sacred,* a series about an iconoclastic, jeans-clad urban priest, written by Jesuit priest Bill Cain, 49. The show was intelligent, well acted, dramatic and believable. But some conservative Roman Catholic groups objected to its portrayal of

TSAR WARS Watch out, Walt: bidding to end Disney's monopoly in movie animation, Fox released *Anastasia,* a cartoon version of the last days of Russia's ruling Romanov family. Disney countered with a re-release of 1989's *The Little Mermaid*—but *Anastasia* won the box-office battle.

STAR WARS Thrilling a generation of younger fans who had only seen their wonders on video, all three *Star Wars* returned to movie theaters—and rode the Force right to box-office heaven.

MEEEP! Robots R2-D2 and C-3PO rode again

the priest (played by Kevin Anderson) as too liberal and too doubting, and they mounted a campaign against the series. Even before the show debuted, a number of sponsors had begged off. Perhaps more threatening to its survival—in a business where only ratings are sacred—viewership of the controversial series remained low.

Women—We Love 'Em!

As the fall '97 TV season got under way, viewership of the major networks' offerings continued to decline. Among the few winners of the new season were shows featuring three women stars: two TV newcomers and a wily veteran. The old hand was Kirstie Alley, late of *Cheers.* Her new show, *Veronica's Closet,* offered Alley as a lingerie mogulette of a certain age, saddled with a philandering husband and cheeky employees who suggested she pose for the company's ads by having her head morphed onto someone else's body. Younger but just as insecure was Calista Flockhart, starring in Fox's *Ally McBeal* as a slightly off-kilter, upper-middle-class Harvard Law grad. To many women, McBeal was quirky and wonderful; to many men, she came off as a simpering drag. But viewers of both sexes seemed to love Jenna Elfman,

CALISTA FLOCKHART: A hit in her television debut

who broke through on ABC's surprise new hit *Dharma & Greg* as Dharma Finkelstein, a ditzy latter-day flower child who marries the ultra-preppy lawyer Greg Montgomery, played by Thomas Gibson.

Men—Who Needs 'Em?

The hills were alive with the sound of women. Riding a surprising shift in audience taste, Canadian singer-songwriter Sarah McLachlan cooked up the summer's musical event: Lilith Fair, an all-female traveling show featuring a rotating line-up of 61 singer-songwriters, including Tracy Chapman, Fiona Apple, Paula Cole and Jewel. Heavy metal was out; heavy mental was in. Rooted in the folk-pop of Joni Mitchell and Bob Dylan, the women's "coffeehouse pop" had a comforting warmth, a topping of sugary froth—and brewed up so much buzz that Lilith Fair's 30 dates were the summer's hottest tickets.

THE BEST OF 1997

MAKERS OF 10-BEST LISTS HAVE TO LOOK BACK, but in 1997 the arts looked *way* back. The pages that follow could be a catalog for Aunt Maude and Uncle Victor's garage sale. Everywhere, yesterday's trash culture was exhumed and hauled to new frontiers. Our critics select a film of a '90s novel set in 1953 and a musical of a '70s novel set in 1906 as the year's best. And what is *The X-Files* if not a cunning updating of '50s bomb sweat? "No matter how paranoid you are," the show tells us, "you're not paranoid enough." And speaking of paranoia: who knows what cultural detritus of 1997 will be embraced in the inevitable retro-future? Cryogenic Spice Girls, anyone?

1 **L.A. CONFIDENTIAL** Everybody knows the rudiments of the classic film-noir manner: chiaroscuro lighting, labyrinthine plots, dialogue written in battery acid. Working up imitations of it has become one of modern Hollywood's minor vices. But at its best it conveyed an idea about how the rottenness of big cities touches everyone, high and low, respectable and raffish. Director Curtis Hanson, working off James Ellroy's bitterly brewed novel about corrupt 1950s cops, gets that wonderfully right in a smart, complex film that exuberantly mixes comic excess, melodramatic pressure, romantic rue and an almost casual murderousness.

8 **Eve's Bayou** "The summer I killed my father, I was 10 years old." With these words, writer-director Kasi Lemmons begins a story of family love, lust and deceit. Samuel L. Jackson and Debbi Morgan shine in—what? The best film ever

made by a black American? Could well be. The year's most haunting family drama? You bet.

2 **Ponette** How can a child cope with her mother's violent death? Little Ponette (the amazing Victoire Thivisol) simply refuses to believe her mother is gone and waits desperately for her imminent return. In a morbid year for films, Jacques Doillon's shattering French drama gets at a rare truth: surrendering to grief can give one a reason to live.

3 **Chasing Amy** Underground-comix artists pair off, then square off in this romantic tragicomedy. He's full of sweetly uncomprehending machismo, she's gay but nervously alert to other possibilities. And auteur Kevin Smith

(*Clerks*) has the best Gen X files in the business, full of compassionate observations on its mysterious manners and morals.

4 **In the Company of Men** Gamesmanship '90s-style: a nasty corporate jock sets up a woman—and his soft-willed colleague—for the betrayal of their middle-class lives. Neil LaBute's Freon-cool comedy, made for a preposterously low $25,000, outraged viewers who didn't get the dark joke or the narrative suavity. See it with someone you're sure loves you.

5 **Oscar and Lucinda** Bold heiress, sensitive clergyman, sinful passion, a trek into the wilderness. Sounds like one of those "classic" novels you'll never get around to. Don't despair. Director Gillian Armstrong and her stars, Ralph Fiennes and Cate Blanchett, find something feverishly unsettling under

the concealing black robes of Victorian propriety.

6 **Face/Off** Action king John Woo harnesses his explosive visual finesse to a mad fable of two men (Nicolas Cage and John Travolta) who become what they most hate: each other. Hollywood high concept meets Hong Kong turbo technique for double the pleasure, double the art. This is Woo's best since *Bullet in the Head.*

7 **Amistad** Again Steven Spielberg enlists his craftsmanship in the service of moral seriousness. Again, in this tale of an authentic slave mutiny and its lingering nightmare aftermath, he creates a gripping portrait of human decency mobilized to help an inhumanly abused

minority. Again he unsentimentally places us in touch with our best sentiments.

9 **Welcome to Sarajevo** War-loving, war weary, a journalist rescues an orphan from the Bosnian chaos but can't explain his sudden fall into grace. Michael Winterbottom's film dares to suggest that small acts of goodness cannot stem the vast tides of historical tragedy. In today's movies, that's an unexpected—and sobering—perspective.

10 **Gabbeh** Tough heroes, winsome kids, things that blow up in the night—can there be another way to make movies? Yes, in this lyrical fable of a woman who literally lives in the weave of a carpet while she awaits her lost love. Iran's Mohsen Makhmalbaf is a weaver too, of sweet dreams, vivid colors and magical filmmaking.

2 ***Ellen: The Puppy Episode*** After the endless media tease, the stakes were high for Ellen's coming-out episode on ABC. To live up to its hype, it had to be a classic—and it was. The hourlong broadcast had wit, charm and great performances by Ellen DeGeneres, Laura Dern and Oprah Winfrey, perfectly cast as a therapist.

3 **Diana coverage** The death of the Princess of Wales was one of those events in which a unified global consciousness is created through television. Billions watched the Queen make her address, the boys walk behind the casket, Charles, Earl Spencer deliver his eulogy. Even in a world of 500 channels, sometimes there is just one thing on.

Buckingham Palace — CNN LIVE

4 ***Miss Evers' Boys*** Alfre Woodard starred in this HBO drama about the scandalous Tuskegee study of syphilis in which black subjects were not given treatment. The script was intelligent; Woodard exquisitely captured the conflicting motivations of a nurse involved in the study; and Laurence Fishburne played her lover with rough charm and wisdom.

1 **FOX'S SUNDAY-NIGHT LINEUP** Everyone talks about NBC and Thursday, but the best night for television in 1997 was Sunday, when you could watch *The Simpsons*, *King of the Hill* and *The X-Files* all in a row on Fox. *The Simpsons* is still the cleverest comedy on TV, and *King of the Hill* creates a world with far more specificity than any live-action sitcom. Both are smarter, funnier and, in fact, more human than *Friends* or *Seinfeld*. Meanwhile, *The X-Files* draws from a bottomless well of inspiration. Two cartoons and a sci-fi show—why are these better than the programs supposedly about real people and real life? Probably because they are imaginative in ways neither possible nor permissible in TV's standard, tired genres.

5 ***Town Under Siege*** This CBS documentary with Ed Bradley was a dramatic, well-argued exercise in muckraking. A little-known loophole exempts oil companies from laws on hazardous-waste disposal, and CBS showed how one poor town suffers as a result. Forget Matt Damon in Hollywood's *The Rainmaker*—the kid lawyer in this case was twice as appealing.

6 ***Everybody Loves Raymond*** In its second season, this CBS sitcom is rapidly coming into its own. The star, Ray Romano, is an amusing, hangdog Everyman, and his relatives are funny oddballs rather than the more typical tiresome ones. Family shows have been done over and over, but *Raymond* can surprise you.

7 ***The Practice*** Set in a small, scrappy law firm, ABC's *The Practice* is a very entertaining melodrama, even if it breaks no new ground. The cast is good, especially Michael Badalucco as a struggling personal-injury lawyer, and the scripts are smartly plotted, with some humor thrown in for relief. As our hero, handsome Dylan McDermott manages not only to have good hair but also to seem genuinely savvy and charismatic.

8 ***The Mill on the Floss*** Ah, if only all Sunday-night TV movies dealing with women in peril could be as subtly haunting as this PBS version of George Eliot's 1860 novel. The filmed story of Maggie Tulliver (played by Emily Watson) features no stalkers, mind you, but it evokes poetically the inescapable dangers of possessing a divided heart.

9 ***The Newsroom*** Its final episodes were too bizarre, but for most of its run on PBS, this Canadian series about the news department of a TV station was balanced perfectly between reality and parody. Filmed in documentary style, it achieved some brilliant moments of deadpan humor, and Ken Finkleman, the creator of the show, played the news director with a wicked combination of egotism, pettiness and desperation. *Broadcast News* meets *Spinal Tap*.

10 ***Buffy the Vampire Slayer*** More than just an action series about a 15-year-old superheroine, the WB's *Buffy* is a wry satire of suburban teenage life (the unhip are described as having discovered "the softer side of Sears") and a postfeminist parable on the challenge of balancing one's personal and work life. Buffy (Sarah Michelle Gellar) has vampires to kill, but she also has to find the time for boys and Ben & Jerry's.

2 The Lion King Disney's justly celebrated stage version of the hit movie gave Broadway an electric shock of excitement. Julie Taymor's design wizardry accomplished the difficult task of satisfying everyone: adults as well as kids, tourists looking for a reason to come to New York City, and serious theatergoers looking for a reason to believe in Broadway again. Don't be surprised if Taymor's vision runs forever.

3 A Doll's House Just when you thought Ibsen's war-horse had breathed its last, director Anthony Page, translator Frank McGuinness and galvanizing star Janet McTeer brought it back to life in a brilliant Broadway production imported from London. Their triumph made us feel the wrenching human underpinnings of drama's most famous feminist battle cry.

4 Space A psychiatrist's comfortable world is shaken when he encounters several patients with similar tales of alien visitation. Writer-director Tina

1 RAGTIME The musical version of E.L. Doctorow's best-selling novel could have been a high-minded bore, another mega-disappointment. In fact, it turns out to be a landmark American musical. Doctorow's turn-of-the-century tapestry, mixing fact and fiction, was expertly refashioned for the stage by playwright Terrence McNally; director Frank Galati showcased it in a crisp and beautiful production; the score by Lynn Ahrens and Stephen Flaherty got better with each hearing. And how many musicals have the audience fighting off tears before the end of the first act? The show would not arrive on Broadway until January 1998, but it's hard to see how the Los Angeles production could be improved on.

able man, played marvelously by Tom Irwin.

5 The Life The spring season was a dismal one for Broadway musicals—the off time between *Rent* and *The Lion King*—but it did produce one

Landau's wondrous production for Chicago's Steppenwolf Theatre is a magical mystery tour, packed with inventive sound and lighting effects, that explores cosmic questions of mankind's place in the universe while staying grounded in the spiritual quest of one highly vulner-

underrated gem, this tale of seedy Times Square before it got Disneyfied. Complain about the clichéd book if you must, but few musicals are this hard-edged and slam-bang entertaining at the same time. And few songwriters can still turn out showstoppers like Cy Coleman.

6 Gross Indecency: The Three Trials of Oscar Wilde Using court records, newspaper accounts, diaries and other historical documents, writer-director Moisés Kaufman re-creates the courtroom battles that destroyed the career (and ultimately the life) of the late-Victorian playwright, wit and homosexual bon vivant. The cleverly stylized history lesson, playing off-Broadway and in San Francisco, is also a poignant portrait of an artist brought down as much by his own hubris as by an intolerant society.

7 The Diary of Anne Frank The hit play from the 1950s by Frances Goodrich and Albert Hackett is back on Broadway, fresher and more moving than one might ever have expected. Credit goes largely to adapter Wendy Kesselman, who has removed some of the sentimental '50s uplift and restored a firm sense of time and place, and to director James Lapine,

who keeps the tension high and emotions real.

8 The Last Night of Ballyhoo Alfred Uhry's comedy-drama could have been written in the 1950s, but that doesn't make its old-fashioned virtues any less appealing. The story of a Jewish family in Atlanta in 1939 has a keen sense of its milieu, raises tough issues of Jewish anti-Semitism and goes for honest sentiment, not theatrical sentimentality.

9 How I Learned to Drive Paula Vogel's brief, intense play explores the complex relationship between a young girl and the uncle who sexually abused her. Unsettling and unsparing in facing up to a difficult subject, this off-Broadway play was an actors' showcase (originally starring David Morse and Mary-Louise Parker) that will surely become a regional-theater staple.

10 Les Misérables After 10 years on Broadway, the Alain Boublil–Claude-Michel Schönberg musical had fallen into serious disrepair. So directors Trevor Nunn and John Caird became their own show doctors, replacing much of the cast and giving the production a thorough overhaul. *Mon Dieu! Les Miz* is back and as rousing as ever. Now for the next patient, *Miss Saigon* …

1 ERYKAH BADU *BADUIZM* (Kedar Entertainment/ Universal) Some singers can break your heart; Badu can put it back together again. Her neo-soul songcraft draws from soul, jazz, blues and hip-hop—but instead of a chaotic swirl of sound, the result is a slow-burning, meditative album that brings all these genres together. This is healing music about magic and love, racism and reincarnation, late-night parties and Afro picks. Badu's voice is a natural wonder, sharp and metallic, wounded and sad, yearning for empathy in one song, decrying injustice in the next. Her brilliant companion CD, *Live*, which captures concert performances of the songs on *Baduizm*, shows she's more than another shallow '90s studio creation. She's the most thrilling new voice in pop music.

2 Anne Sofie von Otter *Schubert: Lieder* (Deutsche Grammophon) The cool radiance of Von Otter's mezzo-soprano voice lights up this cannily chosen, passionately sung program of 18 Schubert songs, stylishly accompanied by pianist Bengt Forsberg. Some *lieder* are obscure, some ultrafamiliar, but either way they are irresistible; even the age-old, much-abused *Ave Maria* sounds brand new.

3 Alana Davis *Blame It on Me* (Elektra) A fresh and uncommonly rich fusion of blues and folk-pop, Davis' debut is a stunningly mature work for a songwriter of just 23. Combining the twang of Bonnie Raitt and the soulfulness of Tracy Chapman, Davis uses her serene voice to breathe light and

life into songs, creating a captivating, genre-bending sound all her own.

4 U2 *Pop* (Island) The Dublin-based rock supergroup replenishes its creative batteries by drawing on the trendy electronic-music scene. The end product is rock charged with lightning, as well as winking cultural commentary that suggests the question: In a world built on images and style, is there anything to hold on to? This is smart, self-aware stuff, acknowledging pop's shallowness while refusing to stop panning for nuggets of truth.

5 Luciano *Messenger* (Island Jamaica) The Jamaican-born Luciano has a baritone voice as warm and deep as Montego Bay, and his songs boast ripe, mango-sweet melodies. His lyrics, however, focus on serious subjects such as poverty, spirituality and resisting oppression. The core of Luciano's brand of reggae is a smiling insurgency.

6 Portishead *Portishead* (Go! Beat/London) Distorted, wraithlike vocals, blaring Big Band noir horns and deconstructed hip-hop beats—

Portishead's eponymous album is both bravely strange and weirdly compelling. This triphop masterpiece is futuristic and cerebral music, but it is always heartfelt. The sound of the next millennium, previewing today.

7 Mary J. Blige *Share My World* (MCA). The woman known as "the queen of hip-hop soul" proves with her most confident, sustained work why she wears the crown. The tracks on this CD are gems: expertly cut, with sparkling vocals. Blige's voice, with its oak-dark shadings and unforced, round-the-way sexiness, keeps it all real.

8 Marc Anthony *Contra la Corriente* (RMM) In this collection, rising Latin star Anthony sings salsa with youthful vigor and old-school showmanship. His voice is a flash of gold, blinding and enticing in its purity. The songs are in

Spanish, but Anthony's raw talent comes through, no translation needed.

9 Leonard Rosenman *East of Eden/Rebel Without a Cause* (Nonesuch) The pick of Nonesuch's impressive new film series, this CD, handsomely performed by John Adams and the London Sinfonietta, contains suites from Rosenman's arresting scores for two of James Dean's legendary films. It's a long-overdue solo bow for one of America's most underrated composers.

10 Matraca Berg *Sunday Morning to Saturday Night* (Rising Tide). This top Nashville composer has the ideal voice to inhabit her best songs. Make that voices, for Berg has a tone for each tune: raunchy for the rockin' *Back in the Saddle*, pained and proud for the elegiac *Back When We Were Beautiful*. Here Berg is possessed by her music: she sings in tongues.

FICTION

1 MASON & DIXON (Henry Holt) Thomas Pynchon's vast novel retraces the progress of the men who drew the line between the colonies of Pennsylvania and Maryland. For all its Pynchonesque tom-fooleries—a talking dog, a four-ton cheese—the tale finally is somber, elegiac. Mason and Dixon come to realize that their triumph means an end to the wilderness, the imposition of civilizing order on "the realm of the Sacred."

NONFICTION

1 INTO THIN AIR (Villard) In May 1996 Jon Krakauer reached the 29,028-ft. summit of Mount Everest. His assignment for *Outside* magazine would, it seemed, end in triumph. But the day did not. A storm arose that killed 11 other climbers. Krakauer's book dramatically reports this calamity and examines the proliferating, expensive tours that offer novices the top of the world. Some of the tenderfeet live to tell their tales.

2 Underworld (Scribner) Don DeLillo's 11th and most ambitious novel takes on no less grand a subject than the buried life of the cold war, the specter of

nuclear annihilation as experienced by a large group of vividly rendered characters. The story begins with a memorable account of Bobby Thomson's famous home run in 1951, then moves back and forth over the following four decades, showing how we all got here from there.

3 Cold Mountain (Atlantic Monthly Press) Imagine Odysseus walking through the blue mountains of North Carolina in the ghostly half-light at the conclusion of the Civil War. Charles Frazier's miraculous first novel is as spare as timeless myth, one man's yearning homeward. Yet its deeply local details, its twiggy smell of roots and solitary eccentrics, evoke the spirit of Thoreau—and the Taoist hermits who

once haunted the Cold Mountains of old China.

4 American Pastoral (Houghton Mifflin) The title is ironic—a Philip Roth specialty. There is precious little rural harmony in this scorching novel about a prosperous New Jersey couple whose good life is destroyed when their daughter becomes a '60s terrorist. In Roth's earlier novels, parents tended toward the comic and repressive. Not here. The author renders the Job-like suffering of a father and mother over a lost child with his characteristic emotional force and verbal energy.

5 The God of Small Things (Random House) Arundhati Roy's bold debut achieves an intensity that will feel familiar to fans of D.H. Lawrence. The author sometimes seems too clever for her novel's good, but her material triumphs. Three small children, a blue Plymouth and the lushness of southern India merge into a gripping story of passion ultimately thwarted by prejudice.

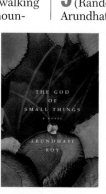

2 A People's Tragedy (Viking) In this tale of what went wrong with the Russian Revolution, Cambridge historian Orlando Figes deals vividly with starvation, disease, tribal hatreds, sociopathic bloodlust, religious mania, governmental terrorism and most of the other sources of human misery. In addition, Figes argues, stupidity ruled the times, quite literally in the stiff presence of Czar Nicholas II. A smarter leader might have led to a better 20th century for all.

3 Legends of the American Desert (Knopf) Alex Shoumatoff, a *New Yorker* contributor, spent 25 years researching and writing this book about the U.S. Southwest. The result is a sometimes bewildering but continually fascinating profusion of stories and themes. Shoumatoff writes knowingly and affectionately about indigenous Indians and those who came later. The scenery is spectacular; there is nothing dry or dusty in this book's desert.

4 Whittaker Chambers (Random House) Historian Sam Tanenhaus rights an old imbalance in this scrupulous biography. For more than 40 years, most discussions of the Alger Hiss–Whittaker Chambers imbroglio focused on Hiss: Was he innocent, as he claimed, or guilty, as Chambers charged? But of the two men, Chambers was by far the more interesting person and tormented soul. Tanenhaus' perceptive illumination of Chambers' sad life also lights up a dark and troubled period of recent American history.

5 Citizen Soldiers (Simon & Schuster) Stephen Ambrose, author of *Undaunted Courage*, last year's best seller about Lewis and Clark, thought there were still some untold stories to tell about World War II in Europe, and he was right. His mixture of narrative and oral histories brings to unforgettable life the G.I.s who slogged through the mess of the European theater.

NOBEL PRIZES
Peace
Jody Williams
For efforts to eradicate the use of land mines worldwide

Literature
Dario Fo
Offbeat Italian playwright-performer and anarchist

Medicine
Stanley B. Prusiner
For his controversial research concerning disease-causing proteins

Economics
Robert C. Merton and Myron S. Scholes
For their groundbreaking work in creating a formula for measuring the worth of stock options

Physics
Steven Chu and William D. Phillips Claude Cohen-Tannoudji
For developing a method to trap atoms

Chemistry
John E. Walker, Paul D. Boyer and Jens C. Skou
For advances in the study of how living cells store and release energy

ACADEMY AWARDS
Best Picture
The English Patient
Best Director
Anthony Minghella
The English Patient
Best Actor
Geoffrey Rush
Shine
Best Actress
Frances McDormand
Fargo
Best Supporting Actor
Cuba Gooding Jr.
Jerry Maguire
Best Supporting Actress
Juliette Binoche
The English Patient

TONY AWARDS
Best Play
The Last Night of Ballyhoo
Best Musical
Titanic

Best Actress, Play
Janet McTeer
A Doll's House
Best Actor, Play
Christopher Plummer
Barrymore
Best Actress, Musical
Bebe Neuwirth
Chicago
Best Actor, Musical
James Naughton
Chicago

HOLLYWOOD FILMS
Domestic box-office leaders
1. *Men in Black*
2. *The Lost World: Jurassic Park*
3. *Liar Liar*
4. *Air Force One*
5. *Star Wars* (reissue)
6. *My Best Friend's Wedding*
7. *Face/Off*
8. *Batman & Robin*
9. *George of the Jungle*
10. *Con Air*

TELEVISION
Fall season favorites
1. *ER*
2. *Seinfeld*
3. *Veronica's Closet*
4. *Friends*
5. *Touched by an Angel*
6. *NFL Monday Night Football*
7. *CBS Sunday Movie*
8. *Home Improvement*
9. *Union Square*
10. *60 Minutes*

BOOKS
Best-Selling Fiction
1. *The Notebook*
   Nicholas Sparks
2. *The Partner*
   John Grisham
3. *Cold Mountain*
   Charles Frazier
4. *The Celestine Prophecy*
   James Redfield
5. *The God of Small Things*
   Arundhati Roy
6. *Plum Island*
   Nelson Demille
7. *London*
   Edward Rutherford
8. *Up Island*
   Anne Rivers Siddons
9. *Sole Survivor*
   Dean Koontz
10. *Airframe*
    Michael Crichton

Best-Selling Non-Fiction
1. *Angela's Ashes*
   Frank McCourt
2. *The Millionaire Next Door*
   Thomas Stanley
3. *Conversations with God: Book I*
   Donald Neale Walsch
4. *Midnight in the Garden of Good and Evil*
   John Berendt
5. *Into Thin Air*
   Jon Krakauer
6. *The Perfect Storm*
   Sebastian Junger
7. *A Reporter's Life*
   Walter Cronkite
8. *Conversations with God: Book 2*
   Donald Neale Walsch
9. *The Man Who Listens to Horses*
   Monty Roberts
10. *Brain Droppings*
    George Carlin

SPORTS
Baseball
• World Series
Florida Marlins
• College World Series
Louisiana State Tigers

Basketball
• NBA
Chicago Bulls
• NCAA Men
Arizona Wildcats
• NCAA Women
Tennessee Lady Vols

Football
• Superbowl XXXI
Green Bay Packers
• College polls
Michigan Wolverines & Nebraska Cornhuskers

Hockey
• Stanley Cup
Detroit Red Wings

Horse Racing
• Kentucky Derby
Silver Charm
• Preakness Stakes
Silver Charm
• Belmont Stakes
Touch Gold

**MARTINA HINGIS:
One short of a Slam**

• Breeder's Cup Juvenile
Favorite Trick
• Breeder's Cup Classic
Skip Away

Golf
• Masters
Tiger Woods
• U.S. Open
Ernie Els
• U.S. Women's Open
Chris Johnson
• British Open
Justin Leonard
• PGA
Davis Love 3rd
• LPGA
Chris Johnson

Tennis
• Australian Open
Martina Hingis
Pete Sampras
• French Open
Iva Majoli
Gustavo Kuerten
• Wimbledon
Martina Hingis
Pete Sampras
• U.S. Open
Martina Hingis
Patrick Rafter

Sources: Facts on File (Nobels, Oscars, Tonys, Sports); Cowles/Simba Information based on New York *Times* Best Seller Lists (Books); Baseline (Films); Electronic Media (Television)

Dark Days for the Clan

More tragedy and more scandals afflict the Kennedy family

It was a bad year to be a Kennedy. Scandals—both recent and long past—continued to plague America's most notable political family, and the year ended with the tragic death of Michael Kennedy, the sixth child of Robert Kennedy. He died after slamming into a tree while playing a risky game of football on skis with members of his family on New Year's Eve in Aspen, Colo., adding yet another sad chapter to the family's growing book of sorrows.

In the third generation of the Kennedy politicians, much of what remains of a once powerful dynasty is good teeth, good hair and the best public relations a trust fund can buy. In 1997 Michael, who once seemed to have his father's quiet passion without the Kennedy sense of entitlement, found himself at the center of a scandal—that he allegedly had a five-year affair with a girl, beginning when she was 14, who baby-sat his three children.

LAST JOURNEY: Michael Kennedy Jr. carries the front of the coffin; Joe Kennedy is at its rear, with mother Ethel behind.

Joe Kennedy II, a six-term Congressman planning to run for Governor of Massachusetts, was crippled by campaign manager Michael's problems as well as by *Shattered Faith*, a new book by Joe's ex-wife Sheila Rauch Kennedy that depicted him as a narcissistic bully who selfishly tried to have their 12-year marriage annulled by the Catholic Church. In August Joe announced that he would not run.

In the fall veteran investigative reporter Seymour Hersh re-raked every smidgen of muck he could find regarding John Kennedy's presidency in a new book, *The Dark Side of Camelot*. Hersh, who won the Pulitzer Prize in 1970 for exposing the My Lai massacre, produced in his long-awaited tome an unrelenting compendium of accusations against the late President, including J.F.K.'s extramarital affairs, his concealed health history, his suspected dealings with known mobsters.

Before publication Hersh had to remove what would have been his most titillating assertion: that the President had signed a contract agreeing to pay Marilyn Monroe $600,000 in hush money to keep quiet about their alleged (and much-rumored) affair. Hersh acted after document experts warned him that the "contract" showed clear signs of being a counterfeit. Even so, the book became a best seller.■

TROUBLED: Left, Michael, wife Vicki and mom Ethel. Right, Joe and first wife Sheila

RUSHDIE: Mystery bride

Cupid's Corner

A '97 report from TIME'S Bureau of Romance: **Salman Rushdie,** still under a Muslim death sentence, wed his girl-friend of three years in a private ceremony; her identity is secret. Talk-show titan **Larry King** married his seventh wife. **Barbra Streisand** and actor **James Brolin** said they hoped to marry. But Hollywood's hottest young duo, **Brad Pitt** and **Gwyneth Paltrow,** called off plans to wed.

KING: Yet another wife!

PITT: Paltrow vows denied

BROLIN: At Barbra's side

Brothers of The Road

FIRST FAN? The Pontiff greets Dylan

What do Pope John Paul II and Bob Dylan have in common? Easy: they both love road trips. Dylan, 56, was hospitalized in May with a potentially fatal heart infection, but he bounced back in time to perform for the Pope at a September conference in Italy. The wandering min-strel then climbed back on the bus to resume his Neverending Tour. Meanwhile, fellow traveler John Paul II, 77, hit the road in his Popemobile to visit six countries in 1997.

A Bounteous Crop in Iowa

THE MCCAUGHEYS: Some Pampers bill!

And this little piggy went to town ... Bobbi and Ken-ny McCaughey had a total of 70 toes to count after Bobbi, 29, gave birth to septuplets on Nov. 19 in Des Moines, Iowa. When fertility drugs worked only too well, concerned doctors proposed "selective reduction"—a euphemism for the aborting of several fetuses so that the others would stand a better chance of survival. But the McCaugheys, who oppose abortion, chose to have all seven babies. The four boys and three girls were all born healthy, by cae-sarean section, prompting an understandable sound bite from Kenny: "Wow!"

After the Fab Four, the Prefab Five

Let's see: from the left, that's Scary Spice, Sporty Spice, Ginger Spice, Baby Spice and ... um ... the other Spice. The career of Britain's saucy Spice Girls took off with the happy-go-lucky trajec-tory of a Mentos commercial, as they topped charts worldwide in January. But before year's end they were booed in Spain, they fired their manager, and they saw their second CD fizzle. British bookmakers began taking bets on exactly how long the chirpy quintet would last.

Bored of The Lord

Michael Flatley is the Mr. Big of the new jig, the center of a surprising cultural phenomenon—a rage for Irish step dancing. As star of *Riverdance*, Flatley helped turn the Gaelic dance troupe into a worldwide sensation. But he left the company in a bitter creative dispute and went on to fashion a glitzy rival to *Riverdance*. But after 18 months of steady touring, fleet-footed Flatley, 38, collapsed of exhaustion in Australia in November. The star, whose love of Irish dance was perhaps exceeded only by his love of Flatley, modestly titled his new extravaganza *Lord of the Dance*.

Broadcaster Blues

Tabloid woes hit two prominent sportscasters. Marv Albert, 53, pleaded guilty to a misdemeanor count of assault and battery in a case brought by a longtime lover. After the trial, which revealed Albert's penchant for cross-dressing and biting, he lost his jobs with both NBC and the New York Knicks. Over at ABC, *Monday Night Football's* Frank Gifford, 67, was snared in a hotel assignation with a temptress who was reportedly paid $75,000 by a tabloid to document their affair on videotape.

Garth in Gotham

Who said an Oklahoma-born country crooner like Garth Brooks couldn't win over Manhattan's tough-minded sophisticates? After all, he always boasted he had friends in low places. When Brooks played New York City's Central Park in August, a crowd of some 300,000 yowled along. Later Brooks rode his new CD, *Sevens*, to the top of the charts; it sold a stunning 897,000 copies in its first week.

Mr. Smith & Mr. Jones

Resuming their love affair with aliens, moviegoers made *Men in Black* the summer's biggest hit. The comedy starred Will Smith and Tommy Lee Jones as members of a crack corps of agents charged with keeping extraterrestrial rascals in line. Following *Independence Day* in 1996, it was the second year in a row that Smith, TV's erstwhile Fresh Prince of Bel-Air, kicked alien butt to win glory, *Variety*-style.

Hail, Hail (to the Chief)—the Gang's All Here

Now here's a happy group! The occasion was the opening of the George Bush presidential library in Texas Station, Texas: hence the faux White House façade with its gleaming hardwood "lawn." Sadly missing from the gathering of First Families was Ronald Reagan, 86, who continued to decline from Alzheimer's disease. The opening capped a big year for Bush, 72, who wowed America in March when he joined members of the Army's élite Golden Knights in a parachute jump from 12,500 ft., recalling his daring leap from a damaged plane in World War II. The one sad note: the Bushes' beloved dog Millie died in May.

Good Sports, Bad Sports

BRETT FAVRE Green Bay's quarterback overcame family troubles and addiction to pain-killers to lead the Packers to a 35-21 win over the Patriots in the Super Bowl. The NFL named Favre its MVP for the second year in a row.

MIKE TYSON The former heavyweight champ and eternal bully bit part of Evander Holyfield's right ear off in the third round of their June rematch. When Tyson bit Holyfield's left ear in the next round, the referee disqualified him.

JIM LEYLAND A manager's manager who had never won the World Series, but had come achingly close three times, Leyland led the upstart Florida Marlins to victory over the Cleveland Indians in a thrilling Game 7 Series finale.

LATRELL SPREWELL The Golden State Warriors' leading scorer throttled coach P.J. Carlesimo in a practice, then returned 15 minutes later to resume the attack. The Warriors fired him, and the NBA suspended him for a year.

Mother Teresa stooped to help the lowest of the low, explaining that she saw her God in every suffering soul

SISTER OF MERCY

SOULS IN SEARCH OF FINAL BLESSING OFTEN came to the temple of a powerful Hindu goddess in Calcutta. But nearby, many discovered another source of solace: a small woman, wrinkled and bent, a willing companion to the dying. She tenderly cared for the abandoned and the sick, washing their wounds, soothing their sores, preparing them for death. "They must feel wanted, loved," Mother Teresa said. "They are Jesus for me." Only physically did Mother Teresa's heart fail her, subjecting her to years of illness that finally led to her death on Sept. 5 at age 87. She had always been adamant about who owned her heart. "People think we are social workers," she once told one of her spiritual advisers, Father

Edward Le Joly. "We are not. We serve Jesus. I serve Jesus 24 hours a day."

She was true to her master through the obscurity in which she first labored, through the acclaim that began in the 1960s, through the sometimes heated denunciation that ensued when she defended controversial church teachings on contraception. For those who believed and perhaps even for those who simply admired her, Mother Teresa was a living saint, and those who loved her have long been murmuring hopeful prayers for her official canonization in the Roman Catholic Church she served so faithfully. That may not be imminent, but for many there can be no doubting it, no devil able to advocate otherwise. Already, her humble ways and the grand religious enterprise she founded are worthy of veneration and emulation.

The woman who became Mother Teresa was born Agnes Gonxha Bojaxhiu on Aug. 26, 1910, the daughter of a prosperous, ethnic Albanian business contractor in Skopje, now the capital of Macedonia. When she was seven, her father Nicholas died during what may have been a Balkan ethnic brawl. At 18, Agnes joined Ireland's Sisters of Loreto, and after a brief period in Rathfarnham, where she learned English at the order's abbey, Sister Teresa sailed for India. She spent the next 17 years as a teacher and then principal of a Calcutta high school for privileged Bengali girls.

It was on Sept. 10, 1946, during a train ride to Darjeeling for a religious retreat, that Teresa received a "call within a call" in which she felt God directing her to the slums. "The message was clear," she said. "I was to leave the convent and help the poor whilst living among them. It was an order." Two years later, after her adopted homeland won independence, Teresa received permission from the Vatican to strike out on her own. Attracting a dozen disciples, she started what she called her "little society." The sisters crept

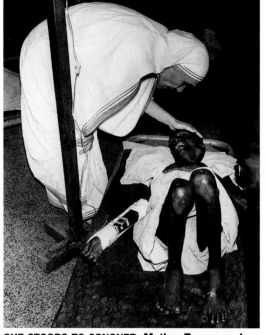

SHE STOOPS TO CONQUER: Mother Teresa made admirers of Popes, Presidents and princesses

along the harsh streets of Calcutta in search of mankind's most miserable; they begged for their own support, even their daily meals. Teresa soon asked the Vatican if she and her followers could take a vow supplementary to those of poverty, chastity and obedience: "To devote themselves out of abnegation to the care of the poor and needy who, crushed by want and destitution, live in conditions unworthy of human dignity."

It took Rome two years to say yes, but in 1950 the Vatican formally established the Missionaries of Charity, and Sister Teresa became Mother Teresa, leading a ministry to

> "I'm only a little wire— God is the power."

the destitute, doomed and dying. One of the missionaries' first projects, in 1952, was to turn a former hostel beside a Hindu temple into a place where the elderly poor of Calcutta, who often died alone in the streets, could at least spend their last hours in comfort and cleanliness.

THEIR HINDU NEIGHBORS GREETED THE NEW Catholic mission with hostility. The temple priests even asked city authorities to relocate the hospice, newly named Nirmal Hriday, or Home for the Dying. But then one of the Hindu priests was found with advanced stages of tuberculosis after he had been denied a bed in a city hospital, reserved for those who could be cured. And so one of the prominent enemies of the Catholic order ended up in a corner of the Nirmal Hriday, tended by Mother Teresa herself. When the priest died, she delivered his body to the temple for Hindu rites. As the story circulated, Calcutta began its long love affair with the sisters.

A 1969 BBC television documentary by Malcolm Muggeridge brought fame to Mother Teresa. In 1979 she received the Nobel Peace Prize; at her request, the traditional banquet was canceled so the $7,000 cost could go to the poor. She won access to global leaders; Princess Diana was a personal friend, and Pope John Paul II valued her as a revered colleague. Today some 4,000 sisters of the Missionaries of Charity pursue her rigorous path, along with 450 brothers in a separate men's order. Their network of 569 missions spreads across some 120 nations, including workshops for the unemployed, food centers, orphanages and refuges for the old and needy.

Mother Teresa did not hesitate to use her fame to speak and act on matters of the secular world. She repeatedly decried abortion. At Harvard University's commencement in 1982 she called it "the greatest evil." A 1995 book by British journalist Christopher Hitchens, *The Missionary Position*, accused her of taking donations from unsavory individuals, including Haiti's former autocrat Jean-Claude Duvalier; of secretly baptizing dying Hindus and Muslims into Christianity; of not providing the dying with pain-killing drugs.

But her accusers were far outnumbered by her admirers. Despite her celebrity status and a flourishing empire, Mother Teresa had a faith that was not of this world. She was intent on saving souls in an era when many people no longer believed souls existed. Yet to millions of others, the rewards of her example were enormous. As hundreds of mourners gathered at the order's Calcutta headquarters to honor her, a weeping Muslim driver said simply, "She was a source of perpetual joy"—a holy commodity indeed. ∎

The Columbus of the Deep

Jacques Cousteau discovered a brave new world beneath the sea

THE WATER MAY BE THE TRANSLUCENT SURF OFF Bermuda, an ice-skimmed quarry in Vermont, the Pacific rolling in majestic rhythm toward the shores of San Diego. Around the world, divers spend hours deep beneath the waves, like spirits through flying an alien realm. That humans are exploring a world long forbidden to man is largely because of the work of a single visionary Frenchman, Jacques-Yves Cousteau, who died in June at 87. Cousteau was at once the pioneer, prophet, poet and foremost promoter of the deep. As the developer of the Aqua-Lung, he set divers free to roam in the kingdom of the fish. As captain of the research vessel *Calypso*, he became a noted international exponent of marine conservation. As an author, filmmaker and expert in underwater photography, he was the dean of ocean explorers.

Young Cousteau graduated second in his class from France's naval academy and, after a car crash left his arms badly injured, spent hours working their strength back by swimming daily in the Mediterranean. In 1935, a fellow naval officer gave him a pair of goggles used by pearl fishermen. Cousteau put his head beneath the surface of the sea and, as he later told it, his life seemed to change almost instantly: "There was wildlife, untouched, a jungle at the border of the sea, never seen by those who floated on the opaque roof."

Cousteau explored the jungle, but he was still tethered to the surface by the need for air. Looking for a way to supply it, he tried an oxygen lung based on a design developed by the British as early as 1878. He almost killed himself. He did not know the fatal flaw of oxygen: it becomes toxic at depths below 30 ft. Twice he had convulsive spasms, and was barely able to drop his weights and return to the surface.

Cousteau allowed World War II to distract him only briefly from his search. Under the eyes of the indifferent Germans in Occupied France, he worked with a brilliant engineer named Emile Gagnon to develop a lung that would automatically feed him safe, compressed air at the same pressure as the surrounding water so that he could swim with both arms. One day in 1943 he waddled out into the Mediterranean under the 50-lb. Aqua-Lung and realized his dream. He was free. "Delivered from gravity and buoyancy, I flew around in space," he said.

Cousteau could scarcely wait for the war to end to develop his new discovery. He sold the French navy on the virtues of the Aqua-Lung and got leave to conduct oceanography sponsored by the government aboard the 360-ton *Calypso*, a refitted World War II British Royal Navy minesweeper. Aboard this ship, he gathered the material for the books and films that would bring him fame, like *The Silent World*, his first book, which sold more than five million copies.

Over the years, his rewards were many: expeditions to study waterways all around the globe, more than 100 undersea documentary films, more than two dozen books, three Oscar awards, induction into the Académie Française. But the explorer also knew tragedy. His son and heir apparent Philippe died in a plane crash in 1979. Later Cousteau parted ways with Jean Michel, his eldest son and close collaborator; their dispute ended in court.

As his knowledge of the oceans grew, Cousteau underwent a final transformation: he became the tribune of the undersea world, the Columbus of the deep. He spent his autumnal years in a different role: as an aging King Canute, defiantly raging against the rising tide of human exploitation of the seas. ∎

JACQUES-YVES COUSTEAU: 1910-1997

"When a person takes his first dive, he is born into another world."

MILESTONES

In a year haunted by the death of a princess and the murder of a designer, an honor roll of other notables who passed from the stage:

EDDIE ARCARO, 81, masterly jockey whose style, spirit and heritage made him the Joe DiMaggio of racing. Only Arcaro rode two Triple Crown horses—Whirlaway (1941) and Citation (1948).

SIR ISAIAH BERLIN, 88, erudite British historian-philosopher. The son of a Jewish timber merchant, Berlin became one of Oxford University's most eminent thinkers. His essays dazzled: ruminating on determinism in *Historical Inevitability,* updating Mill in *Two Concepts of Liberty* or exploring Tolstoy's conflicted nature in *The Hedgehog and the Fox.*

RICHARD BERRY, 61, singer and composer. He wrote *Louie Louie,* the raucous, unintelligible rock-'n'-roll anthem that inspired many risqué versions. In 1956 the Louisiana-born Berry sold rights to his works for $750, but in 1986 he finally regained royalties of some $2 million.

SIR RUDOLPH BING, 95, authoritarian impresario who called the tunes at the Metropolitan Opera for 22 years. Bing moved the company to Lincoln Center, introduced its first black performers and built it into a first-class opera house—though he never quite lived down firing Maria Callas in 1968.

HERB CAEN, 80, classic newspaper columnist. In the brightly written rat-a-tat of the daily column he produced for 58 years, the Pulitzer-prizewinning Caen was raconteur, funnyman, tipster, nightclubber, friend of the powerful and tireless chronicler of "Baghdad by the Bay," the city he loved and that loved him back.

JEANNE CALMENT, 122, officially the world's oldest person. Born before the invention of the phonograph, Calment lived exuberantly, enjoying chocolates, cigarettes and one-liners ("I've never had but one wrinkle, and I'm sitting on it").

ADOLPHUS "DOC" CHEATHAM, 91, trumpeter who understudied for Louis Armstrong, then became a leading sideman of the swing era. In his trademark stance, he held his trumpet high, pointed to the heavens, producing buttery lyricism and witty improvisations.

WILLIAM BRENNAN

In his 34 years on the Supreme Court, William J. Brennan Jr., 91, came to be regarded as one of the most influential Justices in U.S. history. Before Brennan, the Bill of Rights protected people mostly from the Federal Government but scarcely from states and cities. Governments couldn't seize a mansion without a hearing, but they could repossess a car or kick someone off welfare without explaining why. Desegregation was required in principle but not in practice. Sex discrimination was legal. Religious practices could be penalized. Through his 1,360 opinions Brennan changed all that, building an edifice of common sense and uncommon wisdom that transformed America. If John Marshall was the chief architect of a powerful national government, then Brennan was the principal architect of the nation's system for protecting individual rights. Intellectually brilliant, Brennan was animated by compassion, insight and empathy, and a vision of a Constitution of, by and for the people.

GERDA CHRISTIAN, 83, Adolf Hitler's devoted secretary. Christian was on hand at the Führer's 11th-hour wedding to Eva Braun and lunched with him before his suicide, but chose not to take the poison pills that Hitler reportedly gave her as a parting gift.

ALEXANDRA DANILOVA, 93, ballet's radiant empress who left Russia in 1924 but never defected from its classical dance traditions, soaring at the Ballet Russes in the 1920s and '30s and inspiring generations of student dancers at the School of American Ballet.

JOHN DENVER, 53, singer-songwriter who composed sunny anthems to human goodness and nature's wonders. After an early stint with folk's Chad Mitchell Trio, he went solo, charming audiences with a lyrical tenor and country-boy appeal that embodied the peace-loving ethos of the 1970s. He died when a lightweight airplane he was piloting plunged into the Pacific.

JAMES DICKEY, 73, Georgia-born poet whose collection *Buckdancer's Choice* won the National Book Award in 1966. Dickey found a passing Hollywood glamour in the 1970s, when his novel of backwoods adventure, *Deliverance,* became a best seller and a popular movie. Dickey was intoxicated by language and the power of myth; his best work has a virile and transformative splendor.

JEANE DIXON, 79, celebrity astrologer, psychic and widely read syndicated columnist. Dixon's star (she was a Capricorn) began to rise following her 1956 prediction that a young Democratic President elected in 1960 would die in office.

LEON EDEL, 89, the reigning authority on Henry James. Edel's Pulitzer-prizewinning, five-volume biography limned a spirited artist within the façade of the passionless scholar.

CHRIS FARLEY, 33, gifted comic who rose from Chicago's Second City comedy troupe to NBC's *Saturday Night Live* to such Hollywood hits as *Beverly Hills Ninja.* The heavyweight star's image was of the ne'er-do-well party guy, the addled but lovable omnivore. In real life he battled a fierce appetite for drink and drugs that substantially hastened his death.

CURT FLOOD, 59, doughty former St. Louis Cardinal centerfielder. Flood defied baseball's hallowed reserve system in 1969 by refusing to be traded from St. Louis and later, in a case that went to the Supreme Court, sued for antitrust violation. He lost, but his singular challenge paved the way for the 1975 agreement permitting players to become free agents.

SAMUEL FULLER, 85, brassy writer-director of feral, cynical B movies. His life was as convulsive as his films: copyboy for the New York *Evening Journal* at 13, crime reporter in San Diego, Depression-era hobo, a Purple Heart veteran of World War II. Fuller invigorated old genres—war films, westerns and killer melodramas—with a gutsy storytelling sense and a gracefully vigorous camera style.

JOLIE GABOR, 97, matriarch known as Mama Jolie who brought her exotic daughters Zsa Zsa, Eva and Magda to the U.S. from Hungary in the 1930s and presided over their ascent to Hollywood celebrity.

HAROLD GENEEN, 87, empire builder. During his 18 years as CEO of International Telephone & Telegraph (1959 to 1977), Geneen used some 300 takeovers to build ITT into one of the first sprawling conglomerates.

ROBERTO GOIZUETA, 65. As the pre-eminent general in the cola wars, Coca-Cola CEO Goizueta was the ultimate brand loyalist. Born into a wealthy Cuban family, he was raised in privilege and schooled at Yale. He began his Coke career in 1954 as a chemist at the company in Havana. He and his wife fled Fidel Castro's Cuba in 1961, getting out with a suitcase and 100 shares of Coca-Cola, which he never sold. On his watch as CEO, Coke's stock-market value rose from $4 billion to some $150 billion, despite the disastrous 1980s launch of "new Coke." By his death he had become Wall Street's icon of shareholder value.

SIR JAMES GOLDSMITH, 64, billionaire financier who made his nut with pharmaceuticals and groceries and parlayed it into a fortune as a corporate raider in the '80s, acquiring a succession of high-profile targets. Late in life he founded Britain's Referendum Party, which opposes the European common currency. At his death, his warm and very extended family included his third wife, who lives in London, and his second wife, his mistress and their families, who share a home in Paris.

STEPHANE GRAPPELLI, 89, exuberant jazz violinist. America had Ellington, but Europe got the Quintet of the Hot Club of France in the 1930s—the chamber group–cum–jazz ensemble that featured Grappelli and guitarist Django Reinhardt. The Quintet broke up during World War II, but Grappelli played on, recording more than 100 albums.

PAMELA HARRIMAN, 76, vivacious English artisocrat who married some of the most famous men of the century and died as the U.S. ambassador to France. Pamela Digby married Win-

WILLIAM S. BURROUGHS

Novelist, cult figure and in his last years a pop icon, Burroughs, 83, was perhaps the most audacious individual of the Beat Generation. His novel *Naked Lunch* (1959) was a work of genius to some, gibberish and garbage to others. His life involved alcohol, heroin, homosexuality, a famous obscenity trial and, in 1951, the accidental killing of his wife in a "game."

ALLEN GINSBERG

The quintessential beatnik poet, 70, first raged into public view in 1956 with *Howl,* a profane tirade that railed against a conformist society and celebrated his homosexuality. In the '60s and '70s, he was active in both the hippie and antiwar movements. His work embraced protest and psychedelics, yoga, Buddhism, the Torah, mysticism and Walt Whitman.

ston Churchill's only son, Randolph, at the outset of World War II, but conducted love affairs with Averell Harriman, the top U.S. envoy in Britain, and broadcaster Edward R. Murrow during the marriage. After divorcing Churchill in 1945, Pamela moved to France, where she dallied with playboy prince Aly Khan, auto magnate Gianni Agnelli and banking scion Elie de Rothschild. In 1960 she moved to America and married Leland Hayward, the noted Broadway producer. After his death she reunited with the wealthy Harriman and married

him. In the late 1980s she became a powerful figure in politics, raising funds for the Democratic Party and backing candidate Bill Clinton. After his election, he rewarded her with the post of ambassador to France; in Paris her charm, hard work and access to top officials served the U.S. well.

CHAIM HERZOG, 78, urbane, articulate former President of Israel and exemplar of its soldier-statesman tradition. As U.N. ambassador in 1975, Herzog in a debate defiantly tore up the resolution equating Zionism with racism. As President, he worked to broker rifts in coalition Cabinets, isolate some extremists and push for voting reforms.

BEN HOGAN, 84, golf champion whose personality matched his no-nonsense golfing attire— white linen cap, beige shirt and sharply pressed slacks. But Hogan's legend needed no embellishment: he was rightly revered as the greatest shot-maker who ever lived. His fierce will helped him recover from a 1949 auto collision that nearly killed him; he came back to win six of his nine major championships. In 1967, at age 54, he shot a record 30 on the back nine of the Masters.

MICHAEL HUTCHENCE, 37, sultry front man for Aussie rockers INXS, who died by hanging himself. Driven by Hutchence's propulsive, sinewy appeal, INXS scored with the hit *What You Need,* topped by the bravura album *Kick* in 1987. Hutchence and the band had been preparing to embark on a 20th anniversary tour.

NUSRAT FATEH ALI KHAN, 48, mesmerizing singer who brought the mystical music of the Sufis of northern India and Pakistan to a global stage. Khan was a singer in the *qawwali* tradition, a style that built layer upon layer of increasingly intense music that demanded ferocious vocal control and culminated in whirling peaks of ecstasy.

CHARLES KURALT, 62. With his warm baritone and neighborly mien, CBS broadcaster Kuralt traveled America on his long-running Sunday-morning show to discover centenarian entertainers, whittlers, slingshot artists, brickmakers—an astonishing host of the overlooked. Working in the media fast lane, Kuralt erected roadside reminders of a real world with real people in real time.

JAMES LAUGHLIN, 83, maverick publisher who used inherited wealth to found and run New Directions, which published works by such gifted but nonmainstream authors as Ezra Pound, William Carlos Williams and Henry Miller. Laughlin was also a pioneer in sport: he founded Alta, a ski resort in Utah.

BUCK LEONARD, 90, Hall of Fame first baseman hailed as the Lou Gehrig of the Negro Leagues. With flawless glove work and a career batting average well above .300, Leonard anchored the Pittsburgh Homestead Grays from 1934 to 1950.

J. ANTHONY LUKAS, 64, Pulitzer-prizewinning journalist whose scrupulously detailed books explored America's great divides. The individual was the starting point for his work, as in *Common Ground,* an examination of three families linked and separated by Boston's busing initiative. He died by his own hand.

MICHAEL MANLEY, 72, charismatic former Prime Minister of Jamaica. A fiery leftist when he became Prime Minister in 1972, Manley nationalized farms and companies, railed against U.S. imperialism and flirted with Castro. Ousted in 1980 by conservative Edward Seaga, Manley recast himself as a capitalist and returned to office in 1989, only to step down in 1992, citing poor health.

BURGESS MEREDITH, 89, actor who performed the highbrow and lowbrow with equal enthusiasm and success. His Mio in *Winterset* simmered with earnest indignation; his Penguin in TV's *Batman* was gloriously over the top. He played the gentle George in *Of Mice and Men,* the careworn coach in *Rocky* and even did a gravelly voice-over for Skippy peanut butter.

JAMES MICHENER, 90, prolific and peripatetic author who embarked on a lifelong literary tour of the globe. While a Navy lieutenant during World War II, Michener began writing *Tales of the South Pacific,* a collection of stories that won him the Pulitzer and became Broadway's *South Pacific.* "Location, location, location" was his mantra, and he rarely wavered from the formula that sold 75 million copies of his 40-odd books: he traveled to a chosen place, researched it exhaustively, then wrote workmanlike tomes peopled with real and imaginary characters.

WILLEM DE KOONING

A transplanted Dutchman who jumped ship to the New World in 1926, De Kooning, 92, came to love the lushness, the grittiness, the obtrusive weirdness of American cultural vernaculars. A principal figure of Abstract Expressionism, he brought to his best work a wonderful libidinousness, a way of using the body of paint to access and encompass the world.

ROY LICHTENSTEIN

Born in New York City in 1923, Lichtenstein became the most popular of the Pop artists. Despite its studied neutrality of surface, his work fairly crackled with assertion and impersonality, both at once. With good humor and icy elegance, he transformed the commonplace—Benday dots, romance and action comics of the '50s—into the monumental.

MOBUTU SESE SEKO, 66, African strongman and kleptocrat whose 32-year rule of Zaïre finally ended in May. After seizing power in what was then the Belgian Congo in a 1965 coup, Mobutu played the anticommunist, earning an ally in the U.S. He touted nationalization and other economic reforms, but he spent the following decades looting his resource-rich country, leaving it impoverished.

LAURA NYRO, 49, intense and lyrical singer-songwriter whose free-form musical emotionalism captured the passions of the 1960s. Her songs, a unique blend of folk, soul, gospel and Broadway, were turned into hits by other artists. They include *Wedding Bell Blues* (Fifth Dimension), *And When I Die* (Blood, Sweat and Tears) and *Stoney End* (Barbra Streisand).

COLONEL TOM PARKER, 87, Elvis Presley's impresario. The onetime carnival barker discovered Presley in 1955 and masterminded the King's career while taking oversize percentages for himself. After Presley's death in 1977, his heirs sued Parker, and in 1982 the flashy pitchman relinquished all future income from Presley.

V.S. PRITCHETT, 96, writer, critic and all-around British man of letters. Sir Victor (he was knighted in 1975) turned out pithy, highly polished prose in a variety of genres, including travel writing, memoirs, biographies, novels, literary criticism and short stories.

SVIATOSLAV RICHTER, 82, Russia's incomparable piano-poet. Virtually self-taught until age 21, Richter treated the piano like a soul mate, listening for the romance of Schumann or the fury of Beethoven. "I don't consider the public," he told TIME. "My only interest is my approaching encounter with the composer."

HAROLD ROBBINS, 81, narcissistic novelist whose smutty potboilers mirrored his rags-to-riches life. On a wager, Robbins wrote *Never Love a Stranger* (1948), the first of 23 books that sold more than 750 million copies worldwide.

LEO ROSTEN, 88, author best known for his works celebrating Jewish culture. The Polish native's definitive reference work, *The Joys of Yiddish,* published in 1968, introduced readers to colorful and now common terms like schlemiel, schmaltz and chutzpah.

A.L. ROWSE, 93, authority on Elizabethan England and Shakespeare. Known as much for his cranky self-assurance as for his scholarship, Rowse wrote scores of books, including a three-volume *The Annotated Shakespeare.* "This filthy 20th century," he once said. "I hate its guts."

MIKE ROYKO, 64, caustic columnist who ruled the Windy City from his Pulitzer-prizewinning Page 3 pulpit. From high-society dames to low-down pols, no one was safe from Royko's pen, including himself, as he learned when minorities protested his tactless quips. But Royko remained irreverent in his column to the end.

BETTY SHABAZZ, 61, Malcolm X's steadfast widow. She died of third-degree burns suffered in a fire set by her grandson at her home outside New York City. A devout Muslim, she earned a doctorate in education administration and embodied her husband's message of dignity for African Americans.

RED SKELTON, 84, rubber-faced, gentle-hearted clown who always seemed one laugh short of tears. His father, a clown, died before his birth—a mixed inheritance that sent him tumbling from carnival to walkabout, perfecting lugubrious pantomimes and uproarious pratfalls. He landed in such movies as *The Fuller Brush Man* and *A Southern Yankee,* but it was his TV characters like the Mean Widdle Kid and Freddie the Freeloader that made audiences squeal—for mercy and for more. Skelton, too, often dissolved into giggles at his own antics, even after his son died of leukemia in 1958. As he once said, "a clown is a warrior who fights gloom."

SIR GEORG SOLTI, 84, fierce maestro who prodded the Chicago Symphony Orchestra to the front of the world stage. He transfixed listeners, seemingly verging on levitation in his energetic efforts to draw tight phrasing and brilliant coloration from his musicians. The orchestra won 23 Grammy Awards during his 22-year reign.

TOMOYUKI TANAKA, 86, Godzilla godfather who was head of Toho Films in 1956 when, with director Ishiro Honda, he dreamed up the city-stomping marauder. Godzilla was created to express

horror at the bombing of Hiroshima and Nagasaki; he starred in 22 films and will reappear in a 1998 blockbuster.

BRANDON TARTIKOFF, 48, NBC's programming wunderkind who gave the peacock network reason to strut. Only 31 when he became NBC's entertainment president in 1980, Tartikoff turned the struggling network into The Place To Be with such hits as *The Cosby Show* and *Hill Street Blues.*

PAUL TSONGAS, 55, former U.S. Senator and presidential candidate.

ROBERT MITCHUM

"It sure beats working," Mitchum, 79, always said of acting, and his approach was simple: do whatever the job requires, but don't make a big deal of doing something you're being overpaid for. In such signature roles as the private eye in the film noir *Out of the Past,* Mitchum grimly accepted doom as the price of sexual obsession and lighted his passage to it with flaring wisecracks.

JIMMY STEWART

In a lifetime of movies, Stewart, 89, was the goodwill ambassador for a genial, vanishing America. With his stammer, scarecrow physique and gawky stride, he wore his renown as comfortably as a pair of overalls—but to see him in *It's a Wonderful Life* or *Vertigo* or *The Man Who Shot Liberty Valance* was to discover his guilty secret: Stewart was a great actor.

Democrat Tsongas served two terms in the House and was elected to the Senate from Massachusetts in 1978, but when lymphoma struck in 1983 he decided to serve only one term. With the cancer under control, he ran for President in 1992 and won the New Hampshire primary. Although he quit the race a few weeks later, his sobering message about the need for deficit reduction made its mark on the campaign and the country.

TOWNES VAN ZANDT, 52, gifted songwriter whose dark recordings about

life's losers, including *Pancho and Lefty,* a hit for Willie Nelson and Merle Haggard, influenced a coterie of admiring country and rock singers.

GEORGE WALD, 90, politically active biologist whose research on how the eye transmits images to the brain won him a 1967 Nobel Prize. A proponent of "survival politics," Wald was a vocal foe of the Vietnam War and the arms race and an advocate for human rights.

CHRISTOPHER WALLACE, a.k.a. The Notorious B.I.G., 24, rap artist who stood 6 ft. 3 in. and tipped the scales at 300-plus pounds. Wallace rose from slinging crack on Brooklyn street corners to become a major star in the field of gangsta rap, which celebrates outlaw attitudes and behavior. Wallace was shot to death in his truck after a Los Angeles party—six months after the similar shooting of rapper Tupac Shakur. The unsolved murder heightened rumors of an East Coast–West Coast rivalry in the rap world and led to widespread denunciations of gangsta rap.

SCHOICHI YOKOI, 82, die-hard Japanese soldier who emerged from his jungle hideout on Guam 27 years after World War II ended. Counting the years by lunar cycles and crafting clothing from tree-bark fibers, Yokoi honored his pledge never to surrender. Two hunters who stumbled upon him in 1972 told him of Japan's defeat.

COLEMAN YOUNG, 79, feisty five-term mayor of Detroit from 1974 to 1993. The ex–World War II Tuskegee airman became one of the first black mayors of a major U.S. city. Blunt and upbeat, he integrated the police and fire departments and tried to spur development of the waterfront with construction of the huge Renaissance Center.

FRED ZINNEMANN, 89, three-time Oscar-winning director. In such screen classics as *High Noon, From Here to Eternity* and *A Man for All Seasons,* he illuminated the battle between good and evil and evoked a series of finely etched performances from actors.

Credits appear clockwise from top left, except as noted.

Editorial section graphic icons by Brian Cronin.

The Year in Review iv-v Christopher Morris—Black Star for TIME, Joe McNally—LIFE, AFP, Cherrualt—Sipa **1** (top to bottom) Cherrualt—Sipa, Jeffrey Aaronson for TIME, Joan Marcus ©Disney **2-3** Jed Jacobsohn—Allsport **4-5** Remi Berali & Stephen Ferry—Gamma Liaison **6-7** Justin Kilcullen—Trocaire/Sygma **8-9** Wally Pacholka **10-11** courtesy Iowa Methodist Medical Center, *Dateline* NBC (inset) **12-13** Sipa Press **14-15** In the Spotlight illustrations (from left to right): C.F. Payne, Jon Wateridge, Drew Friedman, Ray Bartkus, Glynis Sweeny, Christian Clayton, Thomas L. Fluharty, Mark Fredrickson, Owen Smith, David O'Keefe, Glynis Sweeny, David Hughes, David Cowles, S.B. Whitehead, Hungry Dog Studios, John S. Dykes, Drew Friedman, Glynis Sweeny. All Spotlight illustrations created exclusively for TIME. **16-17** James Keyser for TIME FOR KIDS, John Chiasson—Gamma Liaison, Jack Dabaghian—Reuters, David Burnett—Contact Press for TIME **18-19** John Barr—Gamma Liaison for TIME, Warner Bros. (inset), Cultural Jet Lag for TIME (art), Tom Morillo—Tom Keller & Associates, Cynthia Johnson for TIME **20-21** NBC—Reuters, Bob Hambly (art), George Lange/Outline

Nation 22-23 The Los Angeles *Times* **24-25** San Gabriel Valley *Tribune*, Ron Watts—Black Star **26-27** Patrick Hagerty—Sygma, U.S. Army—Reuters/Archive **28** Brad Markel—Gamma Liaison **29** David Burnett—Contact **30-31** AP, Nelvin Cepeda—San Diego *Tribune* for TIME, AP **32-33** Alexis Rodriguez—Duarte, Bishops School—AP **34** Savino—Sipa, Bill Cooke—Saba for TIME **35** R. Simons—Sygma **36-37** Wichita *Eagle*—Sipa, Thomas Monaster—*Daily News*, Rogelio Solis—AP, Laurie Driver—Sygma, Scott Takushi—St. Paul *Pioneer Press*/Sygma, Schieren/StockFood America

World 38-39 Snowdon—Camera Press **40-41** AP (3), Charles Platiau—Reuters **42-43** Peter DeJong—AP (far left), Stefan Rousseau—PA News, Peter DeJong—AP, Stefan Rousseau—PA News, Francis Dias-Newspix/Saba, Max Nash—AP, Stefan Rousseau—PA News **44-45** L.R.C.—Sipa, Robert Wallis—Saba **46-47** Max Cisotti—Alpha/Globe Photos, Tim Graham—Sygma, courtesy Ronald Reagan Library, Cherrualt—Sygma, PA News, David Jones—PA

News, PA News, Alpha—Globe Photos, Harvey & Stenning—Globe Photos, Tim Graham—Sygma (center, left) **48-49** Tim Graham—Sygma **50** David Caulkin—AP **51** ITAR—TASS/Reuters **52-53** Christopher Morris—Black Star for TIME **54** Jeffrey Aaronson for TIME, Richard Manin—Sipa **55** (top to bottom) AFP, Christopher Morris—Black Star for TIME, Sichov—Sipa **56-57** New China News, China News—Sipa **58** Michael Kramer—AP **59** Ian Leguen—Sipa **60-61** Nate Thayer—Tom Keller Associates, Silvia Izquierdo—Reuters, James Bu—U.N./D.P.I., Les Stone/Sygma for TIME, Vejnovic—AFP (top), Ilic—AP

Business 62-63 Mark Fredrickson (art) **64-65** AP, Gregory Heisler—Outline, Steve Hart for the TIME ANNUAL (chart), **66-67** Charlie Godbold-Gilford—Sygma **68-69** Britain Hill for TIME, Gregory Heisler for TIME, Kim Kulish—Saba, no credit, AP **70** no credit **71** no credit, Milan Trenc (art), Martin Simon—Saba, Steve Liss for TIME

Man of the Year 72-75 photo-illustrations by James Porto for TIME **76** John Meyer for TIME **77** Robbie McClaran for TIME **78** Intel (top left) **80-81** David Burnett—Contact for TIME **82-83** photos by John Meyer for TIME; diagram by Joe Zeff and Joe Lertola for TIME

Technology 84-85 Jim Bourg—Reuters/Archive **86** TBWA/Chiat Day (top), Jim Bourg—Reuters/Archive **87** George Lange—Outline **88-89** Ted Thai for TIME **90-91** James Porto for TIME, no credit **92** Charlie Samuels—Outline **93** Daniel Adel for TIME (art) **94** Philip Saltonstall for TIME **95** Todd Buchanan for TIME, Amy Etra for TIME, Randall Enos (art)

Society 96-97 Lori Grinker—Contact **98-99** Brad Markel—Gamma Liaison, Ron Haviv—Saba **100-101** Steve Adler (art), Terry Ashe for TIME **102-103** Chris Trotman—Duomo **104** Jamie Squire—Allsport (2) **105** Darren Carroll—Duomo **106** Jim Bourg—AP **107** no credit, Bodleian Library/Ontario (center), Bob Mahoney for TIME (right)

Science 108-109 JPL/NASA (2) **110-111** diagram by Joe Lertola for TIME, JPL/NASA **112-113** Frank Zullo—Photo Researchers, diagram by Joe Lertola for TIME **114-115** diagram by Steve Hart for TIME **116-117** digital photomontage by Arthur Hochstein for TIME; Dolly photographed by Robert Wallis—Saba for TIME, diagram by Joe

Lertola for TIME **118** Robert Wallis—Saba for TIME **120-121** Andrew Winning—Reuters, diagram by Joe Lertola for TIME **122** diagram by Joe Lertola for TIME **123** Steve Casimiro—Gamma Liaison, JPL/NASA, Penny Gentieu

Health 124-125 Andrew Tsiaras—Photo Researchers **126-127** Scott Menchin (art) **128-129** David Strick—Outline, Larry Voight—Photo Researchers **130** Sandra Dionisi (art) **131** Hans Reinhard—Okapia/Photo Researchers **132** diagram by Joe Lertola for TIME **133** James Porto, Eric Sanders for TIME, Ed Reschke—Peter Arnold

Arts & Media 134-135 Harf Zimmermann—Ostkreuz **136-137** Amy Etra—J. Paul Getty Trust (2), Scott Francis—Esto (2) **138** David Heald ©S.R.G.F., NY **139** John Chiasson—Gamma Liaison **140-141** Rickerby—Sipa, Peter Nash—Outline, James Bridges, Outline **142** David Strick—Outline **143** Tom Hilton, Chuck Hodes **144-145** ©Joan Marcus, Joan Marcus ©Disney **146** Sonnabend Collection, Greg Gorman—Fox, 20th Century Fox

The Best of 1997 147 illustration for TIME by Chip Kidd and Geoff Spear **148** Peter Sorel—Warner Bros., Trimark, DreamWorks, Miramax, Arrow **149** MSNBC, Photofest (2), Timothy White—ABC, HBO **150** Michael Cooper, Carol Rosegg (2) **151** Danny Clinch—Outline, Dennis Kleiman—Retna, Matt Barnes, Rankin—Camera Press/Retna (center), Jim Rakete—DGG **152** no credit, C. MacKenzie—Woodfin Camp **153** William West—AFP

People 154 Peter Morgan—Reuters (top), Ira Wyman—Sygma (2) **155** Pelletier—Sygma, Reuters—Archive, no credit, Pacha—Corbis, Rickerby—Sipa, Terry Lilly—Shooting Star, Steve Liss for TIME (center) **156** no credit, Rick Elgar—LFI for TIME, no credit **157** Win McNamee—Reuters, U.S. Parachute Association (inset), George Tiedeman—SPORTS ILLUSTRATED, Otto Creile—Allsport, Mike Blake—Reuters, Allen Fredrickson—Reuters

Milestones 158-159 Raghu Rai—Magnum **160** J.P. Laffont—Sygma **161** Sygma **162** Dennis Brack—Black Star **163** K. Simon—Sygma, Howard Bingham **164** Timothy Greenfield-Sanders—Outline, Elena Seibert—Outline **165** UPI, Neal Peters Collection